MORE THAN A PRETTY FACE

MORE THAN A PRETTY FACE

Using Embodied Lutheran Theology to Evaluate
Community-Building in Online Social Networks

Joel Oesch

PICKWICK *Publications* · Eugene, Oregon

MORE THAN A PRETTY FACE
Using Embodied Lutheran Theology to Evaluate Community-Building in Online
Social Networks

Pickwick Publications
An Imprint of Wipf and Stock Publishers
199 W. 8th Ave., Suite 3
Eugene, OR 97401

www.wipfandstock.com

PAPERBACK ISBN: 978-1-5326-1369-2
HARDCOVER ISBN: 978-1-5326-1371-5
EBOOK ISBN: 978-1-5326-1370-8

Unless otherwise indicated, all Scripture quotations are from the Holy Bible, New
International Version®, NIV®. Copyright © 1973, 1978, 1984, 2011 by Biblica, Inc.™
Used by permission of Zondervan. All rights reserved worldwide. www.zondervan.
com The "NIV" and "New International Version" are trademarks registered in the
United States Patent and Trademark Office by Biblica, Inc.™

Cataloguing-in-Publication data:

Names: Oesch, Joel.

Title: More than a pretty face : using embodied Lutheran theology to evaluate community-building in online social networks / by Joel Oesch.

Description: Eugene, OR : Pickwick Publications, 2017.

Identifiers: ISBN 978-1-5326-1369-2 (paperback) | ISBN 978-1-5326-1371-5 (hardcover)
| ISBN 978-1-5326-1370-8 (ebook)

Subjects: LCSH: Theological anthropology—Christianity. | Luther, Martin, 1483–1546—
Anthropology. | Social media—Religious aspects—Christianity.

Classification: BS661 .O48 2017 (paperback) | BS661 .O48 (ebook)

Manufactured in the U.S.A.   06/23/17

CONTENTS

ACKNOWLEDGMENTS

THANK YOU TO DR. Glenn Nielsen of Concordia Seminary St. Louis for his patient critique of my work from outset. I trust his efforts to steer me around dangerous waters have paid off with a text that may have some on-going benefit for the Church.

A special thank you to my lovely and charming wife, Tiffany. She was my sounding board for every idea that required a measured voice of wisdom, often challenging me to consider unique approaches that I had previously left unexplored. Her support, friendship, and patience mean the world to me!

Soli Deo Gloria!

ABBREVIATIONS

AE   *Luther's Works,* American Edition (St. Louis: Concordia; Philadelphia: Fortress; 1955–1986)

LC   Large Catechism

SA   The Smalcald Articles

SC   Small Catechism

1

WHY DOES THE BODY MATTER AT ALL?

AT THE VERY HEART of Christianity is the body. Or, more precisely, *a* body. This particular human body was born of a woman in a small backwater town in the wake of a controversial pregnancy. It is the body of a man who used his fingers to heal the blind, expel the demonic, and break bread with outcasts. It is a body that crumples under the pain of flogging, experiences the agony of crucifixion, and finally surrenders to death. The Easter refrain of, "He is risen indeed!" boldly affirms the physical resurrection of Jesus Christ, the body that was broken and restored for humanity. Ancient Christian witnesses professed that this God-man overcame death in a uniquely physical manner, and, ever since, Jesus' resurrected body has perplexed those who have sought to understand the nature of their own somatic form. In one sense, humanity struggles to come to terms with their post-Fall physicality, bearing first the burden of the curse whereby women experience pain in childbirth and men experience the toil of producing crops. In another sense, God's chosen vessel of redemption for all of creation was the flesh and bones of his son, implicitly yet boldly affirming the dignity of the human experience and its relation to physicality. The material existence of humanity is caught in this tension.

Christian theology has endured a tenuous relationship with the human body. Even a cursory glance at Christian history and tradition reveals a broad spectrum of belief that ranges from outright condemnation of corporeality to the unabashed celebration of human sexuality found in many modern feminist-oriented theologies. It appears that even the patristic fathers could not make up their minds: either praise the body as "very good" or strike it down with a flagellating whip![1] The origins of early negativity toward the somatic form no doubt take their cue from classic Greek philosophy and/or a peculiar reading of Pauline theology in Romans,[2] where the wants and desires of the body were made subordinate to the "life of the mind."[3] This view potentially manifested itself in one of two ways: either the subject pursued myriad opportunities for sensual pleasure under the guise that physical bodies (and all the appetites that emerged therein) were meaningless, or the human body was viewed as a hotbed of temptation and vice, in desperate need of control. Examples of the latter included forms of sexual renunciation, as abstinence could prepare the body best for the reception of divine communication. The apologist Athenagoras, in one example, writes:

> Nay, you would find many among us, both men and women, growing old unmarried, in hope of living in closer communion with God. But if the remaining in virginity and in the state of an eunuch brings nearer to God, while the indulgence of carnal thought and desire leads away from Him, in those cases in which we shun the thoughts, much more do we reject the deeds.[4]

The physical body, in this instance, is portrayed as a barrier to receiving divine instruction or inspiration. These historically pessimistic perspectives have worked their way into the bloodstream of Christian dialogue, prompting Christian authors of the early- and mid-twentieth century to ponder, "For what purpose does my body exist?"

Today, the pendulum of theological reflection has shifted in favor of a more favorable view of the human body. Perhaps this is due to the broader philosophical turn toward an emphasis on bodily experience, as a multitude of academic programs are integrating human sexuality into more traditional disciplines. This suggests that significant confusion exists whenever the body is used as a topic of discourse. What, precisely, does a scholar mean when he/she refers to the body?[5] Allowing for these present difficulties,

1. Brown, *Body and Society*. For a rich historical description of the body-community dynamic, Peter Brown's work in this field is particularly engaging.

2. Romans 8:13–14 often serves as a scriptural vindication for the mortification of the flesh: "For if you live according to the sinful nature, you will die; but if by the Spirit you put to death the misdeeds of the body, you will live, because those who are led by the Spirit of God are sons of God." Saint Jerome treats Paul's words as an imperative for ascetic living, going so far as to connect this theology to his, at times, puzzling views on virginity and marriage. Jerome, *Against Jovinianus*, 346–416.

3. Dyrness, *The Earth is God's*, 21.

4. Athenagoras, "A Plea for the Christians," 146.

5. Bynum, "Why all the Fuss About the Body?" 241, 243. A helpful survey of this philosophical turn can be found in Caroline Bynum's insightful article on the postmodern shift toward embodied experience.

contemporary theologians are less willing to marginalize the physical component of human existence, even if they cannot fully agree as to the nature and scope of the body's relationship to the person in possession of it.[6]

Relatively recent technological advances have prompted new questions. Is corporeality only experienced in individual terms? While not explicitly rejecting corporeality per se, the Digital Revolution has slowly shaped the way society understands the relationship of physicality to the broader community. Somewhat unexpectedly, online social networks (OSNs) accentuate the view that the body, while still necessary as the vehicle for consciousness, is no longer required in terms of *participation within the community*. When this view is pushed to the extreme, the flesh and bones of the individual has no apparent bearing on the person's degree of involvement in social contexts. Yet even in moderate use, the importance of physical presence in these new forms of social life is significantly minimized. Texts, tweets, and Facebook updates have replaced the art of the face-to-face conversation. Rather than fulfilling the foundational needs of sociality with restaurants, coffee houses, ballgames, and late-night talks, OSNs are pressing toward a world where connectivity, entertainment, and information are the locations that people look toward to feel connected and safe. The Christian Church stands at this junction, where the desire of digital natives[7] to stay globally connected often clashes with the call for an embodied presence in the local community.

The term "online social network"[8] is a paradox. It can bring together friends over vast distances and yet, in the immediate sense, causes a certain degree of physical isolation. For that reason, it is quite common to hear someone decry websites such as Facebook as inherently *anti*-social. The standard use of an online social network encourages a participant to spend a significant portion of his/her waking hours in front of a screen, isolated from any holistic, embodied presence within a community. Alternatively,

---

6. N. T. Wright uses the physical resurrection of Jesus as a springboard to his discussions on the resurrection of the dead at the end of times. His work has, to a large degree, reclaimed the importance of an eschatology that appreciates the bodily component to Christian hope. In conservative Lutheran circles, Charles Arand and Jeffrey Gibbs have given voice to the physical form's unique importance albeit from the differing angles of creation and New Testament theology, respectively.

7. Palfrey and Gasser, *Born Digital*. The term "digital natives" refers to those born after 1980, when the earliest forms of online social networking began to emerge. More recently, the term is used to designate young people who have never known a world without personal computers, cell phones, or Internet access.

8. For my purposes, an online social network may be defined as any Internet-based gathering of individuals for the purpose of creating and developing social bonds through shared interests.

a user may be physically present with their companions yet immersed in a digital conversation on their smartphones, making them intellectually and emotionally absent from those they are actually with. This is not to be confused with the claim that meaningful communication or bonding cannot happen across bandwidth, but one can in all confidence suggest that: (1) these modes of social life differ radically from past generations, and (2) the sheer number of media that the average person engages in a day cultivates an environment of distraction. Such activity cannot help but radically shape what it means to be a social creature in twenty-first century America.

My project, in part, argues that the problematic effects associated with online social networks are essentially theological in nature and therefore require a theological response. Traditional forms of community that require a person's physicality are being replaced with digital meeting grounds that no longer generate the benefits of physical presence. Such benefits include non-verbal communication, heightened degrees of empathy and compassion, and the bonding capabilities of simple physical touch. This book introduces a fresh way of looking at OSNs by bringing Lutheran theology to bear on what appears to be an increasingly common assumption built into these technologies: physical presence is an unnecessary component of community. It is my intent to recapture a theology of embodiment which runs deeply in the Christian, and more specifically, Lutheran, theological tradition. The value of this enterprise may exist on several levels. First, the research at hand affects more than just Christians; any person who uses OSNs to facilitate his/her social interactions experience some degree of alienation from broader society. Second, this project may alarm Christians in particular, as they continue to pursue godly living in the midst of a cultural phenomenon that is reshaping what it means to be human. Last, I believe that Christian leaders can use this project as a launching pad for discussions on the appropriateness of present and future technologies in their ministries.[9]

The trajectory of my argument is initiated by a general examination of embodied theology through the use of primarily Lutheran sources. The theology offered will encounter greater precision and cohesion in the writings of Dietrich Bonhoeffer, as his work presents a substantial case for the embodied, and therefore social, identity of the Christian. These texts will bring to light the essential characteristics of depth, local bondedness, and reciprocal trust, which I will, in turn, use to create a criterion by which one can theologically evaluate the variety of effects that come with OSN use.

9. Along similar lines, I will be primarily addressing the concept of *Christian* community. The text will elucidate theological concepts that give better support and definition to this particular form of life together. However, many of the issues I raise will have significant ramifications for a broader, secular understanding of community.

After arriving at some significant conclusions about technology's ability to create and deliver community with the above three markers, the text will conclude with a brief discussion on the future of the Church and outline areas for future research.

Therefore, the chief aim of this book is to explore the significance of physical presence as it relates to the community, present theological concerns that emerge from the uncritical use of online social networks which call into question such presence, and volunteer a distinctively Lutheran framework by which to evaluate emerging forms of digital community.

The Voices in the Fray

The variety of online social networks that are offered for public consumption mirrors the diversity of opinions touting their worth or lack thereof. It may be possible that OSNs offer people a way to experience authentic forms of community without the explicit need for bodily presence, and if this is so, such community experience should be praised as a way to forge lasting social bonds in a remarkably complex world. However, I propose that OSNs more often foster a version of social living that runs counter to the life offered by God in Scripture, a life framed in the preceding pages as an embodied theology. The connected life of the technophile may have the "appearance of authenticity, but in reality, [online social networks] may be a façade to mask the deep sense of loneliness experienced when one is sitting alone at the computer screen."[10] The Internet has become a contributing force to the individualism made front-and-center by modernity. OSNs, more specifically, attempt to mitigate the loneliness of rampant individualism yet often transform the person's desire for community into a quest for something quite different: *connectivity*. If this is the case, certain instances of OSN usage may: (1) offer only a limited portion of the benefits ascribed to traditional physical communities; (2) be rejected as a wholly antagonistic force that resists a godly understanding of human life and community; and/ or, (3) be subjected to a re-ordering, whereby the goods they contribute to society are placed in proper perspective within the whole of Christian life. A criterion for such decisions will conclude this book, but first, it is appropriate to consider the present research efforts directed toward OSNs, which will allow for a balanced view of their benefits and their potential for harm.

Due to the relatively recent phenomenon of digitally-based social technologies, two particular challenges emerge as one attempts to manage the plethora of voices entering the fray. First, several of the scholars

10. Yust, Hyde, and Ota, "Cyber Spirituality," 291–93.

referenced in this text did not live to see the rise of OSNs in their current manifestations. For example, Marshall McLuhan and Jacques Ellul wrote extensively on the relationship between technology and communication, yet neither had the opportunity to address the popularity of online social technologies and their effects. Based on my reading of their respective work, I will take on the challenge to connect their theories (many of which prove to be remarkably prophetic) to the OSN phenomenon. This is a challenging, but not impossible task. Second, the relative youth of the academic subject creates a certain measure of uncertainty when predicting which contemporary thinkers have staying power. The floodgates are opening, and it is my task to discern which writers are proving to be most influential.

To better understand the polarities of thought regarding OSNs and their cultural value(s), it may be helpful to divide the scholarship into two sets, each with two internal distinctions. The first set concerns methodology and scope. On one side, certain authors seek to understand OSNs from a wide angle. They note the broader sociological shifts that result from OSN usage, and to a lesser degree, attempt to discern the culture which brought about these technologies (and their users) into existence in the first place. The authors most concerned with these "macro" issues include futurists Ray Kurzweil and Peter Diamandis as well as sociologist Robert Putnam. While these writers observe the overarching cultural trends associated with technologies, even social technologies, their conclusions differ in substantial ways. Kurzweil and Diamandis envision a future in which social technologies are directed, whether by human or artificial intelligence, to solve some of the world's most enduring problems, from the lack of clean water in the Global South to efficient energy production in urban centers across America. Putnam, by contrast, sounds the alarm that the social fabric of the West is being transformed in ways that erode fundamental civic and social bonds. While he understands there is no going back, Putnam attempts to make plain the changing landscape of civic life, imploring citizens to pursue local, face-to-face relationships.

On the other side, many scholars take a closer look at what OSNs and/ or social technologies do directly to the person on a "micro" scale. Their interest is less concerned with demographic meta-patterns; rather, they attempt to discover changes and transformations at level of the individual. Marshall McLuhan, Albert Borgmann, and Sherry Turkle use this technique to varying degrees of depth. Their observations elucidate how a user thinks and operates in a world of increasing technological pressure. McLuhan and Borgmann focus on the theoretical effects of technology on the individual, while Turkle prefers qualitative data and practical observation, using device-specific examples. This bottom-up approach grounds the world of the OSN in the lives of real people, not disembodied and faceless populations.

The second commonly-used division of scholarship separates authors by their general affinity to online social technologies. While each scholar, no doubt, understands and respects both the benefit and potential harm of OSNs, it is fairly easy to ascertain whether or not they believe that the positives outstrip the negatives, or vice versa. The technophile camp includes those who see the unlimited potential for social and cultural gains, arguing essentially that open connectivity provides the world with its greatest commodity—information. Since the Internet has limited oversight, at least in the Western world, near instantaneous access to real-time events allow for quicker responses in the worlds of politics and medicine. Sociologist Clay Shirky best exemplifies this attitude, as he offers a variety of examples how the collective, when armed with social technologies, can use information to facilitate significant communal improvements.[11] Other scholars are less optimistic, if not downright critical of these cultural shifts. Nicholas Carr warns of physiological changes happening at the level of neurology; the brain's plasticity molds and shapes to facilitate Internet-style information retrieval at the expense of deep, penetrating thought.[12] Neil Postman and William Davidow express concern in our culture's ability to keep up with the radical pace of connectivity in the contemporary world.[13]

Sharp disagreement exists within the church as well. Technophile Leonard Sweet is convinced that OSNs such as Twitter and Facebook can operate as the primary catalyst for a Christian revival, going so far as to list "the five leading ways that Twitter has changed [his] life and made [him] a better follower of Jesus."[14] Pastor and speaker Jesse Rice appears to hold similar affinity for these technologies, noting the "spontaneous order" that has emerged from OSN use.[15] By contrast, theologian Shane Hipps uses McLuhan to resist the accommodationist perspective; his background in advertising informs his caution for all things driven by electronic media. If the media changes, faith itself changes.[16] The battle lines are forming, yet no clear victor has emerged.[17]

11. Shirky, *Cognitive Surplus.*

12. Carr, *The Shallows.*

13. See Postman, *Technopoly*, and Davidow, *OVERconnected.*

14. Sweet, *Viral*, 63.

15. Rice, *The Church of Facebook.*

16. Hipps, *Flickering Pixels.*

17. Chapter 4 will include analysis of each of these authors positions in greater depth.

Embodiment and Presence

If I am to argue that a theology of embodiment serves as a corrective to the misappropriation of social technologies, a definition of the central term, "embodiment," must first be offered. This task requires a good deal of precision and nuance. The body, as a topic of academic discourse, incorporates a vast range of uses and meanings with surprisingly weak inter-connective tissue. The prompting questions are somewhat obvious: when one refers to the somatic form, is the person referring to the physical structures (i.e., actual physiological processes, sensory accumulation and/or perceptions) that make up human experience, or is he/she referencing the social constructs that have grounding in physical structures, since all understanding and interpretation is ultimately mediated by said physicality (e.g., sexuality, gender, and/or race)? Or, something different entirely?[18] Since body talk is found across a wide swath of academic disciplines, the sheer amount of ways the body can be explored is often disorienting. Caroline Bynum goes so far as to suggest:

> "The body" is the wrong topic. It is no topic or, perhaps, almost all topics. As many contemporary theorists point out, we no longer think there is such a thing as the body—a kind of "flesh dress" we take up, or put off, or refurbish according to the latest style . . . no one in the humanities seems really to feel comfortable any longer with the idea of an essential "bodiliness." We tend to reject both a "bodiliness" that is in some way prior to the genderings, sexings, colorings, or handicappings particular persons are subject to and a body that is easily separable from the feelings, consciousness, and thoughts that occur in it.[19]

If Bynum's concerns are fully realized and the body becomes a topic with too much baggage and/or not enough precision, this present discussion risks utterly confusing the topic further with no helpful roadmap out of the wilderness. She observes that current scholarship is hesitant to separate the physical body (i.e., its matter) as an object of academic reflection apart from its social contexts and influences. Others build onto this assessment, noting the role of "perception, cognition, action, and nature" in the formation of

---

18. Defining the body in modern academia could, in itself, be the subject of future dissertations. The amount of writing on the body in all of its expressions and functions is beyond vast. I will use Bynum's article as a simple way to move forward through this haze, fully aware that a full deconstruction of embodied language is a project for another time and place.

19. Bynum, "The Fuss About the Body," 241–42.

the "acculturated body."[20] The present task shall be to present several possible frameworks with which to understand the current state of the topic, move toward a provisional definition of embodiment in light of the positive and negative aspects of these existing models, and then place the definition in conversation with the broader context of this book.

One possible way to understand embodiment language is to separate the body into purely physical versus social distinctions, then decide which category is more appropriate for the present project and proceed under that rubric. A view toward the body that is ostensibly tied directly to the body's material features could provide a narrow understanding of embodiment, particularly valuable for theology when actual physical presence has intrinsic value qua physical presence. The role of the body in Eve's creation, for example, existed as a "pre-socialized" yet meaningful instrument used for God's service; the theological fruit garnered by this creative act of God has significant meaning.[21] The opposing view of embodiment here would be considerably more expansive, speaking of the body in a way that highlights the particular social constructs that make up one's experience of the somatic in all of its cultural interactions. In such an instance, the body is given meaning external to its own direct physicality: the body as property (e.g., Hagar and Ishmael), the body as sacrifice (Abraham and Isaac), the body as temple (Matt 26, 1 Cor 3), and many others. The former approach (i.e., physical-only) might be used to examine the import of Jesus' physical death on the cross, for example, and the latter might shed light on Jesus as the *embodied* victim, a middle-aged rabbi falling prey to Jewish political maneuverings or Roman imperialism. With such a wide degree of difference between these applications, the below definition will attempt to draw positives from both of these approaches without overgeneralization.

An alternate observation is offered by Caroline Bynum, an approach that bifurcates recent body research into two general, but helpful, camps:

20. Weiss and Fern Haber, *Perspectives on Embodiment*, xiii. Full quote: "In the process of critiquing philosophy's own negligence regarding the body, the very expression "the body" has become problematized, and is increasingly supplanted by the term "embodiment." The move from one expression to another corresponds directly to a shift from viewing the body as a nongendered, prediscursive phenomenon that plays a central role in perception, cognition, action, and nature to a *way* of living or inhabiting the world through one's acculturated body."

21. "Pre-socialized" body talk is increasingly rare (or nonexistent) in the fields of social science precisely for the prevailing view that such a body cannot, in fact, exist. Bynum, Weiss, and Haber all allude to this turn. However, theology can and should speak to the reality of this pre-socialized state because God's act of creation in Genesis brings bodies into existence *ex nihilo,* and, therefore, they have a certain meaning and/ or status prior to any socializing or gendering. Perhaps theology is the only academic discipline remaining with the resources to approach embodiment in this way.

body-in-restraint and body-as-potentiality.[22] This separation is more complex yet significantly more useful as a guide to understanding past and present research on the matter. In the first category, Bynum references authors who speak of the body in the language of limitation, where bodily experience falls under some form of restriction, including those restrictions generated by societal mores and norms. "Sometimes *body, my body,* or *embodiedness* seems to refer to limit or placement, whether biological or social. That is, it refers to natural, physical structures (such as organ systems or chromosomes), to environment or locatedness, boundary or definition, or to role (such as gender, race, class) as constraint."[23] Theology can use this approach to great effect. Embodiment, in the body-as-restraint sense, opens a space for discussions on finitude, sin, death, and physicality. Less relevant themes might include the ongoing regeneration of the believer as an agent of restoration and hope in the world, or, perhaps, how the Christian channels the gifts of the Spirit into a life of love and passion.

The body-in-restraint view's circumscription has the advantage of narrowing the field of discussion to a manageable level; with these constraints in place, the subject retains a certain measure of topical integrity without the ambiguity that comes with too broad a term. A second benefit to this perspective is that it rightly points to the body as a *sensory* place; it acts as the spatial location of human experience and interpretation in the world. Ultimately, humans "do not have unmediated access to knowledge, but acquire information *through* their bodies."[24] The body is single-mindedly grounded in its particular physicality, and therefore, this view does not encourage an arbitrary reference point for expansive talk about human capabilities or culturally produced roles within society.[25]

Bynum recognizes an alternate strain of embodiment talk present in academic inquiry. This family of texts uses an understanding of body that rings with potentiality and action, of opportunity and choice, and in this sense, is the polar opposite of the aforementioned approach. This perspective refers "to lack of limits, that is, to desire, potentiality, fertility, or sensuality/sexuality, . . . or to person or identity as malleable representation or construct."[26] This highly sociological view of the body uses the human form

22. Bynum, "The Fuss About the Body," 243. This is my terminology for Bynum's general categories.

23. Ibid. This language is particularly characteristic of Dietrich Bonhoeffer, who often refers to physical embodiment as a limit.

24. Mellor and Shilling, *Re-forming the Body*, 5.

25. One may note interesting lines of affinity with the Enlightenment's push for empiricism, where truth is ascertained by the use of our senses only, apart from metaphysical claims or traditions.

26. Bynum, "The Fuss About the Body," 243.

in loose connections with the person's sense of Self; identity appears to be more grounded in ethereal abstractions. The freedom of the individual is the material principle at play here. The body-as-potentiality view's advantage reminds us that the body is an instrument of *action*, and as such, rejects any overly simplistic attempt to evaluate the body as a static, rather than dynamic, object of inquiry. This view provides an abundance of resources for the activities of sexuality, potentiality, and drive to seek out and fulfill one's capabilities. In theological discussions, such a view might tend to downplay sin's determinative effect on humanity or perhaps change the definition of sin itself. Sin is framed as ignorance or hindrance, not as total rebellion against God, since humanity would retain some capacity/freedom for choosing their own destiny.[27] Instead, the possibilities of the "new Adam" take center stage, where the old is shed and the life of the sanctified believer would offer new vistas for human flourishing in the present world.[28] Yet this view appears to endorse a perspective of human embodiment that could be experienced in virtual or theoretical worlds, even perhaps imaginary ones. The physical body may be a point-of-reference for such actions, but rarely, if ever, stands as meaningful in and of itself as a physical structure.

With the above considerations is mind, this project will put forth an understanding of embodiment that adequately, albeit not comprehensively, addresses the need for both physicality and action. By offering my distinctive approach, I am implicitly rejecting, or at least augmenting, the polarities of thought articulated in the two different forms above (physical-only v. social construct view, body-in-restraint v. body-as-potentiality). First, physical-only view is inadequate for the following reason: such language about the body risks undervaluing the influence the body has on its surroundings. By nature of its very existence, the body necessarily shapes its surrounding environment and vice versa. In other words, embodiment is reduced to individualist, essentialist language about one's own constitution and material processes without any sense of its impact on the environment, particularly the social environment.[29] I argue for the necessary cohesion of embodiment and community. The connection between the two is vital, not

27. This example would not necessarily suffice for Lutheran theologians. The Lutheran commitment to sin's effect upon free will is central to its understanding of God's redemptive act in Jesus. Humanity can only actively reject God's call; it cannot freely choose God.

28. Embodied theology used in this manner could propel a form of "prosperity gospel" or a therapeutic view of faith.

29. Such an approach is more suited for fields of biological science, although even in fields of physical science like physics or quantum mechanics, the role of the observer, formerly thought to be neutral, is now considered to be an active, operating agent in a system.

accidental. Two Christians could be studying in a library together at the same large table, but this does not necessarily lend support to the notion that this act is either embodied or communal. There must be something more to embodiment, at least in the theological sense of the term, than just the structure and bodily functions of a person in a particular space.

Second, focusing on social constructs at the expense of actual physical presence appear to be distracting, or at least de-centering. A definition that only speaks to these sociological accounts of gender or race seems, for the most part, woefully inadequate. Theologically speaking, conversations about race or gender in relationship to the somatic should not be ignored, as each locus brings insights to the common conversation of Christian life and doctrine. To restrict the conversation about the body to this dimension, however, cuts off a good portion of the corporeal dimension of human existence, particularly the theological value of creature language found in Scripture, the writings of the Reformers, and more recent Lutheran works. The social construct view also risks overexpansion of the term, "embodiment," realizing concerns that body talk has no consistent, common ground across all of its uses in academic discourse.

My provisional understanding of embodiment, therefore, takes these two concerns to heart. *My claim is that embodiment is the intimate experience of related creatureliness made most fully possible by physical immediacy or presence.* In this definition, the embodied presence of a person is a necessary, not accidental, characteristic of the embodied life, as the physical form is the location of our experience of the world around us.[30] My understanding of embodiment here leans more heavily into the former category in Bynum's division, where limit language is more fitting. As I continue to use this term, embodiment will first draw from language that directly affirms the physical as essential to our theological identity (both as an individual oriented toward God, and as social creatures oriented toward one another).[31] Second, there must be a modest expansion of the term, "presence," to account for intimacy or nearness of the person in his/her fullness. In other words, physical body creates room for depth and discourages pretension or inauthenticity. Only physical presence can open up such a space in its fullness.

Intimacy springs from a mutual trust; the term implies that presence is parleyed into some form of deeper relational growth, not necessarily all at once, but accumulated over consistent instances of vulnerability.[32] This

---

30. Even if we participate in virtual worlds, our real-life presence is the point of interpretation. In other words, we cannot interpret something wholly external from our bodies.

31. This important point will be more thoroughly explained in Bonhoeffer's social theology. See chapter 3.

32. "Presence" itself is a term that could be called into question here. This project

allows for a social dimension to embodiment without moving wholly into areas of inquiry that appear to lose sight of the physical body's significance—focusing more on the actual than the potential. This text, therefore, will attempt to draw out the features of intimacy, intentionality, and related creatureliness that distinguish an essentially spatial presence from a truly embodied experience.

Embodiment and History

Embodied theology is not, in itself, a novel idea. At various points in the Church's history the banner of physicality has been raised as a counterweight to various doctrinal missteps. Irenaeus of Lyons, in one early example, used a theology of embodiment to challenge the early gnostic heresies that proclaimed a form of salvation that largely included cognitive illumination. Rather than being saved from sin and for a future resurrected life as orthodox Christianity maintained, Gnosticism held that humanity required a deliverance from a more substantial foe: ignorance. In addition, gnostic eschatology by suggests that all people ultimately dissolve into some form of ultimate Oneness, a view that divests the individual of any particular value or substantive eternal meaning. This view of the individual contradicts the words of Paul to the Corinthian church where he posits that each believer has an individual integrity even as he/she participates in the broader Body of Christ. Therefore, the gnostic views on anthropology and eschatology were met with the full force of the early Church fathers. Irenaeus affirmed the body, contra Gnosticism, as a fully-engaged receptacle of life and grace:

> But if they are now alive, and if their whole body partakes of life,
> how can they venture the assertion that the flesh is not quali-
> fied to be a partaker of life, when they do confess that they have
> life at the present moment? It is just as if anybody were to take
> up a sponge full of water, or a torch on fire, and to declare that
> the sponge could not possibly partake of the water, or the torch
> of the fire. In this very manner do those men, by alleging that
> they are alive and bear life about in their members, contradict
> themselves afterwards, when they represent these members as
> not being capable of [receiving] life.[33]

---

will place presence in the context of a spectrum. Light levels of presence could include one's influence or effect, no matter how slight, within a certain context or population. A heavy level of presence necessitates one's physicality, as well as influence. I am proposing an embodied understanding of presence that includes more influence than just bodily nearness.

33. Irenaeus, *Against the Heresies*, 530.

Irenaeus's struggle with those who rejected the importance of the bodily resurrection of Jesus served as the template for the countless future battles drawn along such lines. At one end of the spectrum are those who recognize the somatic as a fundamental feature of Christian identity, and at the other end are those who would offer a compartmentalized view of the Self where the body is marginalized at the expense of the eternal soul or spirit. If the purpose of the body is purely utilitarian and used simply as a means to some transcendent or intellectual end, then the Self is divorced from any true connection to the rest of Creation. The body is reduced to a simple vessel or receptacle for the true, authentic Self seated in the spirit or intellect. On the other hand, if the pendulum swings too far in the other direction and the body is overvalued, the physical form becomes the locus of attention at the expense of the soul and new threats emerge. The spirit, in this case, recedes into the background and human flourishing is defined in vague notions of "health."[34]

Body talk in the early church, as a subject of theological investigation, primarily explored the division of body and soul. I suggest that this is simply a reasonable reaction of the early church to the theological challenges of the day, particularly in the first two centuries as a consensus for orthodox Christian doctrine was developing. In this body-soul tension, what primarily appears to be at stake is the nature of Christian eschatology. Briefly, if the body and soul are thoroughly entwined without clear distinction, there is no philosophical basis for believing that the soul can survive physiological death, and therefore, Christian eschatology is forced to abandon a position of an intermediary state between death and the coming of Christ. On the other hand, if the soul can exist beyond the point of bodily death, the case could be made that the body is essentially rendered meaningless and the final resurrection of the dead offers no particular hope in the here and now. What would motivate Christians to hope for a return to physical life if they were already in the presence of God in some spiritual reality (i.e., heaven)? I will explore the import of this discussion on Christian eschatology in greater detail in Chapters Two and Three.

My project, by contrast, will redraw the lines of the body, not along the old territorial borders of monism and dualism but instead to illustrate the appropriate tension between the individual and the community. This

---

34. Such over-exaltation of the body has led to some objectionable theological positions. Forms of libertinism in early Christianity were characterized by overindulgence in all manners of human appetites. For example, both Irenaeus of Lyons and Clement of Alexandria mention the licentiousness of an early second century gnostic sect, the Carpocratians. The contemporary trend to preach a "health and wealth" gospel might also serve as cautionary example.

is not to say that the aforementioned historical debate is dead or not par-ticularly valuable; this is neither factual nor accurate.[35] Rather, the body's relationship with the community appears to satisfy better the ways in which physical presence impacts the surrounding social environment. The book will provide a venue by which one can evaluate the import of his/her body with a certain sensitivity to how the body functions in this context. With this tension in place, the nature of Christian identity is properly situated in its orientation to the neighbor.

In the halls of modern academia, scholars continue to probe what it means to be human, and these efforts inevitably include a substantial amount of research on the nature of humanity's physicality and how it as-sists the construction of human identity. While the body's value may seem self-evident from a strictly physiological perspective, it is important to speak precisely about its significance beyond the above sociological categories; the conversation must turn to the body's theological value. The worth of the community is lost in the contemporary obsession to find an adequate ex-pression of identity found in the body of the individual. Hence, a theological understanding of the body opens a space for a more holistic understanding of Self, where worth and identity can be experienced in the intentional, pur-poseful relationships native to Christian communities.

Lutheran Embodied Theology

A properly constructed theology of embodiment most clearly demonstrates God's design for his creatures, where the fullness of their identity is found in the embodied partnership of the individual and broader community. The question at the core of this exploration is: How does one properly under-stand the somatic life in the greater context of Christian identity?

I propose that Christian embodied theology is buttressed by the three central themes of common creatureliness, the sacraments, and eschatology. While certainly not the only tools by which an embodied theology could be manufactured, I have selected these categories in order to construct a measured approach to thinking about the individual-community dynamic through the lens of physicality. When received together, these features make for a framework of theology that adequately respects the physical body as an integral part of human identity without ignoring its relationship to

35. The debate between monism and body-soul dualism, while less frequent, still rages on today, the consequences of which will have some impact on my discussion of eschatology in Chapters 2 and 3. For a comprehensive look at the subtleties and chal-lenges of the body-soul dynamic, see Cooper, *Body, Soul and Life Everlasting*.

neighbor. Later in my project, I will draw out a constitutive characteristic embedded in each of these three themes to address more adequately the issues of isolation and self-centeredness. This characteristic may be referred to as the communal aspect. For now, however, let us summarize what each component brings to the whole of embodied theology, and why together they are particularly significant.

Creatureliness refers to the origins (as well as ongoing ontological status) of human existence. This theme serves as a valuable counterpoint to two of the more significant narratives that contemporary humanism has to offer. On one end of a spectrum, the modern scientific and philosophical paradigms push for an atheistic evolutionary worldview particularly concerned with beginnings—the beginning of the cosmos (Big Bang Theory) and the beginning of life (evolutionary biology). By contrast, Christians confess that humans are creatures of the Creator. Designed, not evolved. Purposed, not accidental. From the other end of the spectrum, futurists praise the coming of the post-human age where humanity can transcend their own bodies and exist eternally as consciousness in the "global cloud." The biblical trajectory of the Christian life, however, ends with no such technology-induced elevation. Humanity cannot drive forward the machinations of history external to the ongoing provision of the Almighty, and, like the tragedy at Babel, humanity will be confronted with the reality of their own limitations. Transhumanism and evolutionary biology are merely two sides of the same coin; one assumes the natural (that is, through non-theistic biological processes) development of all things, the other uses technology to drive forward the next step of human development sans God's sustaining hand. Understanding the human as embodied creature allows for an understanding of the body that properly respects its workmanship and its inherent limitations.

Second, the *sacramental* nature of embodied theology is significant. This text seeks to draw out the specific contributions of Baptism and Holy Communion, for they exist as bulwarks against dualist forms of theology. These two means of grace are presented to the believer through the material: bread, wine, water. At its core, the sacraments proclaim a bold counterpoint to a faith that oftentimes slips into "thinking the right things about God," or, at the other end of the spectrum, faith that is articulated as an immediate experience of God grounded in emotionalism. God offers himself through Baptism and Holy Communion, a radical partaking of the divine-human relationship through material means. In addition, participation in the sacraments draws out the importance of sensory experience, a significant feature of the embodied life. Baptism and Communion allows the believer to "taste and see that the LORD is good" (Ps 34:8).

Third, embodied theology looks toward its ultimate expression in the Last Days, and, therefore, it should be considered highly *eschatological*. While this term can be notoriously abundant in its range of definitions, the following work will limit the use of eschatology to the creedal formulation, "I believe in the resurrection of the dead." Just as Jesus resurrected bodily from the grave on Easter as the firstfruits, so Christians receive God's affirmation of bodily existence in the reception of their new physicality in eternity. Any eschatology that reduces Christian hope to some vague spiritual awakening misses the scriptural claim of a distinctly embodied resurrection and new creation. The body is central to the Church's teachings on death, the afterlife, and what happens between the two.[36]

The resurrection of the dead in the eschaton plays a critical role in how Christians live presently, for this theology explicitly affirms God's ongoing purpose for the created order. If the Church lives solely for another spiritual existence, heaven, without participating in the ongoing restoration of this present material world, a life of wanton waste (on one side) or willful disrepair (on the other) inevitably emerge. N. T. Wright's work reminds us that such a position lacks early Christian support. The Pauline epistles, he argues, call for a new creation grounded in the central belief that God's present (and coming) kingdom is bound to the resurrection of the dead.[37]

These three characteristics have clear moments of overlapping, as they all work in concert to demonstrate God's desire for his children to have a rich and holistic understanding of their own bodies as an imperfect mirror of his relational life within the Trinity.[38]

Dietrich Bonhoeffer and the Body

To give detail and expansion to these three themes, the embodied, community-oriented theology of Dietrich Bonhoeffer works as a binding agent

36. Eschatology, for both Lutheran and Bonhoefferian theology, is not isolated to discussions on death and the afterlife. They both stress the eschatological nature of the Christian in his/her daily life; eschatology includes the ongoing cosmic struggle between God and his faithful versus Satan and his forces of evil *in the here-and-now*. This insight may be due to the historical contexts of Luther and Bonhoeffer, respectively, as each theologian witnessed socio-political threats on genuine Christianity as well as threats to their own well-being. This is a valuable insight, yet somewhat tangential to eschatology's relationship to physical embodiment. The bulk of my efforts in eschatology, therefore, will focus on the coming hope of the bodily resurrection of the dead.

37. Wright, *Surprised by Hope*, 18.

38. It is also important to remember that each of these themes has its own complex history apart from any inclusion into embodied theology, and, therefore, I will limit my discussion of these topics to their direct application to my central thesis.

for the embodied life of the individual and corporate life of the Church. Bonhoeffer grounds the embodied life in Christian community to a higher degree than his Reformation-era forebears and provides nuance to the individual's relationship with his/her neighbor. His theology reminds us of the intimacy of shared creatureliness, yet strongly advances the physical immediacy that is necessary for embodied communities to thrive.

Much of Bonhoeffer's conception of the body falls within a broader discussion of the natural life in his masterwork, *Ethics*. The natural life is not to be confused with the created life, that is, the pre-Fall condition of man in which he has unmediated access to God. Rather, the natural life is that which follows—a life of relative freedom experienced in the dignity given to it by Christ. "The natural is that form of life preserved by God for the fallen world that is directed toward justification, salvation, and renewal through Christ."[39] The human body exists within this natural life. It is impossible to separate an individual from his/her body, for it is only in this body that a person has ever experienced earthly life. For Bonhoeffer, the body exists as a means to an end *and* an end unto itself. It can be means to an end when it serves some higher function for the advancement, or preservation, of the broader community. A soldier, for instance, may use his body to absorb the blast of a hand grenade, thus saving his fellow soldiers from grave harm. However, Bonhoeffer would strongly object to any claim that the body exists *only* as a means. The physical life serves as an end in itself. Such an understanding of the body opens a space for Christians to experience the free activity without the constraints of a nobler *telos*.

In *Ethics*, Bonhoeffer lays out his understanding of the human body in both positive and negative terms. Positively speaking, the body "intrinsically bears the right to its preservation."[40] God gives humanity particular physicality, preserves it throughout his existence, and redeems it in Christ; therefore, Bonhoeffer affirms all efforts to protect the body over-and-against the specific abuses of "intentional injury, violation, and killing."[41] Since his theology was situated amidst the backdrop of German National Socialism, this statement provides us with a clear example of Bonhoeffer's bold witness in a world gone mad.[42]

In addition to protection, the body serves as a locus for Christian joy and fulfillment. "If the body is an end in itself, then there is a right to bodily

39. Bonhoeffer, *Ethics*, 174.

40. Ibid., 185.

41. Ibid., 186.

42. Bonhoeffer witnessed first-hand the Nazi abuses of World War II Germany. The well-documented crimes against the Jewish nation, as well as the Nazi cruelty against dissenters, made Bonhoeffer's comments particularly courageous.

joys, without subordinating them to a further, higher purpose."[43] Such joy is found in the simple pleasures of breaking bread together, sexuality (beyond the utilitarian function of procreation), and play. "Perhaps the clearest evidence that bodily life is meant for joy lies in the way that the body, even when it is rightly made to serve a necessary end with vigorous effort, finds joy in such service."[44] The body's purpose expresses God's desire that humanity should find life beyond the rigid patterns of work, eat, and sleep.

Negatively speaking, Bonhoeffer understood the potential harm that could be done to the body. If the body is subservient to the ego and its drive for power, as Bonhoeffer suggests, it could be made to exert its power over another person to devastating effect. One obvious example of such domination would be rape, for it causes the body to "fall under the unbounded power of another person."[45] This may be an example of sin *par excellence* in Bonhoeffer's theology, as it demonstrates the assertion of one will over another through a radical show of power—bodily power, in this case. The right of a person to withhold their own being, including their own sexuality, defies the natural life in its status as gift. Bonhoeffer includes enslavement and torture as other examples of domination that are expressed in corporeal terms, a place "where the bodily strength of one person becomes the unlimited property of another."[46] Again, one can recognize the unmistakable communal component to Bonhoeffer's thought; the body does not, and cannot, exist in isolation to society. Whether it is used for positive or negative ends, the social impact of natural, embodied living exists necessarily and in force.

The three pillars of embodied theology find a comfortable home in Bonhoeffer's theology. In the creaturely aspect of human life, Bonhoeffer uses limit language to express the reality of humanity's standing before God. This is made manifest in two distinct ways. First, Bonhoeffer describes the God-human relationship as a circle, where the appropriate locations of the characters are: God at the center and humanity at the margins, oriented toward God. Only God can fulfill the role of God, and therefore, all creaturely actions that defy God's will concordantly move God from his position at the center. Humanity becomes utterly alone and is *sicut deus*. The embodied life, by contrast, takes joy in receiving God's ongoing provision and recognizes that only the death and resurrection of Christ can free it from this inward, solitary posture. Second, Bonhoeffer describes creatureliness as an experience of limitation, not in a pejorative sense, but as an expression of

43. Ibid.
44. Ibid., 188.
45. Ibid., 214.
46. Ibid., 215.

the solidarity all creatures experience before their God. "The other person is the limit placed upon me by God. I love this limit and I shall not transgress it because of my love. This means nothing except that two, who remain *two* as creatures of God, become *one* body, i.e. belong to one another in love."[47] Embodied living is embodied love. Thus, Bonhoeffer binds the shared creatureliness aspect of our above definition with the purposeful, intimate features that love naturally demonstrates. The relationship of limited, living creatures serves as the foundation for the human experience, not as some sort of vague humanitarian benevolence, but as the embodiment of Christ's love from God to his creatures.

Sacramental theology demonstrates God commitment to the created order. Bonhoeffer understands this fact in two ways. First, he reminds the Christian that God operates through the earthy means of water, bread, and wine to gift humanity with his grace. He chooses the material as the means, not some transcendent experience divorced from the physical world. The presence of the elements combined with Christ's true bodily presence within them coincides with the embodied defining attribute of physical immediacy. Second, Bonhoeffer understands the sacraments as a binding experience. Christians are bound to Christ's death and resurrection in baptism; Christ's redemptive act serves as God's utterly perfect and final Yes to humanity. Sacramental participation unites creature and Creator, while at the same time, bonds creature to creature in the horizontal realm.

Finally, Bonhoeffer views Christian eschatology as the fulfillment of all things. The Last Day, however, is not a solely individual experience whereby an individual waits in lonely dread for the judgment of God. His emphasis always draws the Christian back to the corporate nature of eschatology. The Church awaits her consummation and the individual is only understood within this matrix. In the present time, the body of Christ waits in expectation by participating in the ongoing restoration of the present world, acting as responsible bearers of the gospel.

In chapter 3, Bonhoeffer's treatment of creaturely, sacramental, and eschatological theologies will be drawn out in full and demonstrate his commitment to an embodied theology.

The Three Markers of Embodied Community

Dietrich Bonhoeffer's theology provides us with a necessary link between the life of the embodied individual and that embodied individual's role within the broader community. If God intended for humanity to experience

47. Bonhoeffer, *Creation and Fall*, 66.

life in corporeal form and that corporeality exists in its fullest sense when in community, then Christian life together finds wonderful expression in local parishes. One question remains unanswered, however: What characteristics are *constitutive* to the experience of Christian community? In other words, are there significant markers that can be located in the Christian community, as suggested by the above Bonhoefferian framework? If so, then the absence of such markers will suggest that some current forms of social connectivity may actually undercut authentic community rather than promote it. Derived from Bonhoeffer's theology, I would offer that authentic community exhibits three essential characteristics: depth, local bondedness, and reciprocated trust.[48] Without these features, the potential for community devolves into a simple band of associations that has minimal lasting impact on a person's sense of identity, both as an individual oriented toward God and as a person in relationship with fellow creatures.

Depth

Every expression of community (sacred or secular) requires a certain level of depth. In the world of sociology, this is often referred to as the presence of "strong ties." Strong ties form when high levels of accountability and personal investment are present in interpersonal relationships, providing societies with valuable social capital. Putnam and Feldstein argue that the formation of social capital—a necessary component of any community—not only requires significant time and effort but also comes about by "extensive and time-consuming face-to-face conversation between two individuals or among small groups of people."[49] The depth of any social interaction is a function of each party's willingness to engage in the work of sustained thought and emotional investment toward a common goal in order that both parties may, in some way, benefit from the effort. No short cuts allow social capital to be manufactured instantaneously.

Bonhoeffer understood the necessity of depth in at least two distinct ways. First, he understood that the sins of the individual were simultaneously a communal problem. The fundamental concern with sin is more than a guilty conscience before God; it is the power of the individual turned against his/her neighbor as domination. The drive for power over another person necessarily destroys community; it renders a more complex hamartiology

---

48. These characteristics are far from exhaustive, but they do coalesce several key terms and concepts into broader categories that are useful. Depth, local bondedness, and reciprocal trust are three categories that I find particularly important.

49. Putnam and Feldstein, *Better Together*, 9.

than one that is overwhelmingly located in the individual. Therefore, Christian confession becomes an opportunity to meet the depths of social evil, not just forms of personal evil, with the offer of Jesus' grace. Second, it follows that confession and absolution stood at the center of the Christian community's experience of grace. Bonhoeffer believed that this was most fully experienced on a person-to-person level. The accountability of such a relationship limits the ways in which a Christian brother or sister could be self-deceptive in their everyday life of sin. If person-to-person confession is an encouraged practice of the local church community, then depth is achieved by very nature of the confession enterprise. This act is the intimate experience of shared creatureliness *par excellence*. Confession, by definition, involves personal searching and disclosures that are normally hidden from sight. A self-reflective venture into one's shortcomings is a journey into the depths of what it means to be a repentant Christian.

Local Bondedness

Contemporary scholarship suggests that embodied communities experience greater degrees of commitment and civic participation precisely because they are not spread across vast distances. Namely, "trust relationships and resilient communities generally form through *local personal contact* [emphasis added]."[50] Individuals within communities express their vast web of relationships mostly with people that they come into regular contact with—with "people that they know." This fact serves as a regulator of certain behaviors. For example, people are less likely to be harsh or abrupt in a phone conversation with their banker, if they know that they might run into each other at the grocery store later in the day. Local bondedness assures the citizens of any community that their interests must be shared—they all have "skin in the game"—in order for the community to thrive.

From the birth of Christianity, Christ-followers have claimed a particular unity with one another, not just in their general partnership as Christians but also in their specific associations at the local, congregational level. Paul writes in Ephesians 4, "Make every effort to keep the unity of the Spirit through the bond of peace. There is one body and one Spirit—just as you were called to one hope when you were called—one Lord, one faith, one baptism; one God and Father of all, who is over all and through all and in all" (Eph 4:3–5). For Bonhoeffer, this unity is an ontological reality. A Christian does not choose a church as his/her own; rather, the Church is a reality created by God in which his children necessarily participate.

50. Ibid.

This participation is made concrete especially, but not exclusively, in the local parishes where God's word reaches particular communities of people. Here, the binding "glue" is much more than the shared interests of those included. The bonding of the local community, as articulated by Bonhoeffer, is grounded in Jesus Christ:

> We belong to one another only through and in Jesus Christ. What does this mean? It means, first, *that a Christian needs others* because of Jesus Christ. It means, second, *that a Christian comes to others* [emphasis added] only through Jesus Christ. It means, third, that in Jesus Christ we have been chosen from eternity, accepted in time, and united for eternity.[51]

This bond of unity is expressed in concrete Christian communities: Christians meet each other as mutual bearers of their God-given limitation and as the proclaimers of God's transformative grace. Bonhoeffer also picks up the importance of locality. While it may be easy to create some forms of social bonding across vast distances (e.g., Paul's letter of friendship to the Philippians),[52] community flourishes when it experiences life *together*.

Reciprocated Trust

Trustworthiness is built over repeated engagements that result in the affirmation of integrity (on all sides). It allows, even encourages, a certain level of vulnerability and attentiveness in one-on-one friendships. As participants in such a relationship protect private disclosures from those outside of the defined community, the measure of trust increases and friendship bonds are necessarily strengthened. Yet significant levels of trust are difficult to create outside of a face-to-face relationship. Robert Putnam and Lewis Feldstein enumerate the value of personal contact as it relates to trust-building:

> Written messages lack the physical expressions and gestures that are such an important part of face-to-face conversation, clarifying and deepening the meanings of the words while adding their own unspoken meaning and providing an instantaneous response to what is being said. That combination of spoken language and body language helps us understand the tone and

51. Bonhoeffer, *Life Together*, 21.

52. Paul uses friendship language throughout his letter to the Philippians. Attesting to the social bonding that takes place in this particular letter, L. T. Johnson remarks, "Friendship was a form of equality. So close was the spiritual unity between friends that a friend was 'another self.' Friends were one soul, sharing a common frame of mind." Johnson, *The Writings of the New Testament*, 372.

substance of what is being communicated and also helps us judge whether we should trust the person we are speaking to, and to what degree. In face-to-face conversation, we also get signals we use to judge *our* contributions: whether we are puzzling people or making them angry, boring them or fascinating them.[53]

If words (sans body gestures) are the only thing exchanged in a communication event, discussions become more "fragile," prone to misunderstandings, include extreme or abusive language, and demonstrate a particular quickness to show judgment. To be in a trustworthy community, then, is to rely heavily on the physical interpersonal contact that promotes attentiveness to all of the communication techniques that humans regularly use.

Lutheran theology speaks to the importance of trust as a precondition to communal life together. Confessionally speaking, participants in Christian community encourage one another in the "mutual conversation and consolation of the brethren" (SA III.IV). This mutual bearing of burdens is most fully experienced when two or more are gathered together physically. If sin is the act of domination perpetrated from one person upon another, no reciprocal trust can emerge and human relationships erode into hierarchical power struggles. Conversely, a community of disciples who are fully present with one another in their mutual joy and sorrow expresses God's design for community and is captured in Bonhoeffer's theology. Pastoral theology is heavily based on this theological understanding of presence; the physical immediacy of direct consolation assures the neighbor of God's immanence: through conversation and consolation, by partaking in sacraments, and by his word.

Must these three characteristics of community always manifest themselves in an embodied sense? In short, they do not. This book is not arguing that a certain measure of relational depth cannot be achieved in a disembodied way (i.e., through some form of mediation). However, community is most *fully* realized in both depth and authenticity when it is experienced in the purposeful presence of one another. The common bond between friends cannot reach its greatest potential in situations that do not require concrete presence. Similarly, the reciprocal trustworthiness found in an embodied relationship far exceeds that of a relationship requiring multiple levels of mediation, as language, the primary mode of communication, requires both verbal and nonverbal cues. What is true for individuals, in this case, holds true for the broader community. Experiencing God's design for community requires a certain measure of physical presence, for it is here where some

53. Putnam and Feldstein, *Better Together*, 234.

of God's deepest and most significant gifts are received: Baptism, Communion, and personal confession. Therefore, the above conclusions may be used to test the present culture and its obsession with connectivity, where vast numbers of online social platforms seek to connect the world like never before. What, then, happens to the fuller Christian community if it uncritically uses OSNs as solutions to any sociological need, in spite of its tendency to minimize physical embodiment?[54]

The Rise of Online Social Networks

The aforementioned markers provide us with the resources to evaluate claim of community made by many online social networks, and while the features are not deal breakers (i.e., their absence necessitates full rejection of the technologies or their social goods), they provide the foundation for the criteria which will be offered in the penultimate chapter of the text. The constitutive markers, if found embedded in online social network use, will provide the Christian with confidence that social technologies offer true and restorative forms of community. I argue, however, that these features are largely absent and in some ways directly contradict Bonhoeffer's understanding of Christian community.

To best understand the OSN phenomenon, it is best to determine what OSNs actually *do* to the human being. For the purposes of this work, I have limited the exploration to three fields of inquiry: philosophy, physiology, and sociology. For the latter two fields, I will present some relevant effects

---

54. The terms, "community" and "connectivity," while complementary in most instances, are not to be conflated. Connectivity may be described as the ability to establish contact with another person—contact which has no predetermined form. In other words, connectivity exists whether two people experience it through the medium of spoken language, telephone, computer, sign language, or any other innovation. It simply sets the stage for communication by providing the forum in which to do so. Community, on the other hand, parlays the connectivity just mentioned into the building, strengthening, and ongoing maintenance of relationships. Community forges bonds amidst people who are brought in contact by connectivity. In addition, community necessarily assumes a certain amount of social interaction that connectivity, by definition, does not. For example, an individual experiences connectivity by having a Facebook account; they have the option of reaching out to any number of friends and acquaintances. The option of furthering relationships with these people is available because connectivity exists. Connectivity is the *ability* to reach out and establish meaningful communication, nothing more. Community is the *actual* forging of authentic relationships within a locale. Essentially, the presence of connectivity does not logically necessitate the growth or emergence of any community. These terms can be confused for one another, particularly when they are used in reference to the nature of online forms of sociality.

that may prove useful in our evaluation of OSNs. First, I will lay out some initial philosophical concerns raised by scholars of technology to shed some light on the understanding of these networks. Working forward from Marshall McLuhan's seminal text, *Understanding Media*, it will become apparent that OSNs are not simply a "neutral tool" in the building or decaying of societal connective tissue.[55]

Second, since a person cannot engage the digital terrain without their own physical bodies present (e.g., real fingers are needed to insert keystrokes), it is appropriate to ask what physiological effects such networks have on the body. Recent research in the field of neuroscience suggests that digital technologies, such as OSNs (though not limited to them), are remapping the neural pathways in human brains to be more efficient at collecting disjointed pieces of information at the expense of sustained concentration. In turn, other areas of the brain may experience some decay as long, sustained spells of concentration are less necessary.

Third, using an online social network, by definition, is an explicitly *social* enterprise. Therefore, an explanation of the various ways OSNs impact social life is both necessary and illuminating. Sociologist Sherry Turkle leads the way in this area of research; her work on social media reflects in depth on the issues of isolation, sexuality, anxiety, and social cohesion.[56] Other scholars contribute to the conversation by pointing toward the collapsing distinction of public and private acts, as the virtual identity blends in and becomes indistinguishable from the individual's physical self.

When taken together, these fields of inquiry will provide us with a helpful, albeit not comprehensive, look at OSNs that can then be placed against the features of an embodied theology and the crucial element of community that runs through its veins. The benefits of online social networks are numerous and important to recognize; however, this project will primarily attempt to draw out the potentially harmful results of OSN use and how these results threaten the depth, local bondedness, and reciprocal trust crucial to the flourishing of Christian life together. It is my hope that the criteria I offer will elucidate the Christian discernment necessary to make decisions about these technologies, both now and into the future.

The Outcome(s) Anticipated

The rise of the online social network has forced the Church into a difficult position. On one end of the spectrum, technology apologists attempt to

55. McLuhan, *Understanding Media*.
56. Turkle, *Alone Together*.

calm our nerves by assuring us that technology is: a) here to stay; b) an innovation that may help a church's efforts to stay connected to its members; and/or c) an avenue by which a new generation may hear the gospel "in their own tongue." At the other end of the spectrum, contemporary neo-Luddites shout, "The sky is falling!" They bemoan the way in which an online social network physically alienates people from their neighbors. Human flourishing, they argue, requires personal investment that the digital world cannot provide. Perhaps what is required is an attentive ear to both sides. If criteria could be offered to adjudicate the worth of OSNs, equally accessible to individuals and broader communities (e.g., parishes), the Body of Christ can use these technologies in good conscience for the good of the kingdom yet avoid the severe pitfalls of a belief system that minimizes physicality.

2

THE CASE FOR AN EMBODIED THEOLOGY

ONE POPULAR THEOLOGICAL THOUGHT exercise poses the following question: Does a person with a disability keep their particular disability in heaven? The question stimulates interesting responses because of what is at stake. To answer the question in the affirmative seems to imply that disabilities are not disabilities at all; they are just realities bound up in the flesh just as a freckle or birth mark would be. This answer appears to be inconsistent with the Pauline view of the new creation, where there would be no more sickness or pain and bodies "sown in weakness" are "raised in power" (1 Cor 15:43). Should society cast disability as sickness, or even weakness? If one suggests that such realities are banished in heaven, however, in favor of a resurrection to a "perfected" state, equally problematic conclusions emerge. To say that a person with disabilities somehow "becomes whole" again through death and resurrection is to acknowledge that disabilities somehow create a fractured or incomplete person and that God's purposes for human identity and flourishing in this present life are not to be found in the person's physicality. This suggests that God only cares about the spiritual portion of humanity, causing some significant mixed messages with regards to God's role as Creator.[1] The inherent dignity of God's creation, and perhaps even his will, is thus called into question. This experiment reveals a simple truth about our earthly existence: our identity is radically bound up in our bod-

---

1. For example, if physicality contributes nothing to the human identity or to the God-human relationship, why bestow it to humanity in the first place? God's acts in Genesis affirm his will to create the physical world as something good. The bodily element of humanity, even in its postlapsarian condition, appears to be a part of God's design for creation.

ies. The perception of our bodies, disabled or otherwise, in relation to our identities drives our understanding of the world and our place within it.[2]

The physical body is a ubiquitous topic in the fields of biology and sociology, but how do we speak of the body *theologically*? What follows is a three-part examination of human embodiment located in the themes of creatureliness, sacramental, and eschatological theology. While the sources consulted in this chapter will be varied, I will rely heavily on the work of Martin Luther himself. His writings on all three themes are extensive, and focusing the lion's share of attention on his work allows us to scrutinize an embodied theology that is cut from whole cloth. With Luther's theology as the principle guide, the earlier definition of embodiment will find deep resonance in the above themes and point us toward a view of the Christian which is both necessarily physical and highly communal.

The First Component: Creatureliness

With the dirt of the ground, God formed the flesh and bones of Adam, connecting God's creative action with elements of the very earth. Hans Walter Wolff describes man's physical being as "completely and utterly earthly."[3] The double creation narrative in Genesis 1–2 serves as the foundation for the First Article of the Apostles' Creed, where believers confess a fundamental truth about God's nature: He is the Creator. Rather than augmenting animal material to create a new being in Adam, God chooses the inanimate dirt, making that which what was lifeless now full of God's *nephesh*.[4] Adam and Eve have a dual citizenship, so to speak. They exist as part of the created order and thus share a particular kinship with other living beings, yet in some important ways, remain separate from the world of animals.[5] Genesis, in particular, emphasizes "man and woman's solidarity with the natural

---

2. As with all thought experiments, they often highlight one particular facet of an issue and obfuscate others. I heard this particular thought experiment posed to the audience by Stanley Hauerwas at Fontbonne University in 2011. He offered several potential responses and their respective implications. I am not suggesting that a person with a disability requires said disability for their identity's sake and therefore should, in godly humility, accept their affliction silently. Part of Jesus' earthly calling was to heal the sick and restore sight to the blind; it seems reasonable to assume that such healing is part of God's vision for a new creation. The experiment, however, highlights how closely people associate physicality with the concepts of identity and wholeness.

3. Wolff, *Anthropology*, 93.

4. Dyrness, *Old Testament Theology*, 79–96.

5. Ibid., 79.

order, which they exhibit in their bodily existence."[6] Dietrich Bonhoeffer speaks of the human-animal relationship in familial language, offering that animals are our "brothers."[7] Luther subtly acknowledges this kinship in his Small Catechism when he declares that God has "created me together with all creatures" (SC II, 2).

Yet, by contrast, the human transcendence of the animal order opens the space for God's unique relationship and intent for humanity. They are placed in a position of dominion over creation to cultivate and to tame, all the while bearing the image of God in all that they do (Gen 1:26–27). Humanity's lofty relational status with God is demonstrated initially "in that no other created being is deemed worthy of the divine address to such an extent as man."[8] This tension is the proper starting point for talk of humanity's creatureliness, even as it points us to the broader affirmation of physical embodiment.

Intimately tied to God's identity as Creator is the status of what he creates. In other words, if God actively and intimately creates life with his own hands,[9] then Adam was first understood *as creature*, the resulting workmanship. Creatureliness runs to the very core of what it means to be embodied. Biblical anthropology rejects any and all attempts to make humanity the result of a cosmic accident or the latest result in an evolutionary chain. The Psalmist praises God because humanity is "fearfully and wonderfully made." The intentional, loving action of being "knit together" defies any passive explanation for existence (Ps 139:13–14).

Two observations need to be made at this point. First, nowhere in the earliest two chapters of Genesis is there a direct connection between created physicality and sin. The Hebrew word most commonly translated as "flesh" (*basar*) most often refers to a "characteristic of bodily existence."[10] The flesh might be recognized as "weak and lacking in strength," but this designation is only used to underscore: (1) humanity's need for ongoing sustenance, evidenced by physical hunger and/or soreness, and (2) God's almighty power juxtaposed to the human condition.[11] The "weakness" is

6. Ibid.

7. Bonhoeffer, *Creation and Fall*, 64.

8. Wolff, *Anthropology*, 95.

9. I have used an anthropomorphic phrase here, to be sure. It is helpful, however, to consider the psalmist words in Psalm 8. "When I consider your heavens, the *work of your fingers*, the moon and the stars, which you have set in place . . ." Also, in verse 6, "You made him ruler over the *works of your hands* . . ." My inclusion of this phrase, then, should not be considered a rhetorical device by which to promote an unbiblical view of divine embodiment.

10. Dyrness, *Old Testament Theology*, 87.

11. Ibid.

not to be interpreted as moral frailty or any particular susceptibility to evil action. This Hebrew understanding of the body-as-flesh dynamic stands in direct contrast to many of the theological uses of the word "flesh," particularly when a use is derived from its Greek counterpart in the New Testament (*sarx*).[12] The platonic understanding of "person" considered the body a type of fleshy housing to the immortal soul, opening the door for a view of the body that is somehow lesser than, or disconnected from, an individual's most authentic mode-of-being. This is Platonic dualism in its essence. The Hebrew passage, taken in its proper context, has none of these inclinations. In fact, the author of Genesis 1–2 appears to go out of his way to stress both the materiality of the created world and its inherent goodness. This necessarily includes the creation of the first man and woman. The final analysis is that "the flesh is the physical form of living, never opposed to the self, but rather the proper medium of spiritual and personal life."[13]

Second, an examination of the biblical text clearly reveals a prototype of early community as a function of humanity's creatureliness. Adam and Eve were borne into relationship. God's creation of humanity as "male and female" (Gen 1:27) underscores the complementarity of human life from the foundation of the cosmos. "It is clear that humanity is created as male and female such that each is incomplete without the other and both stand on an equal footing before God."[14] Their relationship includes sexual complementarity bound in monogamy (1:28, 2:24) and sets the stage for child-bearing under the most fundamental social relationship of human life: marriage. God inscribes community into creatureliness, and thus provides a window into the inner workings of the Trinitarian relationship as the ideal form of community.

Luther and the Creative God

The Lutheran understanding of an individual's identity as creature has often taken a back seat to more pressing Christological concerns, particularly during the Reformation, when confessions were being constructed to unify major areas of northern Europe. Many times, the themes of justification

12. Luther, among others, uses the term "flesh" as that which battles against faith in the life of the believer; the term is neither physical (in general) nor bodily (specific). No doubt, he takes his cue from certain portions of the Pauline epistles. However, my intent here is to simply show that the Genesis 1–2 text appears to be committed to the physical understanding of flesh.

13. Dyrness, *Old Testament Theology*, 87.

14. Ibid., 81.

and the means of grace overshadowed more universally accepted Christian teachings, at least when measured by the length of material devoted to such disputations. Still, Martin Luther and other Reformers contributed a surprising amount of material to the proper understanding of humanity's created nature. It is neither necessary nor accurate to say that Lutherans have a bare shelf on the embodied theology front. Rather, resources need to be rediscovered, reinterpreted, and reapplied to the present situation. This task has already begun.[15] The document "Together with all Creatures" (2010), drafted by the Commission on Theology and Church Relations (CTCR) of the Missouri Synod, lays out the various ways humanity has understood its relationship with nature and how this interaction has evolved over the twentieth and twenty-first centuries.[16] These perspectives ebb and flow with the environmental ethic of the day, but the contemporary shift has been to perceive the human-nature relationship in the language of partnership and/ or stewardship. The Lutheran understanding of this partnership requires humanity to first recognize the common creatureliness of humanity and their fellow animals then move toward humanity's elevated position (and by extension, responsibility) within God's creation. The purpose of this framework is not necessarily to build some artificial empathy for the plight of animals in a rapidly developing world. Rather, the shared origins allow the Christian to proclaim God's identity as the good Creator until he returns.

Paul Althaus binds Luther's theology of creation to God's very own identity. "For Luther, being God and creating are identical. God is God because he and only he creates."[17] The significance of this position is amplified in the case of humans. Although humanity shares a kinship with other animals by nature of their shared creatureliness, man and woman were uniquely created after an initial act of deliberate will. In his Genesis lectures, Luther notes that "the [Genesis] text definitely sets man apart when it says that in a special deliberation God gave consideration to the creation of man, and not only that but also to making him in the image of God."[18] God's decisive act brought Adam into existence, fashioning a "living being" (*nephesh hayyah*) from the dust of the ground with the "breath of life" (Gen 2:7).[19] Thus God

15. Lutheran Church—Missouri Synod, "Together with All Creatures," 5. This CTCR document takes great care in describing humanity's relationship to all of the created order and picks up the theme of creatureliness in a highly accessible way.

16. Ibid., 10–29. These designations are distinctly Niebuhrian: Humankind set apart from nature, above nature, over nature, against nature, as a part of nature, with nature, into nature (the wilderness ethic), and within nature (the ecological ethic).

17. Althaus, *Theology*, 105.

18. Luther, "Lectures on Genesis: Chapters 1–5," 56.

19. From Gen 2:7, "The LORD God formed the man from the dust of the ground and breathed into his nostrils the breath of life, and the man became a living being."

unifies life and body in one remarkable stroke. The breath of life imagery coincides with Luther's articulation of God's enduring presence within all people at a permeating, foundational level. God's power is essentially present in every place and creature. "It is God who creates, effects, and preserves all things through his almighty power and right hand."[20] The omnipresence of God upholds life "both in its innermost and outermost aspects."[21] For Luther, human identity appears to be secondary to God's identity *within* the person:

> Therefore, indeed, [God] himself must be present in every single creature in its innermost and outermost being, on all sides, through and through, below and above, before and behind, so that nothing can be more truly present and within all creatures than God himself with his power. For it is he who makes the skin and it is he who makes the bones; it is he who makes the hair on the skin, and it is he who makes the marrow in the bones; it is he who makes every bit of the hair, it is he who makes every bit of the marrow. Indeed, he must make everything, both the parts and the whole. Surely, then, his hand which makes all this must be present; that cannot be lacking.[22]

Luther's concept of the nearness of God echoes Augustine's familiar words, *interior intimo meo*.[23] God essentially permeates, yet somehow is distinct from, his creatures.[24] The concealment of God remains a significant theme for Luther's theology, for it allows all creaturely action (whether fulfilling God's demands or the daily tasks of one's vocation) to be accomplished under God's watchful eye to the advancement of his kingdom. He becomes the source of all good works, for he sustains his creatures to do that which is pleasing to his perfect will. He is the first cause. Gerhard Ebeling argues that this concealment of God, or "mask," has two discrete meanings:

> Firstly, the creation is only a mask, that is, it is not anything in itself or on its own account, but is only the veil which conceals

20. AE 37:57–58.

21. Ibid., 58.

22. Ibid.

23. Augustine, *Confessions*, 62. Phrase loosely translated as "deeper than my inmost understanding."

24. This is an important theme in Scripture. Christians live in the midst of a tension. From one side, God fills the Christian with his presence (Eph 1:22–23; 1 John 4:12) and promises his Holy Spirit in baptism (Luke 3:16). In other places, most notably in Galatians 3:26–28, the believer knows what it is to be in Christ and have Christ in him. From the other side, the Body of Christ is composed of individuals, distinct from God and one another. This concept is expressed rather straightforwardly in 1 Cor 15 where every member has distinctive importance.

the Creator, who speaks to us from it and through it. That is why the true recognition of reality requires a distinction between the creation as a mere mask and the word of God concealed in it, so that the house is not confused with the host, nor the creature with the creator, and honour and faith are accorded to God and not to the creation. But this leads us to the second point. Because of the distinction between God and the creation, between the word and the mere mask, we are required to acknowledge and reverence the creation as a mask, the purpose for which it was ordained by God.[25]

The final conclusion is: God's perpetual acts of creativity fill the earth and animate the human life within it. In response, humanity's creaturely abilities are to be maintained in a state of "active readiness," an open disposition toward the imagination of God.[26]

For Luther, God's nature as Creator appears to be anthropologically motivated. In other words, Luther's interest in the creative nature of God is often paired with an eye toward humanity's fall. Adam "blames God for his nakedness as if He were the Creator of something shameful. Through sin he has become so crazed that he turns the glory of nakedness into a disgrace of the Creator."[27] Luther contrasts the dignity of the initial creation with the radical sin and isolation man feels after the first sin; he is less concerned with demonstrating a broad-based kinship throughout the natural world.[28] By using the pre-Fall condition of Adam as a control, Luther can theologically demonstrate the great depths of man's sin as well as the equally redeeming grace that is offered in Jesus' atoning death and resurrection. His Law-Gospel dynamic, therefore, has been integrated into his understanding of the First Article.

God as Sustainer

Luther, in particular, understands God (and by extension, Jesus Christ) as both Creator and Sustainer. Luther cannot separate these two functions, as one without the other would lead to a self-contradiction. Without God's hand of preservation, all of creation would "go to wrack and ruin in a twinkling."[29] No creature has control over his own creating, yet Luther

25. Ebeling, *Luther*, 198.

26. Althaus, *Theology*, 109.

27. AE 1:176.

28. The common kinship theme is present in Luther's works, to be sure, but its rhetorical function is ultimately to prove the significance of Christ's redemptive work.

29. AE 22:28.

extends this further to claim that no created being can be the driving force behind his own ongoing sustenance and health. The provision an individual has is sourced only in God. Luther, at this point, uses the effective analogy of a carpenter or architect:

> [God] is, however, not like a carpenter or architect who, after completing a house, a ship, or the like, turns over the house to its owner for his residence or the ship to the boatmen or mariners for sailing, and then goes his way. Craftsmen are wont to do this; after doing a job or finishing a task, they leave without any concern for their work and enterprise and without any regard for its maintenance. God proceeds differently.[30]

God's creative activity continues without ceasing, for "if God were to withdraw His hand, this building and everything in it would collapse."[31] Luther's metaphor here is slightly misleading. A building implies that, once erected, the overall structure is essentially complete. Luther, however, understands creation not as a one-time construction project (with minimal ongoing maintenance) but as a bit by bit progression. "His creation is not a one time but an ongoing process."[32] The necessity of ongoing creation and provision emphasizes a fundamental truth about humanity's creatureliness: To be a creature is to be limited. God circumscribes humanity on all sides that all might seek him for daily provision in every area of life.

One expression of this limitation is age itself. In other words, humanity most directly understands its own finality, its own finiteness, by witnessing and ultimately bearing the fact of death by hearing the defining word from God, "to dust you will return" (Gen 3:19), or, as one theologian describes, "[man's] origins also became his destiny."[33] Bearing the curse of death has lost sting in our modern therapeutic, sterilized world of geriatrics, where death is viewed as a welcome transition (even anthropomorphically as a "friend") to another existence. Luther attempted, however, to press home the ultimate horror and evil of death, most notably on his exposition of Psalm 90:

> Nor does one overcome death by disregarding it and by following
> the example of street bandits and soldiers, who think that they

30. AE 22:26.

31. AE 22:27.

32. Althaus, *Theology*, 106. Althaus would certainly recognize that it is both, as the initial creation narrative is a one-time experience. Rather, he is attempting to highlight that the divine work of creation does not cease after the first creative acts in Genesis 1 and 2.

33. Mathews, *The New American Commentary*, 196.

are displaying a great deal of courage when they, even though jokingly, wish upon others pestilence, devastating diseases, and similar misfortunes. No, in order to overcome death and sin one must employ different means and different remedies.[34]

Death is not to be ignored or made light of; it bears the ultimate proof of creation's surrender to the consequences of sin and evil. The remedy of Christ serves as one poignant example of God as Sustainer. The justification offered in Christ's death and resurrection is God's solution to the finality of death and affords the believer the resurrection of their physical form in the Last Days. We will return to Luther's view of death and eschatology later in the chapter.

At this point, one can observe the difficult task of separating God's creative ability with his ongoing provision, if indeed any distinction needs to be made. Since the attributes work in unison, the essential point is that creatures experience the newness of being creaturely in every breath. Luther expresses this newness as something that happens in the here-and-now, not just as a condition to be anticipated in the eschaton. He notes, "Daily we can see the birth into this world of new human beings, young children who were nonexistent before; we behold new trees, new animals on the earth, new fish in the water, new birds in the air. And such creation and preservation will continue until the Last Day . . . Before one creature dies, They supplant it with another, to insure the perpetuity of Their creation."[35] Notice how Luther views the world as a highly dynamic system, in perpetual flux, where God allows for a certain measure of fluidity in the context of a greater equilibrium.

This sustaining power of God expresses itself in both direct and indirect ways. Directly, God provides for the general welfare of humanity in terms of creaturely gifts. Luther charges in his Large Catechism, ". . . that [God] has given me and constantly sustains my body, soul, and life, my members great and small, all my senses, my reason and understanding, and the like; my food and drink, clothing, nourishment, spouse and children, servants, house and farm, etc." (LC II, 13).[36] In concert with these gifts, God indirectly exercises his grace by supporting the structures around humanity; he "makes all creation help" as accessories to the full life of every man, woman, and child (LC II, 14). The sun and moon are governed to provide people with the necessities and comforts of life, for example, just as the pro-

34. AE 13:76.

35. AE 22:27.

36. All quotes from the Large Catechism and other confessional documents found in the Book of Concord are cited from: Kolb and Wengert, *The Book of Concord*.

liferation of plants and animals help support a person's bodily existence, whether Christian or pagan (Matt 5:45). And similarly, humans must rely on God's provision in "earth's bountifulness."[37] This sustenance can be understood in a negative sense as well: God not only provides direct comfort and care (our physical bodies, companions, etc.) as well as indirect support (seasons, environment, etc.), he also actively resists evil and defends humanity against "all sorts of danger and disaster" (LC II, 17). Note that the social nature of creatureliness is quietly revealing itself, as companionship proves to be a crucial way in which God demonstrates his ongoing provision for humanity. For Luther, these elements of Christian embodied living spring from God the Father's role as the Creator/Sustainer, which, in turn, calls forth humanity's proper fear and thanksgiving.

Often lost in the biblical text, as well as classic Luther texts and commentaries on creation, is the presumption and preeminence of community. In God's complete freedom, he could have chosen a solitary life for Adam to take joy in the whole of Garden unencumbered by human companionship. Yet God declares, "It is not good for the man to be alone" (Gen 2:18). God's intent for sociality is demonstrated in three particular ways. First, the nature of the Trinitarian relationship is first made known in Genesis. The economy of God is evidenced in the plural pronouns in 1:26: "Then God said, 'Let us make man in our image, in our likeness . . .'"[38] This well-known reference to the Trinity is typically used as a way to identify the three persons of the Trinity in the Old Testament, often a difficult task. The present goal, however, is to shift the view away from the three-fold presence of God and draw attention to the fact that relationship is at the core of the creative process. God initiates all other relationships out of this primary ontology; he draws humanity into a dialogue, figuratively and literally (Gen 3:9–19). As Paul Althaus recounts, "God 'showers us with his own being.' He gives us what he is . . . The attributes of God are by their very nature creative and are not only his own and remain in himself but are also shared with men."[39]

The second indicator of creaturely sociality in Luther's writings is found in the first human-to-human relationship; not due to the fact that

37. Lutheran Church—Missouri Synod, "Together with All Creatures," CTCR, 5.

38. Many theologians, including Luther, note the Trinitarian nature of this passage. In his Genesis lectures, Luther states, "The word 'Let Us make' is aimed at making sure the mystery of our faith, by which we believe that from eternity there is one God and that there are three separate Persons in one Godhead: the Father, the Son, and the Holy Spirit" (AE 1: 57). Some exegetes question whether or not a Trinitarian presence in this verse is an overreach, but this contention need not prevent us from noting both the presence of the first person plural and Luther's interpretation of the text.

39. Althaus, Theology, 117.

it came to be, but more directly, *why* God brought it into being in the first place. Luther acknowledges that Eve was "created according to a definite plan."[40] His understanding of the Adam-Eve dynamic is highly pragmatic, declaring the relationship to be valuable due to: (1) the mutual benefit of having a helpful partner, (2) the sexual complementarity that leads to the ongoing survival of the species,[41] and (3) the "medicinal" way in which sexual activity prevents the evil of fornication.[42] Eve shares in the burdens of creaturely living: the securing of food and provisions, for example. But her value cannot be reduced to a utilitarian aid of sorts; her life brings about an independent joy expressed in sexuality, play, and companionship. The creation of Eve, therefore, can be interpreted as one manifestation of God's blessing to Adam and the rest of creation. Of essential importance here is the constitutive goodness, pre- *and* post-Fall, of the male-female relationship.

The third and final indicator that creaturely life is inherently social also comes in the blessing given at Gen 1:28: "God blessed them and said to them, 'Be fruitful and increase in number; fill the earth and subdue it.'" The procreation of children affirms the initial partnership between Adam and Eve and fulfills God's design for the propagation of the species. Luther viewed this as a "marred blessing," for he stressed that sin (both original and actual, i.e., lust) so "overwhelmed" this gift that the "act of procreation . . . becomes downright brutish and cannot beget in the knowledge of God."[43] Lost in Luther's analysis of this blessing, however, is God's design for the *expansion* of human relationships; in other words, God's gift of children cannot be isolated as a utilitarian solution to the need for species propagation. Rather, the begetting of children necessarily creates community, both inside of the family relationship and outward toward other families in civic interaction. This community is designed from the outset of God's creation, as the blessing precedes the breakdown of relational life with the Fall.

40. AE 1:115.

41. Luther understands the "good" in Gen 2:18 as the good of "increasing the human race." He certainly believes that Adam, had he remained innocent, would have lived in perpetuity. However, Luther recognized that God's blessing in 1:28 implicitly acknowledges that loneliness begets a certain lacking.

42. AE 1:116. This is a postlapsarian good, though Luther himself calls this particular benefit of marriage "lamentable." Referencing Peter Lombard, he says, "The Master of the *Sentences* declares learnedly that matrimony was established in Paradise as a duty, but after sin also as an antidote. It is almost shameful to say this, but nevertheless it is true."

43. AE 1:71. Luther speaks to the common depravity of man by saying, in classic form, "But, good God, what has been lost for us here through sin!" He also refers to sins related to sexuality as "the leprosy of lust."

What does this component mean for the pursuit of a holistic, embodied theology? First, being a creature effectively confers a special status to humanity. By nature of his created origins, the First Man was bestowed with an original dignity *constitutive to his very body*.[44] God places upon humanity the status of beloved creature, declaring it "very good," and sustains it with daily bread as well as purpose. Therefore, to live embodied is to recognize that humanity has received the dignity of being intentionally and thoughtfully made and preserved.

The Second Component: Sacramental

The sacramental quality of Lutheran doctrine is the second pillar of embodied theology. In the strictest sense, the Lutheran understanding of the sacraments is whole-heartedly incarnational; that is, God gives of himself in the elements of bread, wine, and water. It will, however, be useful to speak about the specific contributions to embodiment found in Holy Baptism and Holy Communion. In Holy Baptism, God binds his word to the water, grafting the believer to the atoning death and subsequent resurrection of Jesus (Rom 6:4–5) and bestowing the Holy Spirit to work sanctification in his/her heart. Holy Communion brings embodiment to an equally impressive dimension; Jesus' bodily presence is offered in the material elements of bread and wine to the community of faith, reconciling the Creator to the creature in an intimate gift of healing. While many ancient religions use the natural world as a medium for divine-human communication, these sacraments are uniquely set apart from other rituals or symbols *in Christian practice* precisely because they bind God's forgiving grace to physical elements. "The sacraments are physical acts, done to our bodies, and in which we participate through our bodies."[45] They exist as God's material offer of forgiveness, nothing more or less.

With this in mind, the fullest expression of the embodied life of the Christian is participation in the means of grace. This position allows for an initial, yet important, salvo against two positions: (1) Gnostic or dualist tendencies which proclaim the material as unnecessary and/or evil, and (2) a theological position that renders the sacraments as symbolic or containing Christ's "spiritual presence only." First, Gnostic philosophies considered the physical form a type of prison for the immortal soul. The flesh, since it was

---

44. Moltmann, *God in Creation*, 39. As Moltmann notes, while it is dangerous to use the original "goodness" of humanity as a proper descriptive for the present anthropological condition, this does not eliminate humanity's status as God's creatures.

45. Althaus, *Theology*, 347.

perishable by definition, existed as an inferior vessel when juxtaposed to the incorruptible intellect or spirit. It would be unthinkable for a Gnostic or mind-body dualist to accept sacraments as a means by which humanity enters into the life of the Trinity; they would see no intellectual or transcendent value in such earthy things. The material, fleshy, all-sensory experience of Holy Baptism and Holy Communion ring with an affirmation of the physical order: God's proclamation of Yes in the water, bread, and wine. For Luther, the elements could be "grasped with the senses and thus appropriated by the heart."[46] Water and word work in concert to speak to the specific needs of one's body-soul dynamic. "Because the water and the Word together constitute one baptism, both body and soul shall be saved and live forever: the soul through the Word in which it believes, the body because it is united with the soul and apprehends baptism in the only way it can" (LC IV, 46). Since physical elements are a prerequisite for sacramental life and have remained such since the formation of the early church, the Gnostic philosopher's only available refuge is to claim that sacraments themselves have no true significance.[47] This position is impossible to maintain in the light of the history and creedal confessions of orthodox Christianity.

Second, the perception of the sacraments as symbol-only fails to grasp the importance of God's grace in the binding of water and word in Holy Baptism and the bodily presence of Christ in Holy Communion. Indeed, symbolism abounds in both systems. For Holy Baptism, the waters of the font point to a washing of the heart; for Holy Communion, the broken bread corresponds directly with Jesus' broken body on the cross. Their primary function, however, is to offer the forgiveness of sins as a means of grace through the binding of the elements to God's own word; they are secondarily symbolic. The Lutheran position stands in direct contrast to Calvinist thought here. At the core of the difference is the Calvinist philosophical presupposition resolutely set against "the idea that an external, physical action can produce spiritual effects, such as the forgiveness of sins."[48] For example, regarding the practice of Holy Baptism, the Calvinist

46. Ibid.

47. For Gnostic forms of theology, the primary anthropological evil is ignorance. The transcendence of the immortal soul through the accumulation of secret knowledge (*gnosis*) drives the individual's efforts on earth. A Gnostic, then, could conceivably hold the tenuous position that sacraments merely remind the individual of the flesh's weakness: baptism reminds us of the body's capacity for filth or communion reminds us of Jesus' weak body on the cross. Clearly, this position completely ignores Pauline commentary on the sacraments and ultimately empties them of their power as means of grace.

48. Sasse, *We Confess the Sacraments*, 40. Luther zeroes in on the Calvinist proclivity toward elevating reason to the level Scripture in the Large Catechism. "Mad reason rushes forth" to support philosophical principles over the words of Scripture. LC IV, 13.

THE CASE FOR AN EMBODIED THEOLOGY

position on election essentially makes the sacrament unnecessary, granting the believer no external benefit that has not already been conferred in full. If the elect are chosen by God from the beginning of time, of what critical use is baptism? To give reason for this practice, Reformed theologian Karl Barth argues that baptism is performed only by a "necessity of command [*necessitas praecepti*], not a necessity of means [*necessitas medii*]."[49] Indeed, the Lutheran understanding of baptism recognizes the command present in Matthew 28:18–20, but it wholeheartedly endorses *necessitas medii*. Paul's explicit connection between Holy Baptism and the forgiveness of sins in Romans 6, as well as the Lutheran contention that grace is offered through material elements, makes the Reformed position untenable. The command to perform sacraments does not and cannot eclipse the actual work that is being done by God in the water, wine, and bread. In Luther's words, "This is the simplest way to put it: the power, effect, benefit, fruit, and purpose of baptism is that it saves . . . To be saved, as everyone well knows, is nothing else than to be delivered from sin, death, and the devil, to enter into Christ's kingdom and to live with him forever" (LC IV, 24–25).

This section will look at both sacraments, first Holy Baptism, then Holy Communion, probing their connections to embodied theology. After demonstrating these deep affinities through the writings of Luther, Herman Sasse, and others, I will then draw out the particularly communal nature of these sacraments.

Baptism and Physical Immediacy

Before claiming that Holy Baptism is an important expression of embodied theology, we first turn to our earlier definition of embodiment. Embodiment is the intimate experience of related creatureliness made most fully possible by physical immediacy. I will give attention to Holy Baptism's relation to "physical immediacy" first, then proceed to argue for its ability to bear the burden as an "intimate experience of related creatureliness."

The physical immediacy of baptism happens in at least two particular ways: (1) The physical element of water itself is crucial as a means of grace, and (2) the drowning of the old Adam directly grafts the believer to the physical death and resurrection of Jesus Christ. As to the first, Herman Sasse evaluates the means of grace in Baptism by locating the Sacrament's efficacy in the binding of the water and the Word. Noting Luther's objection to the Catholic and Reformed positions on Baptism, Sasse reminds us that "with Luther everything depends on *the intimate connection of Word and*

49. Sasse, *We Confess the Sacraments*, 42.

water [emphasis added] . . . [he] has no need to demonstrate first that this presence of God or Christ can be no other presence than that which happens in His Word."[50] This defies any attempt to make Baptism a symbolic representation of what God does with his own will, apart from the actual elements. The water is not an accidental feature or a way by which humanity can better understand a metaphor of washing; rather, Luther drives home the fact that grace is received externally through such means.[51] Therefore, the Sacrament of Holy Baptism is unmistakably incarnational, counting the material element of water as utterly necessary in this particular means of grace. The Word is present with the water, conferring the Holy Spirit upon the baptized in a spectacularly intimate way.

As to the second, Christians confess the direct connection between Holy Baptism and the physical death and resurrection of Jesus.

> Or don't you know that all of us who were baptized into Christ Jesus were baptized into his death? We were therefore buried with him through baptism into death in order that, just as Christ was raised from the dead through the glory of the Father, we too may live a new life. If we have been united with him like this in his death, we will certainly also be united with him in his resurrection. (Rom 6:3–5)

The embodied language here is crucial. Holy Baptism does not unite the person with Jesus' teachings per se, but with his bodily death and resurrection. This unity confers an embodied quality to Holy Baptism beyond the obvious presence of mere water. The effect is doubled when one considers the drowning terminology used in connection with the sacrament. From Luther's Small Catechism, "[Baptism] signifies that the old creature in us, together with all sins and evil desires is to be drowned and die through daily contrition and repentance" (SC IV, 12). The visceral connection between physicality and the benefits conferred at baptism is made explicit.[52]

Baptism and the Intimate Experience of Shared Creatureliness

Holy Baptism, though most immediately experienced at the level of the individual, is a public affair. Witnesses watch the ceremony, the baptized

50. Ibid., 41.

51. Sasse quotes the Smalcald Articles to support his argument. SA III.V, 2–3.

52. The Body of Christ is a body in which we partake by virtue of our baptism. 1 Cor 12:12–13: "The body is a unit, though it is made up of many parts; and though all its parts are many, they form one body. So it is with Christ. For *we were all baptized by one Spirit into one body* [emphasis added]—whether Jews or Greeks, slave or free—and we were all given the one Spirit to drink."

believer is initiated into a broader family of brothers and sisters, and he/she will be permitted to partake in Holy Communion and all other "Christian privileges."[53] In the Lutheran Service Book, the newly baptized are welcomed with the following words:

> A: In Holy Baptism God the Father has made you a member of His Son, our Lord Jesus Christ, and an heir with us of all the treasures of heaven in the one holy Christian and apostolic Church. We receive you in Jesus' name as our brother/sister in Christ, that together we might hear His Word, receive His gifts, and proclaim the praises of Him who called us out of darkness into His marvelous light.
>
> C: Amen. We welcome you in the name of the Lord.[54]

Holy Baptism invites the believer into a set of common responsibilities and/ or privileges: the hearing of the word, the corporate worship of the elect, and the reception of the Holy Spirit's gifts. For Luther, the mere existence of the Church is only possible with the one baptism instituted by Christ, for "without baptism there is no church."[55] The vertical dimension of God's saving action in Holy Baptism necessitates a new reality in the horizontal realm. Baptism marks the ceasing of the individual; he is no longer isolated but "a member of the people of God in which God at all times unites the believers in Christ through the Holy Spirit."[56] The baptism of the believer, therefore, is an introduction into the shared life of creatureliness, where Christians are built up together as a common body for a life of service.

Baptism saves us, Luther announces with great emphasis, yet it holds secondary ecclesial implications within the broader context of Christian life. For example, as part of a broader discussion of Luther's two realms, Gerhard Ebeling notes how the reformer strenuously dismisses the notion that clergy, by virtue of their special religious status, had unique claim to the tasks of God. Baptism was the basis for this assertion. "The fact is that our baptism consecrates us all without exception, and makes us all priests."[57] By virtue of one's baptism, a Christian of the so-called "secular class" may be called upon to perform, in certain circumstances, some ecclesial tasks in the

53. AE 40:239.

54. *Lutheran Service Book*, 271.

55. Althaus, *Theology*, 360. Luther surprisingly spends little effort noting the communal aspects of baptism, focusing more on: (1) its salvific character, and (2) issuing polemics against those who would reject the doctrine of infant baptism. Later Lutheran scholars would bring the horizontal dimension of this sacrament to the fore.

56. Schlink, *The Doctrine of Baptism*, 76.

57. Ebeling, *Luther*, 180.

spirit of "mutual service."[58] The responsibility bequeathed at Holy Baptism becomes a form of community-building in this system.

This community-building aspect should recognize both dimensions of church participation. First, Holy Baptism signifies the reception of the baptized into the worshipping assembly, which has the significant import of receiving the Lord's Supper. Baptismal orders from the ancient church clearly associated first Communion with Baptism, binding the individual's *partaking of* the Body of Christ (i.e., the bread of the Eucharist) with his/her *inclusion into* the Body of Christ (i.e., as the ongoing presence of Christ in the Church).[59] The local parish is "the center of all churchly life" which "defines the concepts of church, the body of Christ, and the spiritual temple."[60]

Second, Holy Baptism binds the believer to the broader Christian community across all time and space. Edward Schlink notes that the definition of the Greek *ekklesia* is not bound to only local parish contexts, but it is used to designate the whole church on earth as well. "The basis for using the same terms for the local assembly and the people of God scattered throughout the world is that in every worshiping assembly the same Christ is present."[61] Jesus remains the centerpiece of the Christian Church at large, yet every particular parish participates in the broader church. Therefore, when Holy Baptism is practiced at the local level, each convert is not *added* to the church so much as he/she is *included* into the church. Ultimately, the communal nature of Holy Baptism binds believers together in unity as they await God's final victory feast. These communal aspects of Holy Baptism are drawn out in much clearer detail in the writings of Dietrich Bonhoeffer, which we will turn to in chapter 3.

Real Presence and Luther's Opponents

Holy Communion serves as an excellent example of embodied theology. Lutheran theology, in particular, recognizes the bodily presence of God and boldly proclaims God's gift of forgiveness in the bread and the wine, much to the dismay of Luther's critics. Few phrases in Scripture have been more scrutinized than Jesus' words in the upper room: "This is my body" (Matt 26:26). Ultimately, the varying Protestant interpretations of Jesus' statement proved to be the irreconcilable difference at Marburg and beyond. Was Jesus referring to his actual bodily self as Lutherans have contended from the first,

58. Ibid., 181.
59. Schlink, *The Doctrine of Baptism*, 73.
60. Ibid.
61. Ibid., 74.

or was this statement merely reinforcing Christ's spiritual presence in the community of believers? Self-admittedly, Luther was under great temptation to discard the doctrine of Real Presence, recognizing the leverage it would create for his rapidly expanding movement against Rome. But rationalizing the doctrine of the Lord's Supper would create similar pressure to rationalize other portions, if not the whole, of the biblical text.[62] The presence of Christ's physical body and blood had to be maintained at all costs to satisfy Luther's magisterial view of scriptural authority.[63] Contra Calvinism, Lutheran theology confidently proclaims a position of *finitum infiniti capax est*, and thus subordinates reason to the authority of the biblical text. As we examine the sacramental quality of the finite elements of bread and wine, this section will first demonstrate Holy Communion's embodied character in Luther's doctrine of Real Presence, then proceed to lay out the communal functions of said doctrine. The social impact of the sacrament not only affects the present-tense binding of believers but also serves as a template from which to understand Christian fellowship in the Last Days.

Luther's position on Holy Communion is best understood through the prism of history. Prior to the sacramental controversies of 1524, Luther's theological target was Rome; his teachings on the sacrament, therefore, reflected that fact. Here, his concern was not necessarily Rome's strict view of the elemental transformation by way of transubstantiation. In fact, he conceded that the Roman Catholic view had more in common with his own than those who denied Christ's bodily presence in the elements, remarking, "Sooner than have mere wine with the fanatics, I would agree with the pope that there is only blood."[64] Rather, Luther vehemently opposed Roman teachings that the meal was a sacrifice of the mass, arguing instead that Holy Communion is God's gift to humanity with no human act contributing to its value.[65] Luther's conservative tendencies cut against his anti-Roman polemics in the case of elemental transformation yet grounded him deeper is his theological commitment to *sola scriptura*. The scripture that reinforces the true bodily presence of Christ's body and blood had nothing to say about the sacrifice of the mass. "This conservatism . . . goes hand in hand with

---

62. Sasse, *We Confess the Sacraments*, 103.

63. Ibid. Hermann Sasse understood the stakes of Luther's commitment: "[Luther] knew that there could be no stronger weapon against the Roman Church than if one could prove that the Words of Institution must be understood in the [Zwinglian] sense." The philosophical rationalization of the sacraments, which Zwingli appeared to be doing, would force the entire word of Scripture to fall under the interpretative authority of reason.

64. AE 37:317.

65. Althaus, *Theology*, 375.

the most serious and unambiguous rejection of everything that contradicts Scripture and is based on tradition only—even the most ancient and venerable tradition."[66] In this case, the re-sacrifice of the mass was ensconced deep inside centuries of tradition and liturgy, a most difficult challenge to overcome. The Roman position ultimately reeked of works righteousness, a significantly more egregious offense to *sola scriptura* and *sola gratia* than the position of transubstantiation. Luther's problem with Rome could be reduced in this way: "The sacrament is really to be understood as God's gift. As a gift it is indeed present for faith, but it also exists independently of and prior to faith."[67] This was, for Luther, a relatively brief battle compared to the theological war he would soon wage contra the radical reformers.

Word and Symbol

As Zwingli's symbolic interpretation of the Lord's Supper grew in influence during the mid-1520's, Luther composed several writings to combat his theological innovations. Here in the bridge between his struggles with the papacy and the intramural squabbles that occupy much of his later life, two characteristics of Luther's sacramental writing begin to surface: the importance of the word and his evolving understanding of symbol. First, Luther stresses the presence of the word in the sacraments, particular in Holy Communion. There is a dual meaning attached to this emphasis: The word of Scripture was the sole guide to Luther's understanding of the sacraments and the Word made flesh is the content of that gift. In the first meaning, Luther stresses the vitality and importance of the actual text of Scripture. *Sola scriptura* had become more than a guiding principle; it had emerged as an unshakable, unbendable framework for Luther's work—even if the resulting theological positions allied him, at times, more closely with Rome than his Protestant contemporaries. For example, Luther resists the temptation to burn further bridges with the papists by claiming a false alliance with the symbolic or spiritual-presence-only advocates. He speaks about the power of the text as his firewall against such a move. Referring to the Words of Institution in his *Letter to the Christians at Strassburg*, Luther confesses, "I realized at this point I could best resist the papacy. But I am a captive and cannot free myself. The text is too powerfully present, and will not allow itself to be torn from its meaning by mere verbiage."[68] The focus of Luther's attention, however, changed during the course of the reformer's

66. Sasse, *This is My Body*, 66.

67. Althaus, *Theology*, 392.

68. AE 40:68.

career, particularly as it related to the Words of Institution. Early on, Luther stressed the "given for you" clause as a way to drive home the central benefit of the sacrament: the remission of sins. He asks, "What then is this testament, or what is bequeathed to us in it by Christ? Truly a great, eternal, and unspeakable treasure, namely, the forgiveness of all sins."[69] By the late 1520's, he redirected his exegetical skills to the phrase, "this is my body," as a way to combat Zwingli and other radical reformers. Here, the emphasis was on the bodily presence of Christ within the elements, not the benefits received per se.

The second meaning is an extension of the first. Luther's understanding of the word present in the sacrament ultimately gave the meal its potency. This was *the Word*. The Word made flesh. The presence of the Word in the sacrament gives the meal its full meaning and power, and accordingly, the elements are only important insofar as they contain the testament of Christ. According to Luther, "everything depends on the Word."[70] This provides us with a glimpse of Luther's theology: The cross of Christ is a clear and present reality within the sacrament; the Word as gospel cannot be excised from Holy Communion. "I will find in the sacrament or gospel the word which distributes, presents, offers, and gives to me that forgiveness which was won on the cross."[71] By connecting the presence of the Word made flesh to the Words of Institution (in the *text* of Scripture), Luther is making an extraordinary link for embodied sacramental theology.[72] The material elements are but a side note to the more impressive embodied character of Christ's immediate physical presence in the bread and wine. It is a dual-fold affirmation of embodiment, to be sure, but the defining characteristic of the sacrament was and is the bodily presence of the Word promised in the word.

The second significant development of Luther's sacramental writing was his use of symbol language. Luther's early theology provided little connection between the promises conferred at Holy Communion and the doctrine of Real Presence. Since Christ's bodily presence was undisputed prior to 1525, Luther could spend his effort on detailing the benefits of the sacrament rather than its essential form. He couched his discussions on the Lord's Supper in the language of symbols and signs, visible marks that

69. AE 35:85.

70. AE 40:214.

71. Ibid.

72. Sasse notes the distinction between Luther and Zwingli on this point: "Here a strong contrast between Luther's and Zwingli's understanding of the Word becomes evident. For Luther the content of the Word is bound up with the letter. The Holy Spirit comes to us in the external word. In Zwingli's opinion, the external word (the letter) in itself has no power over the human soul." Sasse, *This is My Body*, 116.

conveyed God's promises. While Luther held the doctrine of Real Presence throughout his life, his earlier writings suggest that the body and blood of Christ had only "symbolic significance."[73] The sacrament's primary function, in this case, was to offer the participant assurance of God's promises at the table. The sensory person, after all, requires a sensory sign:

> This is what Christ has done in this testament. He has affixed to the words a powerful and most precious seal and sign: his own true flesh and blood under the bread and wine. For we poor men, living as we do in our five senses, must always have along with the words *at least one outward sign to which we may cling and around which we may gather* [emphasis added]—in such a way, however, that this sign may be a sacrament, that is, that it may be external and yet contain and signify something spiritual; in order that through the external we may be drawn into the spiritual comprehending the external with the eyes of the body and the spiritual or inward with the eyes of the heart.[74]

The body and blood of Christ bound in the external elements of bread and wine exist as the promise and guarantee of the forgiveness of sins.[75] Luther's embodied sacramental theology demonstrates the capacity of this "most precious seal and sign": to effect internal or spiritual benefit. God's creatures intimately experience the intentional presence of Christ, guaranteed by the outward sensory sign of the elements.

In Luther's later disputes with Zwingli and others, by contrast, he uses symbol language in the pejorative sense to accuse his opponents of describing the elements in a strictly symbolic fashion; the bread and wine only represented the body and blood. How is this apparent contradiction resolved? The solution requires some nuance as to the object of reference. Luther's early claims about the sacrament's symbolic nature were directed to the sacrament *in toto*, never questioning the bodily presence of Christ. The meal was to be the physical artifact, indeed to serve as a sensory assurance

73. Althaus, *Theology*, 378.

74. AE 35:86.

75. Althaus comments about the theological difficulties that can emerge from this early approach. It is not entirely clear how Luther connected Real Presence to the forgiveness of sins. The efficaciousness of the sacrament, for Luther, was not located in the bread and wine, nor even the body and blood of Christ, but in God's word. Yet if this is true, why would the elements be necessary at all? Or, more specifically, why would Luther need to press home the doctrine of Real Presence? At this point, the best answer may be to recognize Luther's insistence on the words of Christ. Since Jesus speaks to us about the reality of his own bodily presence in the sacrament, we are obligated to believe it, relying on the mystery of his presence to communicate the forgiveness of sins. See Althaus, *Theology*, 376–91.

of God's promise in the forgiveness of sins. His later rejection of symbol language was not about the meal, per se, but about viewing the elements of the meal as mere signifiers of: (1) the body and blood, and (2) God's offer of grace. These latter positions were impossible for Luther, the first because it denied the literal reading of the Words of Institution and the second because it divested the Eucharist of any real power. "[My opponent's] have taught nothing more than that the bread signifies the body and the wine signifies the blood of Christ, just as if one were to take a figure from the Old Testament and say: the bread from heaven which the Jews ate in the wilderness *signifies* the body of Christ or the gospel, but the bread from heaven which the Jews ate in the wilderness *is* not the gospel or the body of Christ."[76] The Zwinglian view, according to Luther, was that the Eucharist represented God's forgiveness of sins without actually conferring it through the material means. Luther stressed, by contrast, that Holy Communion was "a perfect sacrament or sign"[77] and assured the believer that his/her transformation as a child of God was complete, integrating them into "Christ's spiritual body and the community of love."[78]

After 1524, Luther emphasizes the doctrine of Real Presence "over against its abandonment in the symbolic theory."[79] His split with Roman Catholicism now calcified, the new enemy was heresy from within. Zwingli, Calvin, and others began promoting a position of spiritual-presence only, forcing Luther to confront his critics on an important theological battlefield. This confrontation would ultimately be done *in absentia* with the unambiguous confession of faith, The Formula of Concord (1576–77):

> We believe, teach, and confess that in the Holy Supper the body and blood of Christ are truly and essentially present and are truly distributed and received with the bread and wine. We believe, teach, and confess that the words of the testament of Christ are *to be understood in no other way than in their literal sense* [emphasis added], and not as though the bread symbolized the absent body and the wine the absent blood of Christ, but that because of the sacramental union they are truly the body and blood of Christ. (Epitome, FC VII, 6–7)

The movement against the Zwinglians was now codified into a Lutheran confessional work, somewhat free from the overwhelming force of a living Luther's personality and political clout. But what were the theological roots

76. AE 36:279.
77. AE 35:59.
78. Althaus, *Theology*, 377–78.
79. Ibid., 376.

of such a firm position? And how did Luther's own thought develop over and against those who would reject bodily presence in Holy Communion? Since Christ's real presence in the sacrament was no longer undisputed with the rise of Protestant fervor against Rome, Luther used a great deal of effort to swat down such challenges, forcing him to turn "his attention to the objective character of the sacrament."[80]

This particular writing phase of Luther (post-1524) is crucial for our current project because he shores up the connection between the word of Scripture to Christ's own body and blood offered in the sacrament. "Whoever has a bad conscience from his sins should go to the sacrament and obtain comfort, not because of the bread and wine, not because of the body and blood of Christ, but because of the word which in the sacrament offers, presents, and gives the body and blood of Christ, given and shed for me."[81] Once again, Luther's commitment to the Words of Institution is unmistakable here. Christ initiates the sacrament with his words (the consecration of the elements) and becomes the embodied word of forgiveness won on the cross. God's word speaks through the sacrament, communicating the cross of Christ and its conferred benefits to humanity. He insists that the word "brings with it everything of which it speaks, namely, Christ with his flesh and blood and everything that he is and has."[82] Therefore, Luther's *theologia crucis* stands in the middle of his interpretation of the Real Presence. The explicit binding of God's word to the true bodily presence of Jesus, therefore, shows the intimate depth of God's embodied presence in the life of the believer. He meets his creatures not just in some spatial sense (i.e., he is physically present only); rather, God penetrates the sacrament with the cross. The word of God on the cross comes immediately to the believer at the communion rail, a time of forgiveness, intimacy, and grace. When the cross of Christ occupies this central position in Holy Communion, the believer can look beyond to the hope offered in the empty grave. The sacrament offers restoration in the present tense as a means of grace, but also points toward the final victory of Christ, expressed in Isaiah 26 as a banquet of "rich food" and "aged wine." When one eats of the bread and drinks of the wine, therefore, they are given a foretaste of the feast to come in its entire splendor.

Sasse believed that Luther's "great discovery" was that the Sacrament is the gospel.[83] Luther believed this about the Words of Institution; to violate

---

80. Ibid., 380.
81. AE 40:214.
82. AE 36:278.
83. Sasse, *This Is My Body*, 328.

these words beyond their plain meaning would be to violate the gospel.[84] Thus, one could not simply pick and choose the portions of the text that were suitable. Because they are God's presented gospel, one could not "accept the words, 'This is my body', without believing also, 'which is given for you.'"[85] Luther had no choice but to defend the sacrament at all costs, since the very nature and authority of God's word was at stake. To proclaim a sacrament of human works, as it was done in Rome's sacrifice of the mass, would be to pervert the gospel. Sasse sums up the two opposing positions in this way:

> By making the Sacrament of Christ a sacrifice, the Roman church could not avoid placing the human priest side by side with the High Priest, Christ. Zwingli rejected the sacrificial character of the Lord's Supper. But, by rejecting also the Real Presence, he again made the Sacrament a human action, a feast of remembrance and a mere sign of grace. Thus, the two fights belong together.[86]

Luther's Real Presence, therefore, becomes the only available option—and not without its substantial textual support—if the material principle that God accomplishes all the work independent from humanity is to have any force. The fully embodied Lord actively and intimately meets his people with his word, his true body and blood, and his open arms of forgiveness.

Holy Communion and Fellowship: Many Grains, Many Grapes

The embodied character of Luther's doctrine of Real Presence is beyond dispute. The remaining question for this section is whether or not this sacrament, in Lutheran understanding, gives us a richer understanding of the relationship between embodiment and the believer's experience in Christian community. This section will briefly explore two sources that support this position. First, an examination of the relevant 1 Cor 11 text will draw us closer to Paul's understanding of communion as way to participate in godly fellowship. Second, we will examine Luther's own comments on the function of the sacrament as it relates to Christian community.

Of the thirteen letters Paul writes in the New Testament, only First Corinthians addresses the sacrament of Holy Communion.[87] Here we find

84. Ibid., 86.

85. Ibid.

86. Ibid., 328.

87. I am indebted to Michael Middendorf for this particular portion of the chapter.

that Paul speaks directly to the church about the nature and function of Holy Communion. What was Paul's central concern here? The context of chapters 10–11 appears to be connected with expressions of social living in Corinth. For example, Paul is concerned with lawsuits among believers (6:1–11), cases of sexual immorality and immodest dress (6:12–7:40; 11:2–16), and perceptions associated with food sacrificed to idols (8:1–13; 10:14–22). Each of these difficulties exists internal to the church body; Paul is not condemning the general population of Corinth here. Talk about the sacrament, therefore, falls into the broader discussion of how the *Christian* community shall conduct itself.

The introduction to the key passages (10:14–11:34), then, supports this early conclusion. Divisions are emerging when the *ekklesia* shares food and drink, as some are eating more than their share while others go hungry (11:21). Paul warns that individual overindulgence at the expense of the other causes the offender to "despise the church of God" (22). After a recap of Jesus' words, Paul charges that "whoever eats the bread or drinks the cup of the Lord in an unworthy manner will be guilty of sinning against the body and blood of the Lord" (27). The most natural reading of "unworthy manner" would be connected to its immediate context in verses 20–21. Unworthiness comes when the meal is not shared, when it is experienced outside of the *koinonia* of Christian fellowship. To eat of the sacrament worthily, then, would be to gather in unity, providing for everyone who has need. Paul's prescription is for "a man to examine himself before he eats of the bread and drinks of the cup" (28). Through this self-reflection, a participant may properly "recognize the body of the Lord" (29). The two most common interpretations of this phrase are: (1) Paul wants the believer to recognize Christ's true bodily presence in the bread and wine, and (2) Paul desires the participant to recognize the church as the body of Christ and therefore should not be despised through selfish conduct. The first response appears, to me, to be reading Lutheran doctrine into this passage rather than allowing the text to stand on its own. I agree with Middendorf here when he suggests that the most appropriate way to interpret this passage may be through the words of 8:12, "And thus while sinning against the brothers and wounding their conscience, being weak, you are sinning against Christ."

I suggest that Paul's directives about the meal of Holy Communion is less a proof-text for the Real Presence, although it may be implicitly affirmed, and more a meal of unity in Christ. By participating in the Sacrament of the Altar, believers participate in the body and blood of Christ *as*

His unpublished paper "The Lord's Supper and 1 Cor 11:17–34: Questions and Responses" clarified my thinking with regards to the social function of the Lord's Supper in Paul's thought.

one body, one fellowship, one people under the cross (10:16–17). The *koinonia* experienced here comes from the common purpose of the meal ("in remembrance of me" in v. 25) and the creedal action it naturally produces (to "proclaim the Lord's death until he comes" in v. 26). In my reading, Paul's understanding of the Lord's Supper is inextricably entwined with his view of Christian community. The sacrament provides the believer with Christ himself, and in that gift, Christ becomes the centerpiece and reason for the church's ongoing fellowship.[88]

Did Luther himself consider Holy Communion to be an expression of embodied community? His earliest treatises on the subject resound with the affirmative. In fact, he appears to give the community of saints a central role in his sacramental theology. In his *The Blessed Sacrament of the Holy and True Body of Christ, and the Brotherhoods* (1519), he argues for the distribution of both elements because "the sacrament . . . signifies the complete union and the *undivided fellowship of the saints* [emphasis added]; and this is poorly and unfittingly indicated by [distributing] only one part of the sacrament."[89] The connection between the sacrament and its social character was not restricted to symbolism. In fact, the very effect of Holy Communion had a communal character:

> The *significance* or effect of this sacrament is fellowship of all the saints. From this it derives its common name *synaxis* [Greek] or *communio* [Latin], that is, fellowship. And the Latin *communicare* [commune or communicate] . . . means to take part in this fellowship. Hence it is that Christ and all saints are one spiritual body, just as the inhabitants of a city are one community and body, each citizen being a member of the other and of the entire city. All the saints, therefore, are members of Christ and of the church, which is a spiritual and eternal city of God.[90]

This excerpt draws out the one of the ways in which Luther describes the connection between the sacrament and the community of saints: the metaphor of the *polis*. Just as a citizen shares with every other citizen "the city's name, honor, freedom, trade, customs, usages, help, support, protection, and the like," the Christian profits by receiving all of the corporate benefits of Christ's presence in the bread and the wine.[91]

The burdens of fellowship are likewise accorded to the communicant. Just as members of a *polis* provide mutual encouragement in times of

---

88. Elert, *Eucharist and Church Fellowship*, 23–32.

89. AE 35:50.

90. Ibid., 51.

91. Ibid., 52.

hardship, famine, and war, the Christian is called to share in the hardships of his neighbor. God presents the sacrament to the believer to give the person strength in his/her time of trial. Sin, while burdening the conscience of the individual directly, can be confronted by the whole people of God. Luther's classic tripartite axis of evil is referenced here: the flesh, the Devil (in this case, "the evil spirit"), and the world.[92] "All of these afflictions make us weary and weak, unless we seek strength in this fellowship, where strength is to be found."[93] Yet for Luther, this type of Christian fellowship can only be found in the common partaking of the Eucharist. The fact that this feast is celebrated in the presence of human-to-human contact is not of primary significance for Luther. Such a shallow approach would be akin to claiming that embodiment is based solely on spatial location.[94] Embodiment requires a certain measure of shared intimacy, and Luther on this point believes *the object of their common partaking* is of paramount importance.[95]

When one considers that Luther viewed the sacrament *as gospel*, the communal theme is even more pronounced. The cross of Christ comes immediately in Holy Communion, for in the sacrament the remission of sins intimately reunites believers with their estranged neighbors. This forgiveness is achieved only by the work of the cross. Since communion is receiving of the gospel, and the gospel itself is for all nations unbounded by space or time, it cannot be reduced to an individual experience. Indeed, the gospel individually redeems—but the act, and, therefore, the sacrament, must be considered a saving of all humanity, a restoring of God's creatures in their entirety before God in Christ. The banquet of bread and wine foreshadows the epic feast of the new creation. The sacrament as gospel is not isolated to Holy Communion, of course. The command to baptize is for all nations (Matt 28:18–20) equally unbounded by space or time. Each Christian baptism is done in the presence of other believers and, with few exceptions, unites the baptized with a worshipping local community. The communal nature of the gospel *is* the sacramental community of faith, a community that baptizes and communes together.

92. Ibid., 53.

93. Ibid.

94. See chapter 1.

95. Elert, *Eucharist and Church Fellowship*, 4–5 . This view is in opposition to Schleiermacher's view that church fellowship "is created by the voluntary actions of men." For Luther, human action does precipitate one's entrance into the church community. Rather, Luther starts from the ontological reality of the church and proceeds outward to determine the true nature of Christian fellowship. Bonhoeffer will strongly echo Luther on this point. This will be discussed further in chapter 3.

Luther famously describes the sacraments' effect on community by using a metaphor. Just as individual grapes are crushed to make wine and kernels of wheat are destroyed to make flour, so the believer's individual identity is substituted for a more significant reality. They belong under the banner of Christ with one another, sharing in the meal beside one another, all for the purposes of serving one another in their weakness. Or, in the case of Holy Baptism, the waters of the font wash away our former individual identities as broken and lost souls, revealing the new status of being God's chosen. This transformation foreshadows the community of Christ as it is made fully manifest in the eschaton, to which we presently turn.

The Third Component: Eschatological

The third component to the proposed embodied Lutheran theology is the doctrine of eschatology. The study of the Last Things can be interpreted in two senses: the Christian awaits the termination of his/her own existence on an individual experiential level in death, and Christians corporately wait for God's final reign on the Last Day. While the Lutheran tradition is most known for its Christological views on justification, Martin Luther interpreted his socio-political context through the prism of eschatology, imminently expecting the end times. In the previously introduced individual sense, Luther understood eschatology as an ongoing battle that rages from the present to the end times; in other words, the journey of the Christian is itself an arena for issues of ultimate importance. The Christian is caught up in the cosmic struggle between the will of God and the destructive purposes of Satan; the field of battle, for Luther, is in the believer's life of faith. Althaus notes the here-and-now qualities of Luther's eschatology: "Faith is continually attacked by the temptations arising from the contradiction between the reality it sees and the salvation that is present but hidden from sight."[96] Not simply isolated as a doctrine of ends, Lutheran eschatology vibrantly expresses itself in the life of every Christian as a people who experience what it is "to have and at the same time not to have, to be and at the same time not yet to be."[97] Such an understanding naturally intertwines with other portions of Luther's work, most notably with his treatises on freedom and bondage. *The Bondage of the Will*, for example, repeatedly casts the Christian in a position of submission. Free-will has a place for anything "below" the Christian (i.e., the daily affairs of life), but "with regard to God, and in all that bears on salvation or damnation, he has no 'free-will', but is a captive,

96. Althaus, *Theology*, 404.
97. Ibid.

prisoner and bondslave, either to the will of God, or to the will of Satan."[98] For Luther, there is no third option.[99]

In the communal sense, the church must "endure the bitter suffering brought upon it by the pressure and resistance of the world and of Satan."[100] Luther, once again, understood the community to be a collection of discreet individuals; to speak of the community without understanding this fact would be incomprehensible. Therefore, as the individual experienced the battle of God and Satan on the field of his/her own faith life, the broader community experiences a form of spiritual warfare. To press this metaphor further, an army may be charged with the carrying out of warfare, but in reality, the battles in which it engages is strictly done by the individuals therein. Each soldier's efforts are collectively responsible for the well-being of the whole army. Just so, the church is composed of believers across time and space; each individual member experiences spiritual resistance, whether the resistance is direct (e.g., demonic harassment) or indirect (e.g., temptations of the flesh and world).

Luther's views on eschatology were grounded in his interpretation of Christ's resurrection, which he understood to be the total victory of God over death. This same resurrection promised a "bodily resurrection of all who are [God's] own through baptism and faith."[101] The Christian, by virtue of his/her faith in Christ, experiences the new creation in his/her very own self; God restores humanity to a perfected state, body and soul. For this current discussion of embodiment and community, Luther's eschatology is useful in three distinct ways: (1) His theology draws us closer to the biblical understanding of death and resurrection lost in many contemporary ecclesiologies; (2) the reclaiming of this approach gives our death proper biblical meaning, which (3) explains why hope is a present reality as we wait for the resurrection of the dead. In this resurrection the claim of embodiment experiences its fullest support; God acts in the world to bring his personal, life-giving *nephesh* to the destitute body. To support these claims, I will borrow deeply from the work of N. T. Wright, who is today making many of the same assertions about Christian eschatology that Luther did five hundred

98. Luther, "Bondage of the Will," 189–90.

99. Gustaf Wingren adds that vocation itself can be an arena where God's will for the Christian encounters direct resistance from Satan. "[When one presents works before God in the kingdom of heaven] . . . we espy the work of the devil, through which works are forced up to heaven, salvation by the law, which is both blasphemy of God and scorn of one's neighbor, an impure performance of vocation (on earth). *The devil's work is in direct contradiction to God's, and ever competes with it throughout man's world* [emphasis added]." Wingren, *Luther on Vocation*, 13–14.

100. Althaus, *Theology*, 404.

101. Ibid., 410–11.

years earlier, challenging similar opponents with similar arguments. Wright laments, like Luther, the church's loss of proper biblical perspective in the matters of death and physical resurrection. For these two theologians, how people understand eschatology informs every other aspect of their theology and life.

Before one can appreciate Luther's reforming views on eschatology, it will be helpful to provide a brief overview of the biblical-historical perspectives on the two crucial terms: "death" and "resurrection." Since they are connected in Christology, the wise decision would be to survey second-Temple Judaism's beliefs about these terms and their relationship. With a healthy grasp of their meaning in the Jewish context, we may be able to better frame Lutheran eschatology as it aids the embodied theology we are currently erecting.

The Isolation of Death

Death marks the end of the believer's life until the final resurrection. The Old Testament refers to it as the first enemy,[102] while Paul in First Corinthians and John in Revelation, respectively, indicate that it is the last.[103] If we are to understand death in the way that Paul describes it, however, we should return to the socio-cultural milieu in which it was understood. This begins by examining the Old Testament foundations of Jewish thought on the matter. While there was a vast range of interpretations regarding death, from the deceased person's descent into Sheol to restrictions about necromancy for those still living, it could be argued that death itself was no cause for relief or celebration. "Death itself was sad, and tinged with evil. It was not seen, in the canonical Old Testament, as a happy release, an escape of the soul from the prisonhouse of the body."[104] To give one of many possible scriptural examples, the psalmist in Psalm 88 laments:

> For my soul is full of trouble
> and my life draws near to Sheol.

102. Death is the centerpiece of the discussion between Eve and the serpent in Gen 3. Eve reiterates God's warning that the fruit, by tasting or touching, will lead to death. The serpent immediately calls into question God's instruction. Death, to Eve, is an entity that merits avoidance and fear—and even mystery.

103. 1 Cor 15:25–26: "For he must reign until he has put all his enemies under his feet. The last enemy to be destroyed is death." Revelation 21:4, concordantly, describes the New Jerusalem, "[God] will wipe every tear from their eyes. There will be no more death or mourning or crying or pain, for the old order of things has passed away." The New Jerusalem finally fulfills the promise of Gen 3:15.

104. Wright, *Resurrection*, 91.

I am counted among those who go down to the pit;
> I am like a man without strength.
I am set apart with the dead,
> like the slain who lie in the grave,
whom you remember no more,
> who are cut off from your care.

You have put me in the lowest pit,
> in the darkest depths.
Your wrath lies heavily upon me;
> you have overwhelmed me with all your waves.
You have taken from me my closest friends
> and have made me repulsive to them.
I am confined and cannot escape;
> my eyes are dim with grief.

I call to you, O Lord, every day;
> I spread out my hands to you.
Do you show your wonders to the dead?
> Do those who are dead rise up and praise you?
Is your love declared in the grave,
> your faithfulness in Abaddon?
Are your wonders known in the place of darkness,
> Or your righteous deeds in the land of oblivion?[105]

One can notice the psalmist's deep sense of despair as he considers his inevitable fate. There is no textual evidence here to suggest that death acted as a gate into another better existence, even for the faithful. The psalmist emphasizes the isolation, the grief, even perhaps the godlessness of death. This belief conversely coincided with the firm Jewish commitment to the goodness of the God-given life demonstrated in the Genesis creation narrative.[106] To live the life of the creature was a blessing; death was the ultimate stripping of that gift. The general sentiment connected to this gloomy view of the end is that death affords the dead no opportunity to return—at least until the Final Day. To die is to be essentially forgotten.[107] Yet death's impact was not felt on merely individual levels.

---

105. Ps 88:3–12.
106. Wright, *Resurrection*, 91.
107. Ibid., 98.

Death for the second-Temple Jew was of secondary importance to the ongoing fate and survival of Israel *as a people*. "The nation and the land of the present world were far more important than what happened to an individual beyond the grave."[108] A Jew may die as all people must; the promise of God, however, allowed Israel to give death new meaning. As the seed dies to produce the plant, the life of the solitary Jew was subsidiary to the still-preserved remnant. Two implications follow from the above statement: (1) Jesus' death had significance for the whole of the Israelites, not just as a collection of individuals hoping for redemption, and (2) the created world (terrain, plants, animals) had central importance in Jewish thought. The former conclusion requires us to consider Jewish, and, therefore, early Christian, eschatology to be remarkably creaturely *and* corporate in nature. Wright suggests that the topics of death and resurrection are perhaps best understood as extensions of God's promise to deliver his people from hardship to glory, from exile to the Promised Land.[109] Considering that Pauline theology opens the door for Gentile inclusion into this hope, all humanity now can rejoice in this narrative. *We* die presently, but *we* also rise in the Last Day. The latter conclusion reminds us of the overlap between the eschatological and creaturely dimensions of embodied theology. Paul no doubt had this connection in mind when he writes in Romans 8:22, "We know that the whole creation has been groaning as in the pains of childbirth right up to the present time."

Luther and Death

When Luther speaks of death, it becomes quite apparent that he takes it with utmost seriousness. Death is neither a welcome friend to be embraced nor a reality of life that simply must be pushed to the side of one's consciousness. Death is the great enemy.

Luther's theology of death is framed by his understanding of the Law-Gospel dynamic. The Law properly generates a fear of death, for such condemnation represents God's ultimate No against the sin of humanity. Only the Christian can grasp the oncoming locomotive of God's wrath in this way, for only the Christian understands both the demands of the perfect God and the impossibility of perfect obedience. Clearly, the experience of God's rejection in Lutheran thought is immediately and paradoxically coupled with the great and overwhelming Yes that is in the gospel. The acceptance that God offers is radically present in every moment of our lives, although it

108. Ibid., 99.
109. Ibid., 121.

is only received as an expectation grounded in faith. Luther writes, "Where there is forgiveness of sins there are also life and salvation."[110] The "complete, unbroken, uninterrupted, constant, and uncontradictable experience" of this salvation can only be received in the time to come, however. In the present, the Christian can only trust in the promises of God paid in full on the cross.[111]

Still, death for Luther had devastating force; it was the "constantly threatening tyrant."[112] In his commentary on Psalm 90, Luther rejects a view of death that comes by natural processes, as if God intended from creation to set the course of human days. Rather, it is to be treated, as in the psalm, with "the most repulsive colors" and that "God's wrath is the cause of our death."[113] God created humanity to live in obedience under the lordship of the Word and "to be like God."[114] The disobedience that began in the Garden and has been perpetuated through present times necessarily invokes God's eternal wrath, a punishment that is an "inevitable and deserved consequence."[115] This wrath drives the individual to despair. For Luther, death is never considered a way out or God's gift to end suffering; death oppresses the person as ultimate destination of the sinful life.

This termination of life is not to be considered in mere physical categories. Luther realized that if one simply viewed death as a bodily end, some might be compelled to look forward to its coming. "But the fact is that we are subject to eternal death, which it is impossible for us to overcome."[116] This view resonates well with the biblical perspective on death, whereby death affects the whole person, past, present, and future.

The Hope of Resurrection

Only when one perceives death, like Luther, with all of its vitriol can one view the physical resurrection as a truly hopeful experience. If death is simply ignored or redefined in vague categories like "passing over," it still remains a threat to the human condition. Yet the central claim of the New Testament is that death is, in fact, the enemy and will be ultimately defeated in the Last Day. "God's intention is not to let death have its way with us. If

110. Taken from a quote in Althaus, *Theology*, 404.
111. Ibid.
112. AE 13:78.
113. Ibid., 77.
114. Ibid., 94.
115. Ibid.
116. Ibid., 78.

the promised final future is simply that immortal souls leave behind their mortal bodies, then death still rules—since that is a description not of the *defeat* of death but simply of death itself, seen from one angle."[117] For this reason, Jesus' resurrection (the starting point for talk about any resurrection) involved transformation of his physical self. Jesus' bodily life after the grave was totally physical, yet not *mortal*, a distinction we will soon clarify.

Luther's understanding of the Last Things has been lost to the steady cultural pressures of present times, where the bodily resurrection is marginalized in favor of a disembodied, spiritualized version of resurrection, and by extension, heaven. However, this trend is currently experiencing some significant resistance. As a case in point, N. T. Wright begins his exploration into eschatology by noting how the cultural landscape, particularly in the West, has shaped the Christian understanding of death, the afterlife, and the body. Rather than strictly observing a biblical view of the resurrection of the dead, Western culture has created a false dualism that has taken root in nearly all forms of popular Christendom. His argument begins with a critique of the modern theological understanding of God's kingdom. Rather than portraying death as an escape from the present reality into another, Wright stresses that the New Testament pointed "to God's sovereign rule coming" as a full manifestation of his presence *within the created order*.[118] Earth was to be fully restored by God's direct rule, not abandoned. The shift is substantial. A Christian cannot, in good conscience, lay waste to the present world or ignore injustices perpetrated against it by rationalizing that God will eventually destroy it anyway. No, the earth remains as the destination of God's ultimate victory march. The biblical direction of God's kingdom is from heaven to earth; this movement brings the initial victory of Jesus Christ to full fruition at the end of time. God's act of complete restoration includes humanity's very bodies, its communities *in toto*, and its relationship with the natural world.

The trajectory of God's movement toward a new creation climaxes in Revelation 21–22, where John is presented with a vision of heaven coming down to earth. Rather than separating the physical from the spiritual, the New Jerusalem has come in all fullness. Heaven and earth are not diametrically opposed but merged into one as the Lord's Prayer petition of "thy will be done, on earth as it is in heaven" is finally fulfilled.[119] In Romans 8:19–23, the nature of creation's redemption is made abundantly clear:

117. Wright, *Surprised by Hope*, 15.

118. Ibid., 18.

119. Ibid., 104–22.

> The creation waits in eager expectation for the children of God to be revealed. For the creation was subjected to frustration, not by its own choice, but by the will of the one who subjected it, in hope that the creation itself will be liberated from its bondage to decay and brought into the glorious freedom of the children of God. We know that the whole creation has been groaning as in the pains of childbirth right up to the present time. Not only so, but we ourselves, who have the firstfruits of the Spirit, groan inwardly as we wait eagerly for our adoption as sons, *the redemption of our bodies* [emphasis added].

Paul moves in a general-to-particular pattern. By doing this, he connects the liberation of creation with humanity's unique status as embodied heirs of the new creation. No longer is it satisfactory to claim a life of glorious freedom without including the redeemed body.

Before we explore the concept of resurrection in its original context, it may behoove us to consider first what the term *did not* mean, at least in the Jewish sense. First, resurrection, in the New Testament understanding of the word, was not a spiritual ascendency into heaven where the eternal soul finds bliss in the presence of the Trinity. When the Gospels speak of Jesus' resurrection, they did not mean he entered into some form of spiritual power with God in heaven, though he most certainly had such power at his disposal.[120] This view, while popular in many Christian circles, fails to address adequately the tyranny of death over humanity. Such a view would merely re-describe death in a more palatable form without ever striking a blow against it. A spiritually resurrected Jesus flies in the face of the embodied Christ that eats with his disciples (John 21:15), reveals his scars to Thomas (John 20:27), and provides convincing proofs of his newly restored life (Acts 1:3). In the Gospel accounts of Jesus' resurrection, the implication is clear: his crucified body was reanimated into some form of new life. Resurrection, whether referring to Jesus in the particular or Christendom's expectation of the future event, cannot be reduced to a purely spiritual experience based on the biblical evidence.

Second, New Testament Jews did not conceive of resurrection as the ongoing survival of an immortal soul. This view appears to be more of a Platonic relic that gained traction in the second and third centuries, as Gnostic sects began to eviscerate any theology that spoke of the body's inherent goodness. Gnostic mind-body dualism simply posited that since the body can die yet the soul is immortal, only the soul experiences some sort of ongoing life after death. Over time, this "life" was understood as a

---

120. Wright, *The Resurrection*, 204.

resurrection.[121] This philosophy misidentifies immortality as an exclusively spiritual process. To conflate these terms drastically misrepresents the form of the post-resurrected Jesus. The Easter Jesus is fully physical, but in his resurrection, enjoys (in at least one important sense) a radically new state-of-being distinct from his pre-resurrected self in which he cannot die again (1 Cor 15:42).[122] This fact separates the Jesus' particular resurrection from other resurrections in Scripture (Elijah and widow's son in 1 Kgs 17, Jairus' daughter in Matt 9, Lazarus in John 11, et al.).

Finally, resurrection was not considered, in the earliest Christian texts, to be a "one-stage postmortem journey" (i.e., from death straight to heaven or hell); this would devalue the central feature of Christian hope.[123] Resurrection, as a Jewish term, never expresses the state-of-being following death; rather, it is a term for the reality of life *after* life after death.[124] Heaven, by extension, is not a place "where you go when you die." It is, as Wright describes, "the place where God's purposes for the future are stored up."[125] The resurrection image that the New Testament more strongly endorses is the picture of God's reign coming in fullness from heaven to earth, where he restores all of his people into a new bodily life under Jesus' direct lordship. An intermediate time of waiting (i.e., between physical death and the final resurrection in the Last Day) had been largely accepted in Jesus' day, yet this post-death, pre-resurrection period has been mostly lost or misunderstood in our present discourses of the afterlife.[126] I am not suggesting here that such an interim state includes or gives support to the Roman teaching on

---

121. Some might argue that Paul speaks to a clear difference between the mortal body and the spiritual body. However, it needs to be pointed out that the distinction he makes in First Corinthians 15 is between a mortal physical body and an immortal physical body. Wright believes that the initial view (mortal v. spiritual body) imports too much Platonic thought into its presuppositions. Immortality most certainly exists in the physical form, just as the Easter Jesus cannot die yet is embodied.

122. Describing the difference between Christ's pre- and post-resurrection body warrants some caution here. Theologically speaking, Jesus' attributes and power within the Trinity are timeless and constant. One should avoid language that infers some form of Adoptionism. Still, the New Testament text affirms a fundamental change in Christ's physical qualities. He moves from perishable (indeed, he perished!) to imperishable, never to taste death again. I am indebted to the insights of Jeffrey Gibbs on this point; his presentation at the Lutheran Theologians Conference in May 2014 pressed home these nuances.

123. Wright, *Surprised by Hope*, 148.

124. Ibid., 151.

125. Ibid.

126. Luther referred to this period as a time of sleeping or resting in "the bosom of Christ." Althaus, *Theology*, 413.

purgatory; rather, the biblical text simple allows for some sort of restful post-death period in Christ's presence in anticipation of the final resurrection.

So what *is* the resurrection? The Jewish community immediately preceding the Incarnation generally understood resurrection in a dual-fold, and often overlapping, meaning: (1) the restoration of Israel to her land, (2) made manifest by the individual's physical resuscitation from the grave into a new form of life. We will return to the corporate dynamic shortly, but it is presently appropriate to consider the individual experience of resurrection as one's direct participation in God's new creation.

The personal resurrection experience within the broader communal matrix is the beholding of a radically new form of living, a life that includes an intimate relationship with both God and neighbor. God brings death out of life, as only God can. In the totality of death, then, the individual completely relies upon God's good will to restore a person from the grave. Yet this is not a restoration merely in the *temporal* sense, i.e., the body simply returns to function as if death never happened. The resurrection of humanity penetrates at the *ontological* level, where people are "not longer being subject to sickness, injury, decay, and death itself."[127] Using Paul's language in Romans 8:23 as his guide, N. T. Wright stresses that "God's people are promised a new type of bodily existence, the fulfillment and redemption of our present bodily life."[128] The New Testament writers seem to be arguing for a resurrected body that is still uniquely personal yet fundamentally different than its originally created form. This insight would be largely lost or misunderstood in church teaching for the next millennium, until an Augustinian monk would move to reclaim the biblical text.

Luther and the Resurrected Life

Luther understands resurrection to be a wholly bodily experience, falling in sync with New Testament thought. He departed significantly from the church of his era, rejecting the tradition of eschatology that taught the soul immediately beheld the glory of heaven upon death. Taking this position would have divested the Last Day of any true significance, as the soul would have no real need for a resurrected and glorified body. Luther, however, recovered the New Testament tradition of the *physically* resurrected body along with a post-death interim rest in his eschatology. Paul Althaus lays out the reasoning behind this position:

127. Wright, *Surprised by Hope*, 160.
128. Ibid., 147.

> The New Testament idea of the resurrection which affects the total man has had to give way to the immortality of the soul. The Last Day also loses its significance, for souls have received all that is decisively important long before this. Eschatological tension is no longer strongly directed to the day of Jesus' coming. The difference between this and the hope of the New Testament is very great.[129]

Holding this theological stance made Luther a reformer of the highest order once again. His emphasis on the immanent coming of Christ shifted the thrust of Christian hope away from a disembodied life in heaven to the restoration of all things, beginning in the present and experiencing full completion in Jesus' return.

Christian eschatology adds a crucial element to embodied theology. Without a sense of divine purpose, Christians are left with no direction for present living and are forced to confront the meaning of their lives alone. Eschatology, however, points theology toward an end game. It joins together the will of God as he drives forth his purposes throughout the arc of history, making his presence known to his creatures in a supremely intimate and immediate way. As a result, if the end times are misconstrued in a way that encourages a rejection of the bodily, hope is a hollow term and present-day living is nothing but a yearning for something else. Wright urges the Church to return to the Jewish-Early Christian understanding of the resurrection of the dead. The importance of the body in this life is reclaimed, for it is the present in which the Christian works toward the renewal and restoration of all things, including the restoration of the community itself.

Eschatology as a Corporate Experience

Is this undercurrent of community (and its relationship to the body) in eschatology prominent enough to merit an audit of its specific worth? Luther himself understood the link between eschatology and ecclesiology. I suggest that the corporate life of the Christian is most forcefully articulated in this branch of theology, as the Church orients itself toward the final reign of God in the eschaton. For this reason, all Christian theology is ultimately eschatological, as eschatology points the Christian down the path to God's endgame, how history has been, all along, *God's* history. According to Sasse, "[Luther] saw the church as the holy people of God of the end time, attacked by the devil, led by the Antichrist into the great temptation to fall away,

---

129. Althaus, *Theology*, 414.

and protected and preserved by Christ."[130] In Luther's particular context, the struggle was waged against the forces of Rome and their self-aggrandizement, as they attempted to supplant the role of Jesus himself as the sole arbiter of God's grace. The life of the church in Reformation Germany, therefore, regularly invoked the language of eschatology to give explanation to the disconcerting fractures between Rome and the Protestant resistance. If the church is inextricably bound to the life and doctrine of the Last Things, there is no escaping the fact that Luther viewed eschatology as an affair for the whole people of God together, not just the individual parts. Luther had solid biblical foundations for such a position.

The biblical view of death and resurrection could not be compartmentalized into individual and communal categories. In the Old Testament, hope in the resurrection sprung not from an individual's desire to escape Sheol; rather, the biblical concern was for Israel's redemption as a people. As N. T. Wright notes, "The hope of the biblical writers, which was strong and constant, focused not upon the fate of humans after death, but on the fate of Israel and her promised land. The nation and land of the present world were far more important than what happened to an individual beyond the grave."[131] The integrity of the person's afterlife, in this case, recedes against the immeasurably more important destiny *of the people*. When one considers the trajectory of Old Testament theology, this conclusion should not surprise us. The *Heilsgeschichte* brought forth by God's action is the collective story of the remnant, the gathering of a people that God preserves and takes as his own. Many of the great prophetic discourses promise peace and prosperity for the land as well as Israel's place within it.[132] God instructs Jeremiah to buy a field in the midst of the Babylonian exile, for example, promising the survival of the remnant:

> "This is what the LORD says: 'You say about this place, "It is a desolate waste, without men or animals." Yet in the towns of Judah and the streets of Jerusalem that are deserted, inhabited by neither men nor animals, there will be heard once more the sounds of joy and gladness, the voices of bride and bridegroom, and the voices of those who bring thank offerings to the house of the LORD, saying,
>
> > "Give thanks to the LORD Almighty,
> > for the LORD is good;
> > his love endures forever."

130. Sasse, *We Confess the Church*, 116.
131. Wright, *The Resurrection*, 99.
132. Ibid., 100.

For I will restore the fortunes of the land as they were before,'
says the LORD."[133]

God's preservation is oriented not toward the individual's emancipation, but instead, God's provision is promised to the whole of God's chosen people and their relationship to the land. Ezekiel, by comparison, uses the valley of dry bones imagery to reinforce God's commitment to a people wallowing in captivity; Israel will return from apparent national death, united as "one land" with "one king" (Ezek 37:22). The culmination of history from the prophetic perspective comes to fruition in the restoration of the nation. Luther strongly affirms this point. He expected that history itself, which is itself in nothing other than *Heilsgeschichte*, "will come to an end and be completed in the ultimate kingdom of God."[134] Yet this history is not understood in individual terms. The "future renewal of the entire world" is at stake: the universe and all the creatures therein.[135]

But this Old Testament view is slightly incomplete. Despite the wide-ranging meanings that death and resurrection had in the time before the Incarnation, the post-resurrection Church was surprisingly monolithic its belief in the bodily resurrection of the dead, apart from any metaphorical use.[136] This led to a near disappearance of the resurrection as a socio-political analogy for Israel and the Promised Land. Instead, the New Testament letters pressed home the fulfillment of this longing: the Messiah's kingdom has been initiated in the here and now. The triumphant return that "Israel longed for, both resurrection and restoration, [was] already coming true . . . in Christ, empowered by the Spirit."[137] The Christian expectation manifested itself not in politics or economic wealth; the Incarnation inaugurated the full coming of God's kingdom.

Before proceeding to the next chapter, it may be useful to sum up the conclusions of this chapter. Up to this point, my work has argued for a three-pronged defense of embodied theology. First, God the Creator/Sustainer gives a certain measure of inherent dignity to his creatures simply by his act of creating them. Humanity bears the imprint of a Creator God who sought to give them bodily form, as well as gifting them with blessings of a distinctly physical and communal character. Second, the embodied sacraments of Holy Baptism and Holy Communion give Christians God's very own self. The immediate presence of the Holy Spirit works regeneration

---

133. Jeremiah 33:10–11.
134. Althaus, *Theology*, 424.
135. Ibid.
136. Wright, *Resurrection*, 210.
137. Ibid., 218.

through the waters of the baptismal font, and Jesus' bodily presence is given in, with, and under the elements of bread and wine. These gifts are neither accidental nor solely physical; they are embodied. As such, God intimately and intentionally avails himself in the means of grace for the sole purpose of restoring the God-human relationship. Third, I argued that the Church participates in the ongoing restoration of all things, inaugurated by the Incarnation and awaiting full consummation at the end of time. The physical resurrection of the dead plays the central role, both in the present and future tenses. It provides the Christian with a reason to act as agents of grace in their communities now, while it simultaneously points to the hope that comes with a new heaven and new earth. Now we will consider the communal aspect of these pillars in greater depth and detail in the writings of Dietrich Bonhoeffer. If one can establish certain distinctive characteristics of the embodied Christian community, criteria could be offered to evaluate all claims of community, present or future, physical or digital.

3

DIETRICH BONHOEFFER
AND THE EMBODIED COMMUNITY

WHILE EMBODIED THEOLOGY NECESSARILY requires a solid foundation of the creaturely, sacramental, and eschatological components of the Christian faith, it remains incomplete in one sense. A theology that emphasizes the importance of human physicality without linking it more directly to the community as a whole fails to address the aforementioned isolation and/or self-centeredness that may be experienced in many contemporary contexts. This text has already noted, in general terms, how the communal aspect quietly resides within each of the three pillars. Through the theology of Dietrich Bonhoeffer, this connection is crystalized into one cohesive vision of embodied Lutheran theology. The body, as it stands for Bonhoeffer, emerges as necessarily physical and necessarily communal; he explicitly binds the physical nature of human experience to the social reality of Christian community in a helpful fashion.

Dietrich Bonhoeffer (1906–1945) was a Lutheran theologian during the rise of the National Socialist political movement in Germany. Before his martyrdom in 1945, he had successfully demonstrated his theological and ethical prowess in a variety of written works, seasoned by the sociopolitical threats that he was forced to endure. Before one can appreciate Bonhoeffer's writings, therefore, it is important to recognize two things. First, the particular historical era in which the Lutheran pastor stood must be appreciated, for it would be the context that would frame his theology. Second, Bonhoeffer employs several terms which have nuanced meanings rather different from their present definitions. It will serve us to consider these terminology issues before proceeding too far into his theological positions.

1906. His father Karl was a respected psychiatrist, practicing in Breslau during Dietrich's earliest childhood years then later in Berlin, and his mother
Paula was the daughter of a university professor and an educator herself.[1]
One of eight children, Dietrich had affectionate bonds with all of his siblings
yet by all accounts was particularly close to his twin sister, Sabine. The Bonhoeffer household was filled with laughter and joy. Part of the family *ethos*,
however, consisted of the careful use of one's language; Karl Bonhoeffer personally required each child to speak with intelligence and clarity. According
to Bosanquet, "The [Bonhoeffer] children were expected to ignore physical
pain; clear thinking and straightforward expression of one's thoughts were
demanded as a *sine qua non*. Burnt into the minds of all the children was
the positive sinfulness of ever using a 'hollow phrase.'"[2] This was the intel-
lectually-driven family atmosphere in which the young Dietrich Bonhoeffer
would be formed, both as a young man and as a student.

Two formative events would shape the young Dietrich Bonhoeffer.
First, World War I would take the life of one of his older brothers, Walter,
plunging Dietrich into a period of loneliness and introspection. It has been
suggested that this time of grief may have served as a catalyst for the young
Bonhoeffer's "first experience of the mystery we call God, his first encounter
with a reality which bursts the framework of language and is with the greatest difficulty communicated."[3] Despite the family's lack of formal religious
practice, the Bonhoeffer's were deeply committed to a Christian ethic and
"simple piety" within the household. Dietrich now embraced the roots of
this ethic, formalizing his fondness for the topic by enrolling in university
life at Tübingen. This was the second significant marker in his early development as a young man and student. In the midst of his university studies,
he had the great fortune of first-hand interaction with Holl, Seeberg, and
Harnack, each with his own impressive reputation, respectively. Bonhoeffer
was developing a reputation for debating, even contradicting (with characteristic politeness), both the hegemonic theologies of the day as well as

1. Bosanquet, *Dietrich Bonhoeffer*, 24–26. The Bonhoeffer's first residence in Berlin was in Bellevue; their house literally backing up to Bellevue Park where the royal
children found their daily amusement. After four years, they moved to Wangenheim-
strasse in Berlin-Grunewald, also called the "academic quarter." Here their neighbors
included the Adolf von Harnack and historian Hans Delbrück, among others.

2. Ibid., 28.

3. Ibid., 36.

their fiercest apologists.[4] The influence of Karl Bonhoeffer and his insistence upon careful, meaningful words paid dividends: Dietrich was maturing into an original, masterful theologian. Bonhoeffer's academic life, however, must be appreciated in light of the broader socio-economic context of the German nation, a nation in the midst of economic and social turmoil.

The Germany of the early twentieth century experienced a humiliating defeat in World War I, essentially ending the hegemony of the Prussian military machine in Europe. The Kaiser monarchy abdicated its political power at the behest of the Allies in order to prevent a greater disaster (at least in the minds of the German people): the rise of Bolshevism. The resulting piecemeal construction of a democracy convinced most Germans that the worst was over. This proved to be far from the truth. To add even more insult, the Treaty of Versailles in 1919 came down like a hammer. Germany lost territory around the globe; its colonies in Africa and Asia were occupied by French and British troops and later annexed to those empires. In Europe, the portion of Germany that had belonged to the German Empire and its antecedent states were incorporated into Poland, Czechoslovakia, France, Belgium and Denmark.

The German nation's rapid economic decline was exacerbated in the three most despised provisions of the treaty. One, Germany was forced to relinquish the portion of Poland it gained through the Prussian Partition in the eighteenth century, thereby cutting off East Prussia from the rest of the nation. Two, the German people were forced to officially accept all responsibility for the World War. Finally (and perhaps most significant), the standing army was to be reduced to a mere skeleton force. One of these provisions would have severely crippled the economic ability of Germany for years, but when taken *in toto*, the treaty created an atmosphere of uncertainty and vulnerability. Eric Metaxas captures the incredulity of the German people perfectly:

> The outcry from all quarters was great. [The Treaty of Versailles] was intolerable. It amounted to a death sentence for the nation, and that it would prove to be. But at the moment there was no recourse but to accept it and the deep humiliation that came with it. Scheidemann, the man who had thrown open the Reichstag window and fatuously proclaimed the German republic, now pronounced a curse: "May the hand wither that signs this treaty! It was signed nonetheless.[5]

4. Ibid., 60.
5. Metaxas, *Bonhoeffer*, 35.

In hindsight, such circumstances precipitated the proper environment for radicalism to emerge. Germany lacked an identity following the First World War, and the leadership void left by the monarchal system begged for a strong antidote to the bickering factions in the new democracy. This lack of national confidence, in turn, prepared the way for a charismatic, nationalistic leader in Adolf Hitler just a few short years later. His arrival signaled the end of the once-proud but now humiliated age of Prussian influence and marked the beginning of an increasingly isolated Germany, full of nationalistic fervor.

On the religious front, the German Church was heavily influenced by liberal Protestant theology, essentially divesting it of the needed resources to resist the State and the now-common demonization of Judaism.[6] The distinctions between church and state existed not as a protection against government interference in sacred matters, but rather to help the National Socialists maintain heavy control over (or, in many cases, abolition of) community organizations, including the church. Many German Christians essentially accepted the lie that the government simply sought a change of administration.[7] The church, in turn, became a legitimizing force for the Nazi regime. Unable or unwilling to see the contradiction between Nazi party platforms and orthodox Christianity, particularly regarding the philosophical concept of the *Führer*, the German churches became accomplices to Hitler's propaganda against the Jews. Prophetically resisting the now-obvious danger of such a relationship, a group of Protestant Christian pastors and theologians emerged to stand against National Socialism. Key figures, such as Bonhoeffer, Hermann Sasse, and renowned Reformed theologian, Karl Barth, were instrumental in the development of such a foil, the Confessing Church. Central to the Confessing Church's credo was a rejection of any assertion of authority the state held over religious matters. On a practical level, this group dismissed claims by Adolf Hitler that he was the sole authority of the Christian church in Germany and denounced the mistreatment of German Jews. This culminated in the production of the Barmen Declaration (1934), the Confessing Church's public rejection of any secular power that attempted to supersede Scripture and the Lordship of

6. German Liberal Protestantism had several notable characteristics: 1) A belief that the intellectual gains of the Enlightenment (particularly in science) could be applied to a more naturalistic reading of the Bible; 2) the limiting of objective authority in the biblical text; and 3) a tendency to view Scripture as grounds for moral living over-and-against any claim to truth through historical propositions.

7. Hermann Göring famously implored the German people to accept the Führer's leadership in all areas of German life, including matters of the church. This was cloaked in the vocabulary of unity, as Göring attempted to draw all Christian religious groups under this control. See Metaxas, chapter 10.

Jesus Christ.[8] Here begins the struggle for truth between Bonhoeffer and the state.

To divorce Bonhoeffer from his historical context would be a critical mistake. A great deal of his writings directly or indirectly address the situation of the Christian Church in Germany, and his own engagement in German political affairs as a part of the resistance movement frequently emerges as the subject of Bonhoeffer's inner struggles. It is from this sociopolitical milieu that Bonhoeffer's "theology of sociality" takes it form.[9]

Bonhoeffer and Terminology

With a better grasp of his historical context, it is presently important to consider Bonhoeffer's unique use of three terms: reality, freedom, and sin. These concepts reach into various portions of Bonhoeffer's theology and require some nuanced attention.

Like many Lutheran theologians, Bonhoeffer's theology is heavily Christocentric. Not surprisingly, his understanding of the concrete Christian community emerges within a broader picture of who Christ is *as the source of all reality.* This emergence is better understood in light of two important insights. One, reality is only understood through the lens of Christ. He is the grounding of everything that exists—past, present, and future. "The incarnation is the statement about 'objective' reality in the sense that there is a connection between God in Christ and all human life which is all-embracing and ontological and prior to all human thinking, willing, and believing."[10] Christ cannot be separated from the whole of reality, nor be considered a separate province within it. Rather, Christ permeates and sustains the real as its very ground for being.[11] Therefore, no account of true community can exist without the presence of the Incarnation as a fundamental preceding condition. This reverberates with the deep echoes of Luther's notion of God as Sustainer. God holds the world together; it is in him that Christians "live and move and have [their] being" (Col 1:17; Acts 17:28).

---

8. Bonhoeffer gave a radio address on January 30, 1933, against the "Führer Principle." Before he could finish his speech he was cut off, presumably by Nazi censors. For a good description of the principle and an analysis of the events surrounding this day, see Metaxas, chapter 9.

9. Green, *Bonhoeffer.* The term, "theology of sociality," is taken from Clifford Green's seminal work on Bonhoeffer.

10. Moltmann, "The Lordship of Christ and Human Society," 59.

11. Ott, *Reality & Faith,* 186.

Two, Bonhoeffer understands that this "reality" cannot be a retreat into ethical theories or principles. Christ enters into concrete communities of real people; he is not the savior of ideas but of men and women. Heinrich Ott brings this concept home well: "To be conformed with the incarnate is to have the right to be the man one really is. Now there is no more pretence, no more hypocrisy or self-violence, no more compulsion to be something other, better and more ideal than what one is. God loves the real man. God became the real man."[12] Bonhoeffer consistently avoids a theology that rests in principles and disembodied ethics; all Christology must impact the individual, as well as the community, in concrete situations. Therefore, the proper frame of human reference within this concrete situation must first be grounded in the reality of Christ.[13] This includes all social responsibilities and relationships, since identity is constructed, to a large (if not total) degree, by the various associations one holds (e.g., family, neighborhood, and/or ethnicity). Christ makes available these associations and exists as their precondition for existence.

Freedom, as often understood in modern Western societies, is the condition in which non-coerced decisions can be made by the human agent. Freely chosen actions come with minimal, if any, restraint or condition, except in rare cases.[14] Bonhoeffer understands freedom only in the light of his broader understanding of community. Freedom cannot be extricated from its effect on the neighbor; decisions necessarily shape the Other. With this in mind, Bonhoeffer seeks to define freedom as the capacity to serve one another in brotherly love and fellowship. To be free is not license for unrestricted action; it is a freedom that is offered by God for the purpose of strengthening the community in love. The freedom of the "natural life" (that is, a life given by God and oriented toward Christ's return) is not absolute; it has been granted to humanity "for God and for their neighbor."[15] Clifford Green notes that this definition has deep roots in the writings of Paul, Augustine, Luther, and Barth.[16]

Linked closely with the concept of freedom, Bonhoeffer uses "sin" in ways that branch out from traditional Lutheran frameworks. While

12. Ibid.

13. This definition of reality must not be divorced from the understanding of something as *factual*. Rather, there is a fundamental reality that precedes all others. As Ott explains, "The factual is not yet the real but something abstracted from the fullness of the real. This fullness, properly speaking, is God, the reconciliation of the world in him, his reconciling presence." *Reality & Faith*, 175.

14. Such cases might be the threatening of the President or saying "hijack" on an airplane. These are matters that have special security interests involved.

15. Bonhoeffer, *Ethics*, 174.

16. Green, *Bonhoeffer*, 320.

Bonhoeffer certainly would have agreed with Luther that sin emerges from the powers of "sin, death, and the Devil," he generates a hamartiology that is remarkably social in nature. Martin Luther often describes the problem of sin (and by association, the soteriological solution) as a matter of the guilty conscience before a wrathful Judge. For Luther, sin was a part of a broader pattern. Luther knew that he should love and fear a God he intuitively hated, his conscience bearing the burden of this impossible task. This caused Luther to loathe God all the more, exacerbating the distress in his conscience. The Pauline insistence of grace alone through faith alone allowed Luther to escape this cycle, transforming his view of God from vindictive judge to loving father. Christ enters as a one who both performs the perfect sacrifice and releases the guilty conscience as humanity's advocate before God.

Bonhoeffer's view of sin and guilt, by contrast, tends to stress the active characteristics of humanity's rebellion. More than experiencing a guilty conscience before God, Bonhoeffer's sinful person was the individual who asserted the ego in domination of another. All sin, in this sense, is socially grounded. The other person is seen as a means to end, not an end in itself. Here one can see the relationship between Bonhoeffer's notions of sin and freedom. Humanity's most pressing need is to experience the cross of Christ as a freeing force; a person's freedom is not to be exercised as a freedom-for-oneself but as freedom-for-the-other.

This distinction becomes clearer when one applies the Latin phrase, *homo incurvatus in se* ("man turned in on himself"), as a proper expression of Bonhoeffer's concept of sin.[17] Sin drives the ego to assert its own ends, its selfishness, against the other person but remains stridently against any authentic form of community.[18] In order to break this selfishness, this inward turn, God's grace liberates man through Christ's atoning sacrifice and releases the individual to engage others in love. The resulting freedom does not exist to feed individual desires; on the contrary, it allows the Christian to love God and neighbor for the first time. Bonhoeffer adds, "All who countenance that they need only to come to themselves, in order to be in God, are doomed to hideous disillusion in the experience of being-, persisting-, and *ending-up-turned-in-upon-themselves utterly* [emphasis added]—the experience of utmost loneliness in its tormenting desolation and sterility."[19] Bonhoeffer concludes that all human efforts to awaken to some internal

17. This phrase will also shed light on Bonhoeffer's understanding of freedom. Only when a person is broken from this inward curvature can he be free to love God and neighbor.

18. Bonhoeffer, *Ethics*, 178. Bonhoeffer takes this idea to its ultimate conclusion: "Life that makes itself absolute, that makes itself its own goal, destroys itself."

19. Bonhoeffer, *Act and Being*, 42.

capacity to love God results in the opposite effect, the inability to recognize God's gift of himself in freedom and the joy of service to one's neighbor. Freedom and responsibility, therefore, walk hand-in-hand.[20]

Bonhoeffer and the Pillars of Embodied Theology

Earlier in this proposal, I introduced three categories by which one could construct a holistic understanding of embodiment: Creatureliness, Sacramental, and Eschatological. None of these categories, however, are monolithic in nature; they often overlap.[21] These strands, each of particular importance, are best understood in light of their function within the community. Therefore, the final critical characteristic of a robust Lutheran embodied theology is the communal component. This communal aspect functions, in many ways, as the crucial adhesive for the other three components.

The above three strands of embodied theology were well recognized by Bonhoeffer. Humanity, he says, "yearns for the physical presence of other Christians. Man was created a body, the Son of God appeared on earth in the body, he was raised in the body, in the sacrament the believer receives the Lord Christ in the body, and the resurrection of the dead will bring about the perfected fellowship of God's spiritual-physical creatures."[22] Each of the three dimensions is listed (in order, no less); yet Bonhoeffer used these against the broader backdrop of the Christian in life with others. We shall presently consider the communal dynamic at work within each of the three components, noting where Bonhoeffer takes particularly nuanced positions that separate his theology from Luther or at least elaborates on the Reformer's theology. Second, I will note the specific Bonhoefferian Christology which demonstrates the unique disposition of the Incarnation in each pillar.

20. Green, *Bonhoeffer*, 320. Martin Luther used *homo incurvatus in se* to inform his own understanding of sin and soteriology in his Roman lectures. Luther also uses this phrase as the backbone for his treatise *On Christian Liberty*. This is just one of the countless ways in which the Reformer deeply influenced Bonhoeffer.

21. For example, Bonhoeffer will often use eschatological language in his understanding of creatureliness and the sacraments. In addition, I will draw attention to the presence of the Incarnation in all three pillars later in the chapter.

22. Bonhoeffer, *Life Together*, 19–20.

Bonhoeffer and Creatureliness

Bonhoeffer recognized with simple clarity the ontological reality of human creatureliness. The human creature was and is formed by the hands of God to exist in relationship with God himself and neighbor. However, Bonhoeffer uses creatureliness as a way to press home some important nuances in his theology. Creatureliness is the very characteristic that keeps a person mindful of his/her ongoing sinful desire to be *sicut deus*; the limitations of the body properly keep an individual not at the "center" (a place reserved for God alone) but at the boundary, *oriented to the center*. As a proper sounding board for this examination, consider Bonhoeffer's understanding of creatureliness prior to the Fall. The "initial state," or pre-Fall condition, is a demonstration of God's radical freedom as Creator. Bonhoeffer explains, "In the beginning God created the heavens and the earth. That means that the Creator, in freedom, creates the creature. Their connexion is not conditioned by anything except freedom, which means that it is unconditioned."[23] Humanity's primal existence bears the very marks of God's creative act, without compulsion or malice. Bonhoeffer adds that the blessing that God offers to Adam (Gen 1:28) underscores the reality of God's own goodness. God outright "affirms man totally in the world of the living." This affirmation is the totality of the divine blessing: "his creatureliness, his worldliness, and his earthliness."[24] These characteristics are not divorced from Adam's role within community; rather, Bonhoeffer understood this initial state as one of intense solidarity and fellowship intrinsic to his shared condition with Eve.

What is the significance of the prelapsarian body? For Bonhoeffer, the body is absolutely essential to an individual's identity, not in some figurative sense, but as a concrete testimony to the person's status as a "very good" creature. The body bears the marks of God's creativity, and therefore, embodies the divine witness to all of creation. It is worthwhile to quote Bonhoeffer at length here:

> Yahweh shapes man with his own hands. This expresses two things. First, the bodily nearness of the Creator to the creature, that it is really he who makes me—man—with his own hands; his concern, his thought for me, his design for me, his nearness to me. And secondly there is his authority, the absolute superiority in which he shapes and creates me, in which I am his

23. Bonhoeffer, *Creation and Fall*, 16.
24. Ibid., 44.

creature; the fatherliness in which he creates me and in which I worship him.[25]

And, later, he adds:

> Man's origin is in a piece of earth. His bond with the earth belongs to his essential being . . . From it he has his body. His body belongs to his essential being. Man's body is not his prison, his shell his exterior, but man himself. Man does not 'have' a body; he does not 'have' a soul; rather, he 'is' body and soul. Man in the beginning is really his body. He is one. He is his body, as Christ is completely his body, as the Church is the body of Christ. The man who renounces his body renounces his existence before God the Creator.[26]

Note these two important points. First, Bonhoeffer clearly desires to connect creatureliness (and by extension, the physical body) with dignity, a dignity located in an individual's "nearness" to God. Here he echoes Luther, proclaiming a particular joy in the ontological status of his bodily life.[27] Second, Bonhoeffer does not view physicality as one element or component of human existence, as if a human was a machine understood only by its parts. Rather, the body is essentially connected to the person's identity. On this point Bonhoeffer is clearly condemning all mind-body dualist interpretations of human existence. The body expresses itself in two theologically notable ways: It bears witness to a person's "nearness to the Creator" and also indicates his/her kinship with Christ, who himself was "completely his body, as the Church is the body of Christ."[28] Whereas Luther's attention was, at times, heavily focused on the relationship between humanity and God the Father (in both Creator and Sustainer roles), Bonhoeffer is already forming Christological bonds between humanity and its fully divine kin, Jesus.[29] The physical body acts as a visible demonstration and reminder of Christ's solidarity with humanity. In his bodily limitation, Jesus shows humanity another concrete feature of his humiliation.

---

25. Ibid., 50.

26. Ibid., 50–51.

27. It may be useful to recall the Lutheran understanding of death laid out in chapter 2. Bodily death, as the final enemy, stands in direct contrast (even the polar opposite, if you will) to God's declaration of goodness found in bodily life. See pages 57–61.

28. Bonhoeffer, *Creation and Fall*, 51.

29. Luther's work, on the whole, is remarkably Trinitarian. Perhaps this fact is overlooked due to the overwhelming amount of scholarly attention his Christology receives, comparatively speaking.

The body identifies man and woman as creatures of the Creator. This identifying characteristic opens up a fundamental reality: the human person is finite.[30] Bonhoeffer discusses, at length, the nature of human finitude in several of his works, but rather than bemoan the fact that a person has a "limit," he regards this restriction as a positive development within his theology of community. In one sense, this limit is encountered in the very nature of one's bodily boundary; an individual recognizes his/her own limitations *as an embodied being*. In another sense, God's prohibition in Gen 2:17 placed another limit upon humanity; their will and action would not be unbounded.[31] The creation of Eve introduces a third sense of the term, "limit." Here Bonhoeffer stresses the communal aspect of embodied living with great force. Eve's existence forces Adam to consider that this "other person is a creature of God" and as such, limits him. "The other person is the limit placed upon me by God. I love this limit and I shall not transgress it because of my love. This means nothing except that the two, who remain *two* as creatures of God, become *one* body, i.e. belong to one another in love."[32]

Human finitude becomes a means by which God gives grace through community. The relationship of limited creatures, as expressed first in Adam and Eve, stands as one of the biblical foundations for Bonhoeffer's "being-for-others," not as a principle for some vague humanitarian benevolence, but rather, as an embodied expression of Christ's love for humanity. The "community of God in the vicarious action of Christ becomes effective in the vicarious acts of men for one another, in the sociality of being-for-others in the church; in self-sacrifice and love, in intercession and forgiveness of sins."[33] As Luther's was before him, Bonhoeffer's theology is remarkably Christocentric, perhaps even more so, as every creaturely act embodies Christ's life, death, and resurrection by proxy. Being-for-others only exists under the banner of Christ's sacrifice and final victory. Because Jesus gave up his physical life as the perfect sacrifice, men and women exist as embodied creatures that can both praise God for his workmanship and encourage others in their shared limitation.

---

30. Consider the historical context of this position. Nazi Germany pinned much of its anthropology on the superiority of the Aryan race, and by extension, it denigrated the "failings" or "frailty" of other races. Bonhoeffer's own anthropological position of humility runs distinctively against his socio-political milieu in this regard.

31. Once again, it is an interesting contrast between the humility of Bonhoeffer's anthropology and the unabashed optimism of Hegelian philosophy which was so prevalent in German philosophical circles at the turn of the 20th century.

32. Bonhoeffer, *Creation and Fall*, 66.

33. Moltmann, "The Lordship of Christ," 45.

Bonhoeffer's description of humanity's limit allows one to see more clearly his understanding of sin. Sin may be seen as a transgression of the limit existing between two people, or in the case of communal forms of sin, a transgression of one group upon the integrity of another. Whereas before Eve helped Adam bear his own limitations in mutual love, if such love fails or is "destroyed," a person makes a claim upon another. The ego attempts to assert its authority over the neighbor, violating the very boundary which God provides as a place of mutual love and burden-bearing. For Bonhoeffer, the transgression of the limit is when the individual resides at the center, pushing God out to the boundaries. Yet such a person is alone; he/she is *sicut deus*. The limitless individual is fully isolated and the full manifestation of *homo incurvatus in se*.[34] This insight is particularly poignant, considering that the doctrine of the *Führer* outlawed any dissent in Bonhoeffer's Germany. Hitler was in the process of becoming the embodiment of his own age's transgression; he attempted to be *sicut deus* where no charitable view toward the Other could hope to exist. With this frame of reference, Hitler's death by suicide was a foregone conclusion, the logical endgame of radical isolation.

Orders of Creation v. Orders of Preservation

In Genesis 1–2, God elevates Adam and Eve to a special place among God's creatures, having a certain dominion over the natural world along with the power, in Adam's case, of naming his fellow animals: "God blessed them and said, 'Be fruitful and increase in number; fill the earth and subdue it. Rule over the fish of the sea and the birds of the air and over every living creature that moves on the ground" (1:28). And, later in 2:19, "[God] brought [the animals] to the man to see what he would name them; and whatever the man called each living creature, that was its name." Built into the foundations of the natural world, God creates certain hierarchies of responsibility that maintained a measure of societal order.[35] Such structures had a secondary role of restraining rampant evil while setting forth a proper framing of the human-animal relationship. Yet in the hands of a sinful human race, these structures of order could and would be used as tools to manipulate a great evil. The tension between order and freedom would frame

---

34. Bonhoeffer, *Creation and Fall*, 80.

35. See also Paul's commendation of those who "bear the sword" in Romans 13:1–8. He explicitly states that God institutes secular government and that the one in authority is "God's servant."

Bonhoeffer's understanding of creatureliness, both in his writings and his everyday experience in Nazi Germany.

Bonhoeffer's theology never strayed too far away from his historical context. At times, this reality forced him to take theological positions that challenged traditional expressions of Lutheranism. The most significant of these divergences was Bonhoeffer's rejection of the popular understanding of Luther's "orders of creation" [*Schöpfungsordnungen*], the theological perspective that gives a certain measure of natural authority to secular institutions apart from the special revelation of Christ. The tension between the German misapplication of Luther's position and Bonhoeffer's "orders of preservation" [*Erhaltungsordnungen*] provides us with a distinctly rich opportunity to witness Bonhoeffer's theology come face-to-face with his cultural milieu.

Deriving his understanding of the orders of creation from the aforementioned Genesis passage, Luther believed that God's rule on earth was manifested into two distinct *Reichs*, or "kingdoms."[36] God's will is carried out by his direct rule in the affairs of Word and Sacrament, as well as the indirect methods found in governance, peace-keeping, and vocation. In the right-hand kingdom the direction of the relationship is vertical, as God justifies and conforms humanity unto himself. God carries his will forth through his grace, seeking "to convey salvation to human beings through the Gospel."[37] The believer could walk in the freedom of God's love, apart from any rule of Law or condition. This kingdom exists to restore the relationship God has with his people and allows humanity to partake in the blessings of being spiritual creatures.

In the left-hand kingdom, God uses natural structures, or ordinances, by which evil is restrained and chaos is avoided.[38] This realm has a horizontal orientation, as it "includes everything that contributes to the preservation

36. Contemporary scholars are suggesting that Luther's kingdom language has been somewhat misunderstood. This is partly due to the fact that Luther's use of the terms evolves over time. Earlier in his career, Luther sets up the two realms in an eschatological sense; the kingdom of God and the kingdom of Satan are set in perpetual opposition. Later, he takes a broader view on the affairs of the left-hand kingdom and includes the family, marriage, and property. These, according to Luther, have "nothing to do with the fall into sin." Althaus, *The Ethics of Martin Luther*, 52. Luther goes so far as to say that these things are "divine blessings." He writes: "God has a double blessing, a physical one for this life and a spiritual one for eternal life. Hence we say that it is a blessing to have riches, children, etc., but only at its own level, namely, for this present life" (AE 26:250–51).

37. Barth, *Theology*, 318.

38. AE 4:7. The left-hand kingdom is laid forth for a world divorced from the garden of Eden; Luther calls the household, state, and church "inconveniences" that are nevertheless "adorned" with the "brilliant rays of the Word of God."

of this earthly life, especially marriage and family, the entire household, as well as property, business, and all the stations and vocations which God has instituted."[39] Justice, for example, is only achievable in this world because God institutes and sustains these hierarchies. Luther believed that God provided "three divinely ordered institutions in which people participated during their lives in this world."[40] These natural hierarchies were: (1) daily life grounded in marriage and domestic affairs; (2) the government or state; and (3) the church itself. "By this threefold authority God has protected the human race against the devil, the flesh, and the world, to the end that offenses may not increase but may be cut off. Parents are the children's tutors, as it were. Those who are grown up and are remiss the government curbs through the executioner. In the church those who are obstinate are excommunicated."[41] These institutions, known as "orders of creation," allow the civil authorities to enforce laws that promote the ongoing maintenance of society under the assumption that such agents have God-given legitimacy.

In Nazi Germany, Bonhoeffer was deeply concerned that the government would manipulate this legitimacy and claim a God-given authority to rule those of who were perceived to be the weaker or lesser class, whether by ethnicity or by social status. Luther's two-realm theology could be incorrectly applied to give unimpeded sanction to the government to assert its own ends. Since the two kingdoms provided different benefits and were to remain distinct, secular structures like the state could administer justice (and punishments) to the people without any direct oversight by the church. In fact, the church was obliged to allow the state the freedom to administer justice since God himself authenticated their authority to do so. But such an interpretation of Luther's work would have horrified the reformer. Luther, in many instances, excoriated government authorities when they strayed from their godly responsibility to serve the general populace.[42] Still, a secularized orders of creation threatened to justify the widespread governmental powers in Nazi Germany, manipulating the understanding of the two kingdoms toward the end of isolating God in the right-hand realm and government in the left.[43]

---

39. Althaus, *The Ethics of Martin Luther*, 47.

40. Wright, *Two Kingdoms*, 130.

41. AE 3:279.

42. AE 45:112–13. In this particular instance, Luther calls those princes who would confiscate the New Testament from their subjects "tyrants" and "murderers of Christ."

43. A helpful guide in this discussion is Kolb, "Luther's Hermeneutics of Distinctions," 168–84.

Early in his theological career, Bonhoeffer noticed the immense danger lurking beneath the surface of such a theological point-of-view. The underlying feature of this theology is the presence (or absence) of an accessible natural knowledge of God. During the early parts of the twentieth-century, two theologians brought this particular theological point-of-interest to the forefront of Protestantism, Emil Brunner and Karl Barth.[44] These two titans engaged in a now-famous debate which found its genesis in Barth's outright rejection of natural theology; he took the staunch position that no reliable knowledge of God could emerge apart from the revelation of Christ himself. Brunner, by contrast, insisted that such knowledge was possible albeit incompletely known as a result of human sin.[45] This knowledge was afforded to humanity by virtue of its elevated status at creation and the witness of the individual's conscience. Not to be outdone, Barth responds to the critique with his own reply, *Nein!*, claiming that Brunner's challenge was ineffectual and ultimately destructive to the Church.[46] Supporting his opponent's posi-

44. The substance of this critique can be found in Brunner's article, "Nature and Grace," and in Barth's final reply, "No!" Both are collected in the following source: Brunner and Barth, *Natural Theology*. These articles, written in 1934, were first published together in 1946.

45. Ibid., 15–64. Brunner's critique of Barth had several components to it, but let me give attention to the two most central. First, Brunner argues that man retains, at least in the formal sense, some measure of the *imago Dei*. That is, by virtue of their "superior position" in creation, humanity retains its "special relation to God" (23). "This *function* or calling as a bearer of the image is not only not abolished by sin; rather is it [sic] the presupposition of the ability to sin and continues within the state of sin" (23). Materially speaking, the image is destroyed where no part of the sinner "is not defiled by sin" (24).

Second, Brunner rejects Barth's contention that "every attempt to assert a 'general revelation' of God in nature, in the conscience and in history, is to be rejected outright" (20; this is Brunner's summary of Barth's position, not a quote from Barth himself). Here Brunner argues that God leaves certain imprints of his goodness throughout creation; this remnant, if you will, allows humanity to recognize his goodness as a form of general revelation. In addition, Brunner says that people know the will of God innately, so that "they are without excuse . . . Only because men somehow know the will of God are they able to sin" (25).

46. Barth believed Brunner's argumentation to be riddled with contradictions and inconsistencies. God's creation, for Barth, cannot exist as a precondition to Christ nor is it recognizable as a gift without the grace of Christ (83). He asks, "How can the preservation of man's existence and of the room given him for it be understood as the work of the one true God unless one means thereby that man is preserved through Christ for Christ, for repentance, for faith, for obedience, for the preservation of the Church? How can it be understood unless baptism is taken into account? How can one speak of these things unless the one revelation in Christ in the Old and New Testaments is taken into account?" Barth insists that such a position would be to defy the Reformation's insistence on *sola scriptura* and *sola fide*. Grace outside of the person of Jesus Christ was, for Barth, an impossibility.

tion would be tantamount to claiming that all societal relationships exist as a part of God's established order at creation. Therefore, in Brunner's natural theology, history and nature retain some autonomous authority as sources of revelation, something Bonhoeffer (let alone, Barth) could not abide. Bonhoeffer was deeply impacted by Barth, both as a mentor and as a theologian, and so it is no great surprise that Bonhoeffer himself rejected Brunner's position on general revelation.

Bonhoeffer had good reasons to side with Barth on this issue, both theologically and pragmatically. Knowledge of God through exclusively natural means would further a *division*, as opposed to Luther's desire for a *distinction*, between the right-hand and left-hand realms, essentially allowing an opportunist government to claim a divinely-appointed mandate apart from Christ himself. More specifically, any political or economic power could use the orders of creation as a means to justify any action the state deemed necessary. As Clifford Green describes, "A theology which developed 'orders of creation' gave, at the very least, an opportunity for reading off from nature, history and society the divine will for the state, family, economic organization, and so on."[47] The ultimate ideal running through this doctrine was the belief that "with the help of 'unbroken orders of creation' the possibility is opened up for man to return into a sinless world, thereby making Christ's death upon the cross superfluous."[48] This utopian disposition has significant national implications. Obedience to the orders of creation, argues Bonhoeffer, leads to the following conclusions: "Because the nations have been created different, each one is obliged to preserve and develop its characteristics. That is obedience towards the Creator. And if this obedience leads one to struggles and to war, these too must be regarded as belonging to the order of creation."[49] This "obedience" cuts two ways. In one sense, the nation must obey God to fulfill their divine-given destiny, even if that leads to radical race-based policies (internal) or warfare (external). But, secondly, this sense of duty is also communicated to the people; the government, in their obedience to God, demands the absolute obedience of its citizenry. Any form of individual dissidence can be construed as a rebellion against God's will for the *Volk*.

If the strong were mandated by God to rule the weak, then those in power could use any resources at their disposal to either exploit their weakness for the ongoing consolidation of their power, or even worse, demand an accounting of the weaker person's very existence. Internally, the Nazis

47. Green, *Bonhoeffer*, 203.
48. Weissbach, "Christology and Ethics," 134.
49. Bonhoeffer, *No Rusty Swords*, 165.

worked toward the implementation of the Final Solution, whereby all Jews were subjected to labor and death camps, all the while assuming that this was their God-given obligation as their stronger race. Externally, they could justify large-scale wars against their European neighbors under the guise that God's will was being carried forth on the backs of German panzers. The presence of Hegelian philosophy in such a belief is unmistakable.[50] The use of this ethos was not motivated by any attempt to understand the biblical concept of orders of creation, nor Luther's particular interpretation of it. Luther firmly held that all government action is subject to the Word of God; if Christ is defied in a state action, the government loses its legitimacy. Bonhoeffer's hope was to divest the National Socialists of any theological justification for the above abuses, recognizing as well that many of Hitler's actions had support in the writings of pro-Nazi theologians in German Christian churches.[51]

Bonhoeffer understood that any attempt to construct natural hierarchies of power (whether familial, national, or racial) apart from the revelation of Christ would be doomed to fail. Here he sounds distinctively like Karl Barth in his rejection of a natural theology, or general revelation, understood apart from Christ. "Every place as well as every situation is qualified only by the call of Jesus Christ."[52] And, more often than not, deriving direct, natural human-to-world relationships as the will of God (apart from the revelation of Christ) would lead to the widespread exploitation of the many at the behest of the few.[53]

So what is Bonhoeffer's response? He offers an alternative to Luther's nomenclature, replacing the reformer's "orders of creation" with his own "orders of preservation" [*Erhaltungsordnungen*]. God's rule in the world is not an authorization for the state to institute their will over and against those it would oppress; rather, the state is created by God "to *preserve* the life which the Creator continues to affirm as Preserver."[54] Bonhoeffer acknowledges that, "preservation is God's act with the fallen world, through which he guarantees the possibility of a new creation."[55] In this way, the state

---

50. The nineteenth-century German philosopher Georg Hegel believed, among other things, that progress was both inevitable and an intrinsic good. He understood this as a historical phenomenon, where the progress of humanity could, and would, be ultimately embodied in the Prussian State.

51. Green, *Bonhoeffer*, 217.

52. Weissbach, "Christology and Ethics," 134.

53. Green, *Bonhoeffer*, 323–24.

54. Ibid., 204.

55. Bonhoeffer, *No Rusty Swords*, 167.

has power only insofar as it acknowledges the source of its authority and remains submissive in its obedience to the will of God:

> The kingdom of God assumes form in the state insofar as the state acknowledges and maintains the order of the preservation of life, and insofar as it holds itself responsible for protecting this world from flying to pieces and for exercising its authority here in preventing the destruction of life. Its function is not to create new life, but to preserve the life that is given.[56]

Bonhoeffer stresses that God's design in the midst of a fallen world is a community that prevents destruction, resists arbitrary rule, and protects the people from the "lust for power."[57] The orders of preservation openly defied Nazi attempts to subdue the Jewish people. He recognized with clarity, from the Third Reich's very beginning, that when an order prohibits the proclamation of the gospel, it can and must be dissolved.[58]

Bonhoeffer used the orders of preservation as a way to bring Christology back into the understanding of sanctification that includes a space for creaturely obedience. Prior to his theological innovation, Protestant theologians largely accepted that God's commandments to his creatures could be hidden in nature. If the person (or nation) discerns God's will from the design of the created world, they may act toward the fulfillment of those commands. Yet Bonhoeffer understood that sin had overtaken creation to such a degree that the two were hardly distinguishable; certainly no person could "separate the one from the other."[59] No, the commandment of God must be revealed in Christ:

> From Christ alone must we know what we should do. But not from him as the preaching prophet of the Sermon on the Mount, but from him as the one who gives us life and forgiveness, as the one who has fulfilled the commandment of God in our place, as the one who brings and promises the new world. We can only perceive the commandment where the law is fulfilled, where the new world of the new order of God is established. Thus we are completely directed towards Christ, towards the new creation.[60]

Two distinct thoughts begin to coalesce for Bonhoeffer: (1) Christ as the only ground for reality and (2) the creaturely limitation of humanity. The

56. Bonhoeffer, "Thy Kingdom Come," 40–41.
57. Green, *Bonhoeffer*, 204.
58. Ibid.
59. Bonhoeffer, *No Rusty Swords*, 166.
60. Ibid.

definition and purpose of creatureliness cannot be discerned in some vague natural order; sin makes this impossible. For the Christian, the ontological reality of being a creature necessarily compels one to follow Christ. Christ's presence in the world opens up a path for godly obedience and mutual bearing of responsibility. The intimacy of community is made possible because it requires each person to embody Christ to one another in acts of restoration and mutual limit-bearing. Christ stands as the origin and fulfillment of this being-for-others; his command is the command to participate in the community of the gospel towards the preservation of the world.[61]

To be creaturely under the Bonhofferian model means that each Christian is a responsible agent tasked with bringing the gospel and restoration to the weakest members of the community. This task is given authority and value from outside itself, from Christ, as the act of restoration points to the new creation. Bonhoeffer's orders of preservation, then, serves to reinforce the communal nature of his work; the community is strengthened in its cooperative efforts to uplift the weak through service and hospitality.

Bonhoeffer's work on creatureliness, in summation, points to Christ as the source and exemplar of the creaturely experience. First, Jesus makes himself nothing in the Incarnation, yet in his humiliation displays an intense solidarity with humanity; this provides humanity with an assurance of God's Yes. God's nearness to his creatures cannot be understood in theologically abstract concepts like omnipresence; nearness requires a certain physicality and depth of relationship. The divine nearness is most fully realized in the Incarnation. Second, this solidarity manifests itself in the mutual bearing of one another's limitations. Each act of being-for-others is only made possible by the cross, as the sacrifice for all humanity is both embodied here and frees humanity from its inward turn. Finally, Bonhoeffer points us to a theology of preservation. His stance rejects a natural order to creation apart from the Incarnation. Jesus, as the sole grounding for reality, not only gives humanity a bearing toward the good but also inaugurates the coming of a new creation in which his creatures can participate. This eschatological reality points humanity toward a common hope for the future under the cross and the empty tomb; a hope, Bonhoeffer reminds us, that is intensely communal in nature.

61. This is not to say that Bonhoeffer would suggest that non-Christians cannot participate in the order of society. Preservation, for the Christian, is an explicit charge with which to confront and restore the world with the word and sacrament. For the non-Christian, he/she can serve God's will indirectly in affairs of the left-hand kingdom as this realm preserves the given life of the individual and serves as a protector of the "community order." Godsey, *Preface to Bonhoeffer*, 42.

Bonhoeffer understands human creatureliness to be, at its core, an expression of God's design for community. His language of limitation provides a clear picture of God's intended design of mutual love and gives insight into his understanding of human sin. These insights provide substantial resources to the Christian parish that seeks to mitigate much of the hardship imposed on society from intrusive government, unrestrained business, or other matters of social justice. God's solution in the Incarnation had to effectively counter the human proclivity to dominate their fellow creatures which had disrupted God's design for community.

Bonhoeffer and the Sacramental

The bodily presence of Christ in history and in the ongoing life of the Church meet the modern believer in a particularly unique way—the sacraments of Holy Baptism and Holy Communion. Here at the font and table, the nearness of God is expressed in a radical demonstration of embodiment. The physical means of grace offer the believer an intimate form of participation within the life of Christ.

How do the sacraments function in Bonhoeffer's theology of sociality? First, the sacraments of Holy Baptism and Holy Communion are wholly passive experiences of God's grace. Bonhoeffer echoes Paul as he speaks of baptism. At the font, Christ unites himself to humanity by taking on all humanity's sin at the cross and lifting all believers up with himself in the resurrection. "But if Christ is in you, your body is dead because of sin, yet your spirit is alive because of righteousness. And if the Spirit of him who raised Jesus from the dead is living in you, he who raised Christ from the dead will also give life to your mortal bodies through his Spirit, who lives in you" (Rom 8:10–11). Since baptism is understood as a dying to sin, one cannot "achieve his own death." This death is only accomplished in Christ as the free gift of God, and as such, it can only be received external to the self.[62] The action of Christ on the cross as well as his victory at the empty tomb binds the believer to himself without the individual's own merit, and, therefore, "baptism means sharing in the cross of Christ."[63] But one cannot choose the manner of his/her death. A person cannot self-baptize. It is a wholly passive experience. In similar fashion, Christ gives the individual his own body and blood; the gift of reconciliation is received only, not something that is chosen or attained. Reconciliation itself implies an external participant; the term acknowledges, by definition, a broken relationship in need of restora-

62. Bonhoeffer, *The Cost of Discipleship*, 257.
63. Ibid., 258.

tion. Since a person is incapable of self-reconciliation (i.e., reconciling his own conscience), the presence and initiative of God is required to make right the divine-human relationship.[64]

Second, the sacraments are the true gift of God to humanity; he is both the giver and the content of that gift. At Holy Baptism, the Church confesses that the Holy Spirit fills the baptized with its presence. In the case of Holy Communion, believers receive the fullness of the Incarnation in the bread and wine; in both cases (Holy Baptism and Holy Communion), the Church confesses neither a symbolic presence nor a mere spiritual presence. As Bonhoeffer argues, "The Word in the sacrament is embodied Word. It is not representation of the Word." The Word of God makes the Eucharist what it is because "God, by his Word, addresses and hallows the elements of bread and wine."[65] Here Bonhoeffer strongly affirms the Lutheran doctrine of Real Presence; he avoids speaking of Jesus' manifestation in Holy Communion in any way that would lessen Jesus' corporeal presence found there. But how is this concretely understood in Holy Baptism and Holy Communion?

Bonhoeffer understands the sacraments to be embodied experiences of God's grace. Starting with baptism, its embodied features go beyond the material presence of water. Baptism, for Bonhoeffer, engrafts the Christian into the bodily life, death, and resurrection Jesus. In this sense, the believer's embodiment is a function of Jesus' own physicality. Without the real physical death of Jesus, the death of sin enacted at baptism loses its force and becomes a metaphorical (and, therefore, disembodied) expression of some psycho-social change of heart. Similarly, only the actual bodily resurrection of Jesus gives the believer the assurance of God's grace, the guarantee of his/her future resurrection. The resurrection of the body, in Paul and in Bonhoefferian thought, then, contributes heavily to the understanding of the new creation. Christians are connected to Christ's body, both in death and in resurrection.

In Holy Communion, by comparison, the Church experiences an embodied Savior that meets the community in its own concreteness. Bonhoeffer structures his understanding of communion by first acknowledging the unique creatureliness of man as both necessarily spirit and body:

> Man as man does not live without God's Spirit. To live *as man* means to live as body in Spirit. Escape from the body is escape from being man and escape from the spirit as well. Body is the existence-form of spirit, as spirit is the existence-form of body. . . The human body is distinguished from all non-human

64. Bonhoeffer, *Sanctorum Communio*, 244.
65. Bonhoeffer, *Christ the Center*, 53.

bodies by being the existence-form of God's Spirit on earth, as it is wholly undifferentiated from all other life by being of this earth.[66]

If the body is essential to the constitution of the human being, then God enters into that physicality to wholly redeem it, not just in the Incarnation proper, but through Christ's presence specifically in the body and blood of Holy Communion. Clifford Green sets forth Bonhoeffer's distinction of sacrament from proclamation by saying, "While the one, whole Christ is present in the sermon as in the sacrament, yet the sacrament is a specific form of Christ, for here the Word is enacted *in corporeal form* [emphasis added]."[67] Therefore the body of Christ in the sacrament serves as the "form" in which the Logos rescues the *Natur* of man, his body.[68] God "enters into the body again" in the form of the sacrament as a way to meet the broken. The body and blood "are the new realities of creation of the promise for the fallen Adam."[69] One can see how multiple facets of embodied theology come together in Bonhoeffer's work, in this case, tones of creatureliness and eschatology become more apparent in his discussion of the sacraments.

At this point, Bonhoeffer's theology mirrors that of Luther. One of Luther's greatest contributions to sacramental theology, as noted earlier in chapter 2, was his view that the Sacrament of the Altar is the gospel. Holy Communion is essentially indistinguishable from God's Word embodied in the Incarnation:

> It is impossible to accept Luther's attitude toward Rome and to reject his attitude toward Zwingli. The confessor of Worms is also the confessor of Marburg. In both cases he confessed the Gospel which comes to us in the Word and in the Sacrament. It is really true that the Sacrament is the Gospel, and the Gospel is the Sacrament . . . Here is God who became man; here is Christ in his divinity and humanity. Here is the true body and blood of the Lamb of God, given for you, present with you. Here forgiveness of sins is a reality—and, with it, life and salvation. This Sacrament is the Gospel.[70]

66. Bonhoeffer, *Creation and Fall*, 52.

67. Green, *Bonhoeffer*, 217.

68. Ibid.

69. Bonhoeffer, *Creation and Fall*, 52.

70. Sasse, *This is My Body*, 328–29. Perhaps a clearer definition of gospel is required at this juncture. Sasse, I think correctly, suggests that Luther equates the gospel with the physical reality of the Incarnation, the tangible Word, not as a synonym for grace or as a reference to the Gospels proper.

Bonhoeffer picks up on this theme early in his career and elaborates upon it. For Bonhoeffer, "the sacraments, both eucharist and baptism, have the same social character and intention as the Word; they also, of course, have the same content, purpose, and function as the Word."[71] What exactly does this mean? In my view, Bonhoeffer is driving at the inseparability not just between sacrament and gospel (as Luther would have it), but also the inseparability of the church-community (*Gemeinshaft*) from the other two. The reality of the Incarnation is proclaimed by the church-community; the sacraments are only performed in the midst of the church-community. The social character of the Body of Christ now exists as a precondition to human interactions with the Word.

Sacraments are certainly embodied and necessarily social. Each sacrament, however, expresses this sociality in specific ways. Bonhoeffer's view of baptism falls squarely into the context of Lutheran orthodoxy. He stresses that baptism is a means of grace; the spiritual death experienced in baptism "means justification from sin."[72] But contrary to the erroneous view that baptism is primarily an individualistic experience, Bonhoeffer understands the sacrament to be, at its core, grounded and realized in Christian community. For this reason, he approved of infant baptism only in the midst of a surrounding body of believers "which remembers Christ's deed of salvation wrought for us once and for all."[73] Such a narrative can only be produced with other believing Christians. Yet Bonhoeffer presses the role of the church-community even further. Since he believes that the "sacrament demands faith" and an infant is incapable of articulating the presence of such faith, the faith present at Holy Baptism must be that of the entire body of believers:

> Through baptism [the church-community] incorporates the child in faith into itself; but since the whole church-community is present wherever one of its members is, it follows that *the faith of the child is that of the whole church-community* [emphasis added]. Baptism is thus, on one hand, God's effective act in the gift of grace by which the child is incorporated into the church-community of Christ; on the other hand, however, it also implies *the mandate that the child remain within the Christian community* [emphasis added]. Thus the church-community as the community of saints carries its children like a mother, as its most sacred treasure. It can do this only by virtue of its

71. Green, *Bonhoeffer*, 59.
72. Bonhoeffer, *Discipleship*, 258.
73. Ibid., 261.

'communal life'; if it were a 'voluntary association' the act of
baptism would be meaningless.[74]

The community bears the corporate responsibility of faith at a child's baptism, not simply the burden of instruction and encouragement as the child
grows. Bonhoeffer expands on the Lutheran understanding of baptism
beyond its classic use as a means of grace; he adds the social gift of church-
community to the personal gift of the remission of sins.

    In light of Bonhoeffer's attention to confession and absolution, per-
haps he envisions the church-community as the ultimate manifestation of
sacramental life. The church-community experiences Christ in the sacrament and simultaneously bears Christ to one another. The question is: Is
the church-community of believers to be equated with the actual presence
of the risen Christ, or is it simply the vehicle for the proclamation of the
Incarnation's presence in word and sacrament? Bonhoeffer proposes that
Christ cannot be considered solely as the subject of proclamation or the
content of the sacraments; he mysteriously exists as church-community.[75]
In his Christology lectures, Bonhoeffer offers the formula, "Christ existing
as a Community," in various permutations:

> Christ is not only the head of the community *but also the com-
> munity itself* [emphasis added]. Christ is head and every mem-
> ber . . . the head means the Lordship, but the two expressions do
> not contradict one another.[76]

And, elsewhere:

> Just as Christ is present as the Word and in the Word, as the
> sacrament and in the sacrament, so too *he is also present as com-
> munity and in the community* [emphasis added]. His presence in
> Word and sacrament is related to his presence in the community
> as reality is to figure. Christ is the community by virtue of his
> being *pro me*. His form, indeed his only form, is the community
> between the ascension and the second coming. The fact that he
> is in heaven at the right hand of God does not contradict this;

74. Bonhoeffer, *Sanctorum Communio*, 241.

75. This theological feature is distinctive Bonhoefferian. Early in his career, Bonhoeffer establishes the social character of the human person. The individual is necessarily social and cannot be conceived apart from his/her relationship to other human
beings. Christ, as the representative of all humanity (*Kollektivperson*), frees the sinful
and isolated individual to return the community—to their essential humanness. This
Kollektivperson concept will be revisited in Bonhoeffer's treatment of eschatology. See
Green, *Bonhoeffer*, 234–37.

76. Bonhoeffer, *Christology*, 61.

on the contrary it alone makes possible his presence in and as
the community.[77]

Finally:

> What does it mean that Christ as *Word* is also community? It
> means that the *Logos* of God has extension in space and time
> in and as the community. Christ, the Word, is spiritually and
> physically present. The *Logos* is not only the weak word of hu-
> man teaching, *doctrina*; he is also the powerful Word of cre-
> ation. He speaks, and thus creates the form of the community.
> The community is therefore not only the receiver of the Word of
> revelation; it is itself revelation and Word of God.[78]

Bonhoeffer asserts that church-community, by virtue of Christ's identification as the creative Word, holds distinctively sacramental characteristics.
Yet for Bonhoeffer, this does not prevent Christ from confronting the
community externally; Christ both *is* community and *comes to* the community with his justice and mercy. Bonhoeffer sees no contradiction in this
position. Christ restores the fundamental social nature of humanity. When
Adam sinned, his failure destroyed the communal nature of the human
being (to be *sicut deus* is to be completely alone); this isolation creates a
self-contradiction.[79] Jesus Christ, as the embodiment of the new humanity (and, by extension, the church-community) restores by his resurrection
the true social character of the human creature. Fellowship is restored, and
the contradiction is no more. Bonhoeffer affirms the point that fellowship
is only experienced in the Body of Christ, and no communion can exist
outside of his Body, "for only through that Body can we find acceptance and
salvation."[80] Bonhoeffer's emphasis on community and its attachment to
the word of the gospel is so fundamental that it becomes difficult to ascertain any true boundaries between the two.

The formation of the Church itself relies on baptism. In this act, God
in Christ "invades the realm of Satan, lays hands on his own, and creates for
himself his Church."[81] A new order is established in which Jesus serves as
mediator; the world-community of sin is replaced by the church-community. Bonhoeffer understands this transition in a way that preserves both com-

77. Ibid., 59–60.

78. Ibid., 60.

79. For Bonhoeffer, the human cannot be understood apart from his/her relationship to others. When this relationship is excised by sin and isolation, the human embodied a self-contradiction.

80. Bonhoeffer, *Discipleship*, 267

81. Ibid., 256.

munal and individual integrity. "God does not desire a history of individual human beings, but the history of the human *community [Gemeinshaft]*. However, God does not want a community that absorbs the individual into itself, but a community of *human beings*. In God's eyes, community and individual exist in the same moment and rest in one another."[82] This is yet another example of overlapping themes within embodied theology, where the church-community formed by baptism (sacramental) leads to a new world order in which Christ is the head (eschatological).

In the case of Holy Communion, its social importance is no less than the culmination of Christian community; it serves as a feast of grace and reconciliation for believers. "The fellowship of the Lord's Supper is the superlative fulfillment of Christian fellowship."[83] At the table feast, Bonhoeffer envisions an embodied form of the new community to come, a unified body that perfectly participates in the joy of Christ. The communal gift of Holy Communion is made manifest in at least two distinct ways: (1) Christ's presence gives community with himself, and (2) Christ's presence renews the church-community for its ongoing benefit.[84] First, Christ's work on the cross imputes righteousness to the community which imparts both a gift and a responsibility in the eyes of Bonhoeffer. With the Lord's Supper, "Christ gives to each member the rights and obligations to act as priest for the other, and to each Christ also gives life in the church-community."[85] The mutual bearing of one another, formerly expressed as a function of his/her creatureliness, is made possible in the reconciliation offered at the Lord's Table. By Jesus' "self-giving," Christ provides the strength necessary to uphold the priesthood of all believers as they offer communion and absolution to one another.

Second, Christ's presence renews this church-community both in the present and into the future. The sustaining power of God is not restricted to his creation. Jesus Christ as God renews the vitality of his Church, mirroring the Father as the source of all life and reality. Yet Bonhoeffer extends this relationship considerably deeper. "Jesus Christ is at once himself and his Church."[86] It follows then that baptism unites the Christian with Christ in a bodily way, for each baptized believer is brought into the fundamental reality of God's Church. Since Christ, by his very nature, cannot cause himself harm or decay, the Church thrives as the ongoing bodily presence of Christ

82. Green, *Bonhoeffer*, 43.

83. Bonhoeffer, *Life Together*, 122.

84. Bonhoeffer, *Sanctorum Communio*, 243.

85. Ibid.

86. Bonhoeffer, *Discipleship*, 269.

in the world. As Bonhoeffer notes, "We should think of the Church not as an institution, but as a *person*."[87] The new humanity, therefore, is the Body of Christ that has experienced Jesus' life, death, and resurrection. Just as the resurrected Jesus cannot die so the Church experiences the ongoing life and freedom of Christ's presence.

The presence of the Incarnation is unmistakable in Bonhoeffer's sacramental theology. The Incarnation exists as both the content of the sacrament and the ultimate way in which God provides for his people through embodied means. In other words, God's love to humanity is demonstrated in sacramental fashion: the physical character of Jesus Christ is offered in its entirety for the good of God's creatures. Bonhoeffer's view of the sacraments is nothing, if not doggedly Christocentric and remarkably social:

> The entire building begins and ends with Christ, and its unifying center is the word. Whereas baptism signifies the will of the church-community in its most comprehensive form to spread God's rule, which for us implies the fact of a *church-of-the-people*, the church addressed by preaching consists of those who are personally faced with the decision whether to accept or reject God's gift, and is thus both a *church-of-the-people and a voluntary church*. In the Lord's Supper the church-community manifests itself purely as a *voluntary* and as a *community confessing its faith*, and is summoned and recognized by God as such.[88]

For Bonhoeffer, Christ's embodied presence in the sacrament animates the church-community as the source of the church's vitality and simultaneously becomes the "focal point into which all its life flows."[89] This presence has a certain historical import. On one hand, believers today are bound to and have common kinship with the believers throughout time; this includes the first disciples. On the other hand, a contemporary believer's experience of Christ's bodily presence in the sacrament exceeds that of the first disciples. Bonhoeffer believed this to be true due to the exalted form of the resurrected Christ: "Our communion with [Jesus] is richer and more assured than it was for [the disciples], for the communion and presence which we have is that of the glorified Lord."[90] The depth of this reality is profound. Christians encounter the full power of the resurrected Incarnation in each encounter with the Lord's Supper, not as a superficial relationship that needs

87. Ibid.
88. Ibid., 247.
89. Ibid.
90. Bonhoeffer, *Discipleship*, 263.

to be reenergized but as the full meeting of the resurrected and glorified Lord with his flock.

The sacramental feature of embodied living finds beautiful expression in the writings of Bonhoeffer. The sacraments function as the place where the Logos is present, offering grace and a new status as participants in his Body through the Church. Yet this central truth is often underappreciated in many parishes, as the means of grace is viewed in individualistic terms: The participant receives grace for their personal sins, yet little is communicated regarding the interpersonal reconciliation that Holy Communion offers. Likewise, Holy Baptism not only serves as a means of grace for the individual recipient; its waters claim the baptized as a newly initiated member of the Body of Christ. For Bonhoeffer, the communal experience must stretch both vertically (i.e., toward God) and horizontally (i.e., toward our neighbor). The sacraments open up these vistas of healing, but they do so in the context of the church parish, here-and-now. What of the embodied, social character of Lutheran theology that ultimately transcends space and time in the age to come?

Bonhoeffer and the Eschatological

Eschatology is the study of ultimate things. In practical terms, eschatology refers to the culmination of God's *Heilsgeschichte* on earth, his judgment of all things, and the existence of a new creation under the lordship of Jesus.[91] The central feature of this new creation is humanity's physical resurrection of the dead. Perhaps the events of World War II led Bonhoeffer to interpret his political milieu through the prism of eschatology, as Luther most certainly did in his own socio-political context. To be sure, Bonhoeffer's theology of sociality regularly ventures into the reformers understanding of God's new creation, both as a present unfolding reality and as the final culmination of all history. While Bonhoeffer's attention to eschatology has been somewhat minimized in the past, recent scholarship has offered a reading of his works with eschatology occupying a more central position.[92] Eberhard Bethge, Bonhoeffer's closest friend and confidante, remarks that "those who came in contact with [Bonhoeffer] were often astonished by the passion with which he treated eschatology as a serious contemporary issue, particularly in his sermons and catechism." Bethge further explains that

91. This is my definition, although I am aware of the difficulty in defining this term. N. T. Wright reminds us that there are at least ten distinct definitions of eschatology in Scripture. Wright, *Resurrection*, 26.

92. Lindsay, "Bonhoeffer's eschatology," 290–302.

eschatology dominated much of Bonhoeffer's thought during his *Disciple-ship* period, later receding in order to avoid an impression that eschatology served as a false crutch against his "desperate situation."[93]

Bonhoeffer lays out his eschatology by using the language of *fulfill-ment*, God's bringing of all things into full account or development. This language is manifested in two ways. First, it binds the coming of the end times to the experience of God's people as a whole; the arrival of the eschaton was not to be an exclusively personal experience. In *Sanctorum Communio*, he writes, "Christian eschatology is essentially *eschatology of the church-community [Gemeindeeschatologie]*. It is concerned with the fulfillment of the church and of the individual within it."[94] While this definition holds for the duration of his theological career, he clarifies his understanding of eschatology in his unfinished masterpiece, *Ethics*. He avoids suggesting that the individual's final hope lies in the ongoing existence of the Church and his participation within it. Rather, *Ethics* points to an end times in which the whole of God's creation, individual and corporate, sits at the feet of God and hears God's grace pronounced upon it all. In this case, God's grace at the end of time fulfills his project of reconciliation that began in the Garden.

Bonhoeffer understands such eschatology in the light of his famous categories, "ultimate" and "penultimate." The ultimate is the final voice of God, where he declares a justification by grace that supersedes all things prior. Nothing lies behind this declaration, nor follows it; "it is the irre-versibly ultimate word, the ultimate reality."[95] In a sense, God's mercy is the utter realization of eschatology; it is *das Letzte*. This word fulfills the promise of God's own making in Genesis 3. The penultimate, however, is that which marks the journey to the ultimate. For Paul, it was a "glorying in the law and the ensuing enmity to Christ."[96] For Luther, it was the experi-ence of a distraught conscience in the depths of an Augustinian monastery. The penultimate includes "action, suffering, movement, intention, defeat, recovery, pleading, hoping" as the presupposition of justification.[97] Accord-ing to Bonhoeffer, "there is no Lutheran or Pauline method for attaining the ultimate word, the ultimate reality."[98] None of these positions remain in the presence of God's judgment, nor should they, as each human attempt to reach or understand God ultimately fails.

93. Bethge, *Bonhoeffer*, 87.

94. Bonhoeffer, *Sanctorum Communio*, 283. Author's emphasis.

95. Bonhoeffer, *Ethics*, 149.

96. Ibid.

97. Ibid., 150.

98. Ibid., 149.

However, Bonhoeffer offers a certain measure of dignity for the penultimate, lest it be destroyed by God's justifying word and the individual with it. By Christ's presence as the "incarnate, crucified, and risen God" the penultimate is "neither sanctioned nor destroyed." It must be "respected because it is 'preserved and sustained by God for the coming of Christ.'"[99] Bonhoeffer is not trying to discount the concrete experiences of the person; he simply gathers together all things under the all-encompassing lordship of Christ. The Christian retains his/her integrity, *as a creature made by God to live in the world.* As individual or as community, a person can only set aside the penultimate for God's final declaration of humanity's own ontological reality: a forgiven creature. After all, "justification presupposes that the creature became guilty."[100]

Bonhoeffer's theology of sociality exists as a partial glimpse of future glory and looks with great expectation to the ultimate end when Jesus returns to enact his reign "on earth as it is in heaven." Much of Bonhoeffer's thought on eschatology is couched in language of the new creation, both as an ontological reality in the justified Christian here-and-now as well as the redemption of the entire cosmos at the end of time.

Although the kingdom of God is both "here and now" and "not yet," Bonhoeffer did not envision the realization of some manmade utopia to usher in God's reign. His staunch rejection of idealism is critical and particularly Lutheran. Until the final day comes, a person is still a sinner. Bonhoeffer rejected utopian idealism because it threatened the very essence of community located in the confession and absolution of sins. The confessional call to participate in the mutual conversation and consolation of the brethren recedes and the deep community of trust that practices such important affairs necessarily dies. Those who attempt to construct a perfect community based on some idealized model erodes the truthfulness that is necessary for men and women to fruitfully coexist. Bonhoeffer, in this case, seeks "disillusionment" from idealism:

> By sheer grace, God will not permit us to live even for a brief period in a dream world. He does not abandon us to those rapturous experiences and lofty moods that come over us like a dream. God is not a God of the emotions but the God of truth. Only that fellowship which faces such disillusionment, with all its unhappy and ugly aspects, begins to be what it should be in God's sight, begins to grasp in faith the promise that is given to it.[101]

99. Weissbach, "Christology and Ethics," 122–23.

100. Bonhoeffer, *Ethics*, 151.

101. Bonhoeffer, *Life Together*, 27.

Casting aside the "wish dreams" of a utopian Christian community allows the real work of grace to begin; sinful people confessing to one another the truth of their condition breaks open the floodgates of healing.[102] For Bonhoeffer, "every human wish dream that is injected into the Christian community is a hindrance to genuine community and must be banished if genuine community is to survive."[103] The believer must embrace Christian community as it is in its concreteness, lest he/she substitute an empty mirage of "visionary dreaming" for truth and depth. Again, Christ stands at the center of Bonhoeffer's logic. As the way, the truth, and the life, he grounds and sustains the church-community, not as some disembodied representation of what the perfected community can or should be. Rather, he presents himself as the "honest and earnest and sacrificial" savior who all Christians can claim and emulate; in this way he opens a space for reciprocal trust within the church body.[104]

History, the Incarnation, and Eschatology

The features of eschatology, whether general or Bonhoefferian, point toward the Incarnation just as the themes of creatureliness and sacramental theology did the same. Jesus becomes the enabler of a new creation as well as the central feature *of* it. Christ *is* the new creation, both in his resurrected body and as the church-community (the Body of Christ). To fully understand how the incarnational aspects emerge in Bonhoeffer's eschatology, one must go beyond Bonhoeffer's Christocentric definition of reality laid out above and get a firm grasp on his understanding of the Incarnation itself. Jesus Christ, for Bonhoeffer, stood as the God-man in both history and doctrine. One cannot isolate the historical understanding of Jesus from the doctrinal formulations about him. The Gospel message of the New Testament is fully expressed in Christ's life, death, and resurrection. "Here there is no difference between doctrinal texts (in the Epistles or in the sayings of Jesus) and the historical texts. Both are equally witnesses to the unique Christ."[105] Bonhoeffer further acknowledges that the self-revelation of God in Jesus could come equally from an account of the miraculous (e.g., the wedding at Cana) or through the discourses of Jesus (e.g., the Sermon on the Mount). The full testimony of Jesus Christ in word and deeds bears witness to the unique messianic event; doctrine and history both proclaim that Jesus is the

102. Ibid., 26.
103. Ibid., 27.
104. Ibid.
105. Bonhoeffer, *No Rusty Swords*, 317.

Son of God.[106] This stands against a theologically abstracted Christ divorced
from history, a view that would render Christian eschatology as a theological construct, not a future historical certainty.

Bonhoeffer describes the Incarnation in two ways. First, Jesus Christ
existed incarnationally in his *own self*; he came as a flesh-and-bones individual in history. The very purpose of Jesus Christ was to be the bodily vehicle
of God's reconciliation to his people. "God takes humanity to himself, not
merely as heretofore through the spoken word, but in the Body of Jesus."[107]
The "true bodily form" of Jesus takes upon itself the burden of "our entire
human nature with all its infirmity, sinfulness and corruption."[108] Bonhoeffer stresses that Jesus bears all sinful flesh upon his body, pressing home the
point that salvation is not an exclusively cognitive or transcendent affair, it
is grounded in the understanding of a wholly physical resurrection of the
dead.

Second, Jesus Christ exists as the incarnate *Kollektivperson*; he represents the whole of humanity, both as a sacrifice for all sin and as the
embodiment of the new creation.[109] Jesus vicariously represents every individual before God as an advocate; however, he also represents humanity
as the recipient of God's unqualified Yes. This *Kollektivperson* concept was
not restricted to Jesus alone; Adam represented the whole of created and
fallen humanity as *Kollektivperson*, as well. Because of Adam's failure in the
Garden, "genuine humanity" is destroyed in both individual and corporate
ways; humanity's ego is asserted against one another as domination. Jesus,
as *Kollektivperson* for the new humanity, brings all humanity back into the
"dignity of the image of God."[110] By using this terminology, Bonhoeffer is
able to articulate a soteriology that accounts for multiple dimensions of
human sin, as he certainly wanted to avoid a reduction of sin's impact by
couching it in solely individualistic terms.[111]

106. Bonhoeffer affirms this position elsewhere, most notably in *The Cost of Discipleship*. "The Jesus of the Synoptics is neither nearer nor further from us than the
Christ of St. Paul. The Christ who is present is the Christ of the whole scripture. He
is the incarnate, crucified, risen, and glorified Christ, and he meets us in his word."
Bonhoeffer, *Discipleship*, 255.

107. Ibid., 264.

108. Ibid., 265.

109. The term, *Kollektivperson*, is borrowed from chapter 3 ("The Primal State and
the Problem of Community") in Bonhoeffer's dissertation, *Sanctorum Communio*.
Bonhoeffer, *Sanctorum Communio*, 58–86.

110. Green, *Bonhoeffer*, 155.

111. Bonhoeffer would have considered this inconceivable. The sins of the German
people, as a whole, were appalling to him; they were sins he himself claimed a certain
responsibility for as a German citizen. To reduce all sin to individual human decisions

Before proceeding any further, it will be useful to give nuance to this important term in Bonhoeffer's thought. Bonhoeffer believed "in a divine guiding of history." As scholar Herman Ott notes, "For [Bonhoeffer] there is a meaning and a goal, a judgement and a grace of God in world history, and these are for people and not only for individuals."[112] The key feature here is that the collective people hold a separate integrity from the individual. History tells the story not only of important individual people, but also, the history *of peoples*. Humanity as a whole has a collective history and, in a remarkable Bonhoefferian stroke, *a collective ethical personality*.[113] The individual is known by their associations with the collective (e.g., families, communities, ethnicities), and while this does not destroy his/her individual agency or integrity as a "free moral subject," Bonhoeffer reinforces the point that an individual cannot be divorced from their membership within these associations.[114] This allows him to make some significant historical claims. A German citizen does not have the ability to absolve himself from the sins of the nation; Bonhoeffer himself knew that the crimes of the Nazi party were his responsibility based simply on his association with the collective German people.[115] Membership in various forms of community, even ones that come unchosen or unwilling, necessarily create an identity that exists vis-à-vis the neighbor:

> As a historically existing individual I participate in one or more collective persons, and I exist historically as an individual only by virtue of this participation. I am a member of a family, of a people and of humanity. But this participation is not so simply personal to myself as is the colour of my eyes or the abilities of my intellect. It is given to me and laid upon me as a constant *claim*, that I should know myself and regard myself as in solidarity with the collective person, because and in so far as I begin by being in such solidarity.[116]

Ott's observations here draw us back to Bonhoeffer's *Kollektivperson* as it relates to the imputed responsibility of people for communal sin. The

---

would have effectively exculpated the Germans for the sins of a few Nazis. This was not acceptable in Bonhoeffer's eyes.

112. Ott, *Reality and Faith*, 207.

113. Ibid.

114. Ibid., 209.

115. Ott rejects the notion that faith is a precondition of such responsibility. A person, for example, can summon a sense of guilt for the actions of their community with or without belief in God. Ott, *Reality and Faith*, 208.

116. Ibid., 210.

collective has a claim upon a person that includes all action; one's solidarity with any collective is neither a la carte nor piecemeal. Therefore, the sin of the many imposes a collective guilt on the whole as well as the multitude of individual guilt(s) that exist within it. This particular hamartiology offers us a better understanding of Christ's redemptive work in two ways. One, he is the Savior of all history, including the divinely-led histories of collectives, big and small. Two, Jesus' work on the cross redeems the totality of sin (individual and collective), and therefore, offers the individual the distinct authority to confess *on behalf of* the collective.

The *Kollektivperson* language has the added benefit of being naturally eschatological. In Bonhoeffer's words, "every act [Jesus] wrought was performed on behalf of the new humanity which he bore in his body."[117] The restorative acts of the Incarnation both as the Jesus of history and as the reigning Son of God usher in the new age. He eradicates the collective guilt of humanity transforming God's people into a resurrected community of peace. By representing all of humanity before God, Jesus reclaims the initial dignity bestowed in the Garden and imputes this honor upon humanity permanently on the Last Day.

How does this "recovered dignity" express itself in the time between Jesus' ascension and the eschaton? For Bonhoeffer, the Body of Christ continues to be embodied in the life of the Church. "The Body of Christ is identical with the new humanity which he has taken upon him. It is in fact the Church. Jesus Christ is at one himself and his Church."[118] This identification is not to be thought of in the metaphorical sense, as Bonhoeffer argues stridently that baptism unites Christians to Christ's bodily resurrection, just as it connects the believer to the Church. Without this connection to the body, the individual stands alone and without any hope for salvation. For Bonhoeffer, the ongoing presence of Jesus in the Church, yet again, demonstrates humanity's fundamental sociality. "No one can become a new man except by entering the Church, and becoming a member of the Body of Christ. It is impossible to become a new man as a solitary individual."[119] Here the incarnational aspect of embodied theology weds perfectly with the presence of the community. The result is a God who "comes to a person not as an idea, a philosophy, a religion, but as a human being in the Christian community of the new humanity."[120]

---

117. Bonhoeffer, *The Cost of Discipleship*, 265.

118. Ibid., 269.

119. Ibid., 271.

120. Green, *Bonhoeffer*, 158.

The Body of Christ expresses itself not only as an ontological reality but also as a practical agent of the gospel. In the Christian community, for example, Bonhoeffer believed that confession and absolution resided at the very center. A community of forgiveness built on "costly grace" manifests Jesus Christ to one another and to the broader world as witness.

L. Gregory Jones notes that Bonhoeffer was convinced "that God's forgiveness is decisively enacted by Jesus, who is not merely illustrative of a more general human capacity and desire."[121] Both Bonhoeffer's use of Christ and his description of forgiveness were, again, rooted in his understanding of reality. Theology was never supposed to be divorced from the real situations humans faced, and, therefore, Christian forgiveness needed to address the very brokenness that existed in concrete communities. Only then could the Church be a truly eschatological community; the resurrected relationship of reconciliation mirrors the promise of a physical resurrection. Bonhoeffer sharply criticized how forgiveness in German churches evolved into a therapeutic, psychological remedy.[122] If sin was merely a matter of psychology, the church had no resources to draw from when trampled underfoot by the slow, evil march of National Socialism. Indeed, there could be no "evil." Rather, the ongoing consolation of the brethren identifies and remedies the sinful state of humanity in the building of trustworthy relationships that lead one another to word and sacrament.

It makes sense, then, that Bonhoeffer was an emphatic proponent of an embodied form of confession; he strongly encouraged his seminary students to take on confessing partners. Bonhoeffer recognized the very presence of the Incarnation in such a confessing act; it required the Other as a proclaimer of grace. "[A Christian] needs his brother solely because of Jesus Christ. The Christ in his own heart is weaker than the Christ in the word of his brother; his own heart is uncertain, his brother's is sure."[123] Here the embodied presence of Christ in the Christian brother exists as a bold manifestation of incarnational living. This posture is required until the eschatology of God is fully realized and the uncertainty of one's standing before God is effectively abolished. The direct reign of the Lamb over the new creation transforms confession into celebration, uncertainty into faith fulfilled.

Based on the above evidence, one can only come to the conclusion that Bonhoeffer's vision of the new creation was borne from his commitment to Christology; this produced an eschatology where embodiment

121. Jones, *Embodying Forgiveness*, 9.

122. Ibid., 17.

123. Bonhoeffer, *Life Together*, 23.

and community play central roles. In his classic *Life Together*, Bonhoeffer issues a startlingly clear statement on the nature of Christian community. "Christianity means community through Jesus Christ and in Jesus Christ. No Christian community is more or less than this."[124] By virtue of his bodily existence in history as the God-man and his vicarious representation of all humanity as the *Kollektivperson*, Jesus Christ defines human existence as a spectacularly social experience from birth to grave to life again.

Once again, Bonhoeffer's eschatology has fruitful implications for the life of the visible Church. A parish that appreciates the presence of Christ among itself is more prone to recognize, even cherish, the weak among them. Forgiveness and grace are practiced as the concrete expression of Jesus' sacrifice at Golgotha, the place where he, as *Kollektivperson,* claims humanity as equal beneficiaries of his death. As a result, the body of believers finds a common bond in the mutual consolation of the brethren, where the cross of Christ unites men and women as brothers and sisters, even co-heirs. Jesus' presence in the Church serves as a unifying force and foundation for local Christian communities.

Even in his eschatology, Bonhoeffer forcefully argues that all history moves toward a picture of embodied sociality where Christ's authority is made immediate to the world to restore all relationships unto himself. The neutral observer is left with two inescapable conclusions: First, the theology of Dietrich Bonhoeffer is embodied to the core. Second, this particular theology binds together embodiment with the community such that one is not recognizable without the other.

Before laying out the final portion of this chapter, let us first review the unique contributions of Bonhoeffer's theology to the present discussion on embodied theology. With regards to the creaturely component to embodied living, Bonhoeffer affirms the goodness of the human bodily form. The body not only exists as the product of God's creative activity, i.e., the divinely chosen way for humanity to interact in the world; the body becomes the centerpiece of God's redemptive work in Christ. For Bonhoeffer, physicality is essential because it is the means by which the church-community receives Christ and understands itself in relation to one another. While Luther rightly acknowledges God's creative and sustaining power in his Genesis lectures, Bonhoeffer moves one step further: The *body* of Christ is the impetus for all reality, reconciliation, and history. The sustaining power of God is more than an animating force (*nephesh*) or God's way of making himself known in the concrete world, *his sustaining bodily presence defines reality itself.*

124. Ibid., 21.

God affirms this creaturely reality by the following progression. First, he blesses his creatures with inherent limitations. Bonhoeffer stresses this fact to highlight how grace moves through community; Christians limit one another in order that their provision might be sought only in God. This provision includes the grace that people offer to one another in the bearing of mutual limitation. Now the person is directed toward God (at the center) and neighbor (at the boundary mutually oriented to the center). Bonhoeffer rejects a view of the creaturely that allows a person or group to access some natural relationship to the created world, thereby creating hierarchies apart from Christ, what Luther termed, "orders of creation." Rather, Bonhoeffer argues that the intimacy of common creatureliness that is found in the here-and-now (as opposed to prelapsarian natural relationships with the world), including the commonality Christians experience with the Incarnation. Trusting in the provision of God, their *modus operandi* is a life of mutual bearing and restoration. Christ, as the source of the Christian's strength, draws believers into a life of preservation where all people can hear the Yes of God in the cross and empty grave. He, as the embodied Son of God, demonstrates his solidarity with humanity in the most intimate of ways: he lives, he dies, and then he rises. The community of believers partakes in creaturely existence to frame their own lives yet share the responsibility of preserving all creation for God's purposes. All forms of communal identity (national, racial, political) become subservient to the call of preserving the one form of human association that is universal: Being human!

Bonhoeffer also sheds new light on the social functions of sacramental theology. Luther took great pains to distinguish the biblically sound doctrine of Real Presence against his detractors, but spent relatively little effort communicating the ways in which Holy Baptism and Holy Communion strengthen the community *qua* church-community. Bonhoeffer builds on Luther's contention that the sacraments are the gospel by stressing that such a connection exists only in the midst of the church-community. Baptism, for example, places the believer into a church-community; by Bonhoeffer's own admission, an isolated individual could not possibly experience new life in the Body of Christ.[125] Church membership itself (in the broad sense) was a matter of salvific importance. For Bonhoeffer, the Confessing Church preached the Jesus of the Bible, not the German church; to knowingly divorce oneself from the Confessing Church was unthinkable. "The question of church membership is the question of salvation. The boundaries of the church are the boundaries of salvation. Whoever knowingly cuts himself off

---

125. Bonhoeffer, *The Cost of Discipleship*, 271.

from the Confessing Church in Germany cuts himself off from salvation."[126] It is unclear if Bonhoeffer believed that localized parish membership (official association with the local congregation) held salvific value. Corporate participation in the reality of the Church renders any claim of a solely individual faith obsolete, even non-existent.

A second significant sacramental contribution is Bonhoeffer's insistence that: (1) The capacity for fellowship is only through Christ's body, and (2) the Lord's Supper, in particular, exists as the culmination of the Christian community. First, any form of community that a Christian experiences comes directly from his/her participation in Jesus' body; this, for Bonhoeffer, is effectively mediated by the two sacraments.

> How then do we come to participate in the Body of Christ, who did all this for us? It is certain that there can be no fellowship or communion with him except through his Body. For only through that Body can we find acceptance and salvation. The answer is, through the two sacraments of his Body, baptism and the Lord's Supper . . . *The sacraments begin and end in the Body of Christ, and it is only the presence of that Body which makes them what they are* [emphasis added] . . . Baptism incorporates us into the unity of the Body of Christ, and the Lord's Supper fosters and sustains our fellowship and communion (κοινωνία) in that Body.[127]

Holy Baptism "gains the redemption which Christ wrought for us in his body" as the Christian is grafted to his bodily dying and rising.[128] Meanwhile, Holy Communion is a voluntary feast where believers, in faith, gather in a public setting to receive Christ's body and blood. The presence of the Incarnation at the table guarantees the Yes of God experienced individually as grace and corporately as the ongoing fellowship of believers. The essential Bonhoefferian contribution can be summed thus: "All men are 'with Christ' as a consequence of the Incarnation, for in the Incarnation Jesus bore our whole human nature."[129] He is with us, for us, and in us through the power of his bodily presence in the sacraments.

Second, Bonhoeffer's understanding of the Lord's Supper proceeds further than that of Luther's in at least one important way. The culmination of Christian fellowship exists at the sacramental feast. Rather than dwell on

---

126. Bonhoeffer, *A Testament to Freedom*, 169.

127. Ibid., 266–67.

128. Ibid., 267.

129. Ibid., 267–68.

the doctrine of Real Presence,[130] Bonhoeffer claims nothing other than the highest praise for Holy Communion's social function. Christian fellowship reaches its pinnacle at the Lord's Table, where Christians simultaneously receive the means of grace and experience the reconciliation that comes with the physical presence of the brethren. The unity found at the table foreshadows the eschatological unity in the procession of saints; Holy Communion is the "superlative fulfillment of Christian fellowship" precisely because it is an *eternal* fellowship.[131]

Finally, Bonhoeffer provides a distinctive picture of Lutheran eschatology, particularly as it relates to the unique bearing of community by Christ as the *Kollektivperson*. He does this by driving home the picture of a community that hears together God's ultimate word of grace. The penultimate things of this world, the entire experience of the human race individually and corporately understood, recede into the background. They are not unimportant as human experiences per se, they simply offer the person no respite from God's direct word. Yet Bonhoeffer stresses that this final word is not the condemning word of a wrathful Judge; God instead proclaims grace in all its force. Nothing else remains. The promise of a new creation is fulfilled and the human-divine relationship is forever restored. The Christian experiences the resurrection of the dead as direct evidence of God's Yes in Christ.

Jesus Christ replaces the *Kollektivperson* of Adam by being the one who would bear all of humanity's sin on the cross and conquer death's tyranny over all humanity in the resurrection. What would remain would be a true community of peace. Ultimately, this community is the picture of the new creation Bonhoeffer has in mind: The resurrected community of saints living joyfully in God's kingdom of peace.[132] This kingdom of peace, however, was not a superficial attempt to preserve community for the sake

130. Bonhoeffer certainly affirmed Real Presence, but the theological landscape of his day required less a logical or textual proof of Christ's bodily existence in the elements (denominational positions had long been since established) than a proper framing of Holy Communion as a means to God's vision of a grace-filled community.

131. Bonhoeffer, *Life Together*, 122.

132. The "community of peace" phrasing comes from Bonhoeffer's paper for the World Alliance in 1932. His understanding of peace is deeply connected to the socio-political context of the day: "The broken character of the order of peace is expressed in the fact that the peace commanded by God has two limits, first the truth and secondly justice. There can only be a community of peace when it does not rest on *lies* and on *injustice*. Where a community of peace endangers or chokes truth and justice, the community of peace must be broken and battle enjoined. If the battle is then on both sides really waged for truth and for justice, the community of peace, though outwardly destroyed, is made all the deeper and stronger in the battle over this same cause." Bonhoeffer, *No Rusty Swords*, 168–69.

of community alone. In other words, Bonhoeffer's work regularly condemns the temptation of unionism; deep theological foundations supersede the need for accord.[133] The true eschatological-minded church-community shuns lies and injustice for the truth of God's justifying word. The justice of God is meted out to Christ as the collective and the mercy of God is received by Christ in the same fashion.

133. For example, upon visiting the United States Bonhoeffer notes that American Protestants claimed the right "to forgo the final suffering in order to be able to serve God in quietness and peace" (102–3). The central ethos of American Protestantism was borne out of the desire for religious freedom. By fleeing to America as a sanctuary, Christians "forfeited the right to fight" and essentially created an atmosphere of toleration. Theologian Stanley Hauerwas elaborates on Bonhoeffer's insights by concluding: "In America, in the tension between the attempt to say the truth and the will for the community, the latter always prevails. Fairness, not truth, becomes the primary commitment necessary to sustain community for Americans." See Hauerwas, *Performing the Faith*, 66–67.

Luther's eschatological beliefs were essentially built on a similar confrontation. He saw the truth of the gospel being perverted into the lie of Roman Catholic authority over all matters spiritual. The spirit of the Antichrist (in his view, the Pope) was a spirit of falsehood whereby the keys of the kingdom were not won on the cross by Christ's sacrifice but rather distributed at the arbitrary will of the local church. Such lies and injustice, in Luther's view, signaled the coming of the end times.

4
_____

LIVING EMBODIED IN THE AGE
OF EXCARNATION

THE ABOVE EXPLORATION OF Dietrich Bonhoeffer's theology has yielded a
view of embodied theology that is essentially and remarkably community
oriented. The definition of embodied theology offered in chapter 1 is affirmed. The intimate experience of related creatureliness is made manifest
in the believer's body in his/her participation at the font and table and
in his/her experience of the ultimate word of God. The present task is to
concretely describe the essential features of Christian community using
Bonhoeffer's theology as guideposts. Based on the above discussion, I offer
three critical markers that comprise Christian community. These markers
will supply the content for a necessary rubric to evaluate alternate claims
of community, including those claims that might be mediated in the digital
world. The absence of any single marker might not disqualify a certain gathering of Christians as community per se, but the presence of all three allows
one to confidently proclaim its presence. The three markers are depth, local
bondedness, and reciprocal trust. These characteristics are constitutively
built into the most authentic forms of Christian social life. They also afford
Christians the resources necessary to assess OSNs. If the target is embodied
Christian community, these three markers make for a fine quiver of arrows.

The Three Markers of Embodied Community

Depth. Throughout Scripture God calls the believer into relationships of
depth and accountability. The Christian community strives, albeit imper-
fectly, to foster a type of relatedness that values forgiveness over rejection

and responsible love over superficial acceptance. As its model, the Gospels consistently portray Jesus as a savior who exhibits a love that meets the fullness of needs that every person has by virtue of his/her sin; his love penetrates the whole person. In one of many instances, Jesus heals the paralytic in Mark 2 only after he first addresses the more substantial problem of sin. While the physical healing is by no means a trifle, the depth of Jesus' love for the broken man pushes to a far greater level, saving the paralytic from those unseen afflictions which affected his eternity. Communally speaking, the early Christian church in Acts demonstrated that depth comes not by simple association but also by mutual bearing, acts of service, and hospitality. The believers "had everything in common" while maintaining their sense of togetherness in teaching, fellowship, breaking of bread, and prayer (Acts 2:42–47; 4:32–35). The regular patterns of the Christian life fostered the sense of responsibility each member felt toward one another, not allowing any individual to experience the hardship of neediness or hunger. An intentional progression may be seen here: God initiates the relationship between himself and us in Jesus and this becomes the source and model for the relationships that exist within Christian community.

Depth implies intimacy, and intimacy develops out of a community's willingness to know the other and be more fully known itself. Presence together does not, by itself, form communities of commitment and intentionality. Presence is the *precondition* that allows creatures to enjoy the full measure of deep communal love with their fellow brothers and sisters. In the presence of other Christians, the needs of the community are made visible. The Bonhoefferian community thrives on the depth that comes via this presence. In the creaturely sense, the human creature yearns to be known as an end, not a means. The individual seeks out relationships that afford a measure of respect and dignity to each side, and when these qualities are achieved through conversation and/or mutual experience, a relatively safe atmosphere grows in which to test further personal disclosures of depth. Relationships only exist when a certain dignity is given to each side, and relationship is achieved only when both sides are willing to be moved by the other.

The divine-human relationship is pinned on the fact that God allows for a deep integrity to exist within his creature. This integrity is expressed in the presence of soul, of creative agency, of the *imago Dei* imputed upon Adam and Eve. God creates, then models, the type of embodied relationship that he intends for humanity. First, God receives the prayers and petitions of his creatures, listening as a father would receive the requests of his children (Luke 11:9–13). Second, Jesus exhibited trust relationships with his disciples. His love for them was not abstract or distant. He experienced the manifold emotions of being fully human, including participation in local Galilean social life. The Christian church-community, in turn, witnesses this embodied, trusting relationship and enfolds it into life of worship and fellowship.

At the font and table, the Christian is confronted with God's presence, an affirmation of the divine-human relationship. This relationship models authenticity, intimacy, and accountability to the ongoing church-community, as they partake together in the deep bonds that come from receiving (and then offering to one another in reciprocal fashion) grace. In the sacramental sense, God gives his son as the solution to humanity's innermost needs. Where formerly the sinner sits in the center as *sicut deus*, the forgiven creature now receives the bodily presence of Christ. The disposition is transformed into a movement of two sorts: toward God in the center of all being and simultaneously outward toward the neighbor. The cure for sin reaches the depth of the believer's heart in the sacrament. Again the source of all depth begins with God's self-revelation. In this case, the sacraments operate as the full imparting of God's presence to humanity; this relationship creates and models the possibility for human-to-human depth. Neither sacrament, for Bonhoeffer, was symbolic. Each had the unmitigated presence of the Incarnation moving in it and through it.

Eschatologically speaking, Christians experience the depth of relationship most fully at the end of time. Here God makes himself known as a lover of men and women as ends, not as means. The whole of creation is caught up in God's restorative act so that the relationships he formed from the beginning (human-God, human-nature, God-nature) meet their eternal condition—healthy, intentional, joyful, communal. God's act of restoration in the end times cannot be described as a superficial restoration; it is unlimited in its transformative power. All humanity, all creatures, the very universe itself experiences a depth of community only approximated in the here-and-now under the hands of a God who makes *all things new*. The contentious relationships of the past are given a new ontology, as "the wolf will live with the lamb, the leopard will lie down with the goat, the calf and the lion and the yearling together" (Is 11:6). The new Jerusalem is united and presented as the glorious bride (Rev 19:7–9; 21:2) coming down from heaven. Believers join one another in the rich celebration, equally dignified by God's invitation: "Blessed are those who are invited to the wedding supper of the Lamb!" (Rev 11:9).

Local bondedness. Many theologians fall into the temptation of making grand statements about God and Scripture with little attention to how such insights relate to local communities of faith. Not so with Bonhoeffer. His efforts consistently return to the concrete ways in which the person experiences God, whether as a free moral agent or in the context of his/her memberships in various collectives (e.g., family, parish, community). The Body of Christ, in the broad sense as Christendom, receives due attention and most certainly exists under the lordship of Jesus, but Bonhoeffer's sense of embodied community is primarily conceived as a local body of believers bound in common daily fellowship. The daily bearing of limitations, for example, happens through immediate physical presence, as a spatially distant relationship necessarily reduces the sense of shared responsibility for the neighbor. Strong neighborhoods are valued precisely due to the local-ness of the relationships; bonds develop between community members who have vested interest in the immediate environment. "Here" is more valuable than "there." Once again, God enters into the church-community as the initiator and model for local bondedness.

Sacramentally speaking, Holy Baptism and Holy Communion are remarkably social—a sociality that begins with the divine-human interchange of grace and ends with the mutual bondedness of the church-community. Of course, the believer who receives a Christian baptism is borne again into the common kinship of all believers; likewise, the believer participates in the body and blood of Christ with other Christians throughout time and space. However, the immediate experience of the sacraments necessarily requires a fellowship of *local* believers. To accentuate this point, the Christian neither self-baptizes nor consecrates his own bread and wine and self-distributes. Each sacrament is a sharing event, where humanness is reaffirmed and understood in light of the individual's relationship with the other participants in the Christian church-community. In other words, the bondedness that happens at the font and table happens not simply because other people have to be present. Rather, God draws his people into a particular type of community, one with its unique languages, customs, and rituals that unite the local church with the historical faith unbounded by time. The sacraments bind the local believers together in fellowship and simultaneously bind the participants to the invisible church in common celebration of Jesus' death and resurrection.

Even eschatological communities are local. "Communities of peace" look forward to the final coming of Christ, the Prince of Peace, and so they consist of individuals who share in the common collective responsibility of restoring God's kingdom. This obligation is yet another application of Bonhoeffer's deep respect for the mutual conversation and consolation of the brethren. The local *confessing* body is also the local *absolving* body. Such a community parleys the arrival of God's kingdom into a forgiving disposition toward the Other, participating in the advancement of God's rule on earth until the Last Day.

Reciprocal trust. If a community of peace is to exist, truth and justice must be explicitly present and practiced. Such qualities cannot be imposed externally on a community; they must emerge from within. Bonhoeffer locates truth and justice in the Christian practice of confession and absolution. "There is a community of peace for Christians only because one will forgive the other his sins. The forgiveness of sins still remains the sole ground of all peace."[1] The consoling words of the Christian brother or sister remind the believer that no person stands before God unscathed and without sin. The solidarity of humanity as creature is penetrated by the Incarnation who, becoming physically human himself, transforms people's primary identity as sinners to that of priests. Bearing the forgiveness offered in Christ, for Bonhoeffer, allows for the community of peace to develop as trust serves as the necessary precondition to consolation.

From a sacramental point-of-view, the fellowship experienced in both Holy Baptism and Holy Communion is impossible without a sense of reciprocal trust. This is not to say that either sacraments' efficacy comes from the bond that exists between administrator and recipient—or the level of trust that exists between them—but rather, partaking in the sacraments involve a series of reciprocations once again expressed from the divine-human relationship first and proceeding to the human-human relationships that exist in the local church-community. The person comes to the font and table trusting that God's word is true and faithful, and God fulfills that trust by offering his unconditional Yes found in the forgiveness of sins. Similarly, a measure of reciprocal trust exists in the relationship between distributor and recipient, where the latter expects that the former will execute the sacraments faithfully and in good order. Finally, the trust between parishioners is present as each sacrament is received in a common posture of humility and thankfulness. The embodied community invites the recipient into the life of the truth-telling, forgiving Body of Christ.

Finally, Bonhoeffer's eschatological vision once again relies on the foundation of trust. In this case, trust fulfilled to the utmost. Christian hope is built on the relationship between God's promises and his people; as his promises are fulfilled, Christians recognize that the hope-giver is worthy of trust and praise. The return of Christ in the Last Day is the gold standard of this relationship. God fulfills his final promise in the eschaton, validating the trust of the believer completely and excising all remaining doubt. The endgame of Christianity no longer requires faith in Christ, as the believer immediately and directly dwells in his presence and love. Hope, too, becomes a relic of the past as Jesus completes that which is hoped for. In

---

1. Bonhoeffer, *No Rusty Swords*, 169.

the here-and-now, God remains faithful and imparts upon community the model of reciprocal trust needed for human relationships to flourish. In the midst of everyday fears, God imparts us with communities of reciprocal trust where, once again, he serves as the creator and exemplar. He is the object worthy of human trust as the God who fulfills his promises in history; he also invites the Christian to call upon him in times of need, individually and corporately.

The State of the Church

As the next chapter will demonstrate, the rise of the online social network has forced the Church into a difficult position. On one end of the spectrum, technophiles attempt to calm frayed nerves by assuring that technology is: a) here to stay; b) an innovation that may help a church's efforts to stay connected to its members; and/or c) an avenue by which a new generation may hear the gospel "in their own tongue." At the other end of the spectrum, contemporary neo-Luddites shout, "The sky is falling!" They bemoan the way in which an online social network physically alienates people from their neighbors. Human flourishing, they argue, requires a physical investment that the digital world cannot provide. What is required is an attentive ear to both sides.

Even if one accepts the neo-Luddite critique in principle, OSNs afford their users opportunities to connect with other people in ways previous generations could not have imagined. These connections, regardless of how initially shallow they may or may not be, occasionally take root in the virtual world and lead to embodied relationships that foster the type of depth that physical closeness makes manifest. OSNs may be able to spur interest in local issues and be a tool for communication and action that helps generate, but not take the place of, local bondedness within our physical communities. Finally, OSNs may be used as a space to test out trust and honesty in an unthreatening environment, potentially allowing two acquaintances to safely interact without the pressure of physical presence. They *may*. Ultimately, society will be forced to live with the types of community it creates. Whatever version of social living emerges, then, will shape the way Christianity is proclaimed from the pulpits and in the streets.

Much is at stake for the parish. Each congregation will be forced to navigate the range of responses to the Digital Age. The steadily increasing influence of social networks and digital technologies will prompt parishes to confront questions ranging from church structure to evangelism to the nature of fellowship. Can/should the parish model the church community after digital examples which have proven to capture the public's imagination, but perhaps losing some significant features of traditionally physical community? Shall the local congregation reject certain (or, perhaps, all) features of the virtual community ethos, risking its relevance in a world that has embraced such a medium? Many congregations will attempt to strike a proper balance between embodied community and the connectivity offered in modern social technologies and do so with varying degrees of success. Therefore, in this chapter, I will suggest a discerning way forward that will attempt to harness the goods that OSNs provide while actively promoting the essence of the physical yet communal Christian life. Such criteria could potentially serve local parishes as they maneuver through this difficult terrain and provide a strong theological foundation for a discerning disposition toward online social networks.

Criteria for the Proper Ordering of Online Social Networks

For the foreseeable future, online social networks are here to stay. Therefore, a framework for evaluating these networks as they either complement or resist embodied theology could be beneficial to the Church. If the use of an OSN reinforces the characteristics of an embodied community as manifested in depth, local bondedness, and reciprocated trust, Christians can joyfully participate in the goods they offer, using them for the purposes of furthering holistic relationships with God and neighbor. Conversely, if these core characteristics are not present, Christians can appropriately express caution regarding the use and function of these technologies. A potential way forward would be to ask two essential questions: (1) How are Christians (whether individually or corporately) to effectively evaluate OSNs, and (2) based on this evaluation, how should they be used or not used within the parish?

I propose three criteria that assist the Christian in determining the potential value/harm of any online social technology, framed by the three aforementioned characteristics constitutive to Christian community. Each criterion will contain both a negative and positive formulation.

Regarding the Nature of "Depth" in Christian Community

The use of an online social network that values superficiality at the expense of deep, accountable relationships cannot be defined as community-building. Embodied communities experience depth in a multitude of fashions. The sacraments, for example, bind the believer to the broader community of saints at an eternal level, not simply by shared temporal interests. While OSNs can place God's word before a user in non-traditional ways, the digital interface cannot fully offer the forgiveness of sins through the means of grace located in Holy Baptism and Holy Communion. Other vital Christian disciplines are threatened, as well. Confession, in particular, the penitent sinner is called to lay their shortcomings before God and each other; it is difficult to argue that such authenticity and depth emerge when the physical presence of others is absent to hear a general confession. Embodied community provides the picture of a God who fully redeems humanity in the depths of their sin. Jesus, both literally and figuratively, descends into hell to accomplish this feat. The complete justification of humanity is not a superficial mark of God's approval; it is the complete and total transformation of the believer's whole being. Far from useless, however, OSNs can be considered as tools that facilitate such deep bonds by affording the participants ways to physically connect with one another. Meetups are a collection of social websites that exist for that very purpose; they connect strangers for the explicit reason sharing physical time over shared interests (e.g., Mom's groups, bicycle clubs, wine tasting, just to name a few). The OSN is used for initial contact. After that, the participants can determine the depth of all future interactions, often leading to lifelong friendships. A discerning congregation may seek to use such networking tools in good conscience knowing the end is the formation of person-to-person relationship building. *Therefore, online social networks are used in a good and trustworthy manner when they are used to affirm humanity's capacity for depth and accountability in all of its relationships and supplement the face-to-face interactions that facilitate such depth.*

Regarding the Nature of "Local Bondedness" in Christian Community

The use of an online social network that supplants, rejects, or minimizes the importance of local relationships, or suggests face-to-face interactions have limited benefit, cannot edify the community qua *community.* The World Wide Web casts an enormous shadow. While interpersonal connections can be made across the globe by any person with an Internet connection, the strong ties that bind local communities are much more difficult to maintain. Commitments can be accepted and cast aside as easily as closing the box of an Internet browser. The strong ties that serve as the adhesive for authentic communities are often absent in the malleable associations offered by OSNs. By contrast, the Body of Christ unifies Christians in spectacular ways. They

are one in spirit in several ways: (1) They share a kinship with all humanity, as well as other animals, by virtue of their common creatureliness; (2)
together they partake in the waters of Holy Baptism and the bread and wine
of Holy Communion; and (3) they participate in the restoration of all creation and look forward to the Last Day, when every creature proclaims, "To
him who sits on the throne and to the Lamb be praise and honor and glory
and power, for ever and ever!" (Rev 5:13). Yet each of these bonds finds its
clearest expression in local, concrete communities of faith.[2] These embodied communities eschew any form of utopian dreaming, yet experience the
joys of bearing a common limited nature together, oriented to God as the
source of their life together. *Therefore, online social networks are used in a
good and trustworthy manner when they seek to unite members of particular
localities, helping them forge bonds through a common love for the neighbors
in their midst.*

Regarding the Nature of "Reciprocated Trust" in Christian Community

*An online social network that is used to intentionally deceive or mislead an-
other person should be considered a threat to authentic community and, therefore, should be vigorously challenged.* The ubiquity of virtual identities in the
online world suggests that anonymity may be the preferred *modus operandi*,
and while this may not be necessarily problematic, a vigilant participant
should recognize the radical difference between an online presentation of
one's self and the reality of physical presence. This disconnect limits the degree of trustworthiness possible in an online interaction. By contrast, trust
emerges when the mutual conversation and consolation of the brethren is
present. In the Christian's freedom-for-the-other, the will to dominate other
people recedes by the power of God's grace. What remains is a Spirit-driven
willingness to engage the neighbor in their weakness, in the mutual bearing
of creaturely limitations which sow the seeds of reciprocal trust and respect.
Furthermore, trust is present when Christian brothers and sisters work side-
by-side in the restorative work of God's kingdom in anticipation of God's
final victory on the Last Day. Such an attitude discourages any claim of special privilege before God; rather, the work of restoration naturally promotes
trust through the common humility of knowing that Jesus owns all claims

---

2. These communities are not to be strictly limited to individual parishes. One
could consider other expressions of Christian community, as well, including Christian service organizations, cohorts of congregations, and/or faith-based educational
institutions.

to lordship. Trust, then, allows for humans to be submissive to the ultimate will of the Father, relying on his provision for all things good and beneficial. *Therefore, online social networks are used in a good and trustworthy manner when they foster an environment of authentic communication, where each participant speaks truth in humility.*

Supplementary Language vs. Substitutionary Language

In the proposed criteria above, I have noted the threat of OSNs insofar as they represent a *substitution* for embodied community. My hope is that the proposed framework will act as a supplementary aid to the physical relationships that already flourish in the life of the Christian. However, it is often difficult to ascertain the degree to which OSNs maintain a hold on the individual's social life. The key question becomes, "Am I using OSNs as a *supplement to* or as a *substitution for* embodied life?" This section will attempt to clarify this crucial distinction and encourage Christians to embrace the supplementary role of OSNs. To be sure, there are some simple nuances to keep in mind that can free a person from taking an overly dogmatic position. OSNs have the unique ability to foster relationships that do not have the luxury of physical proximity; platforms such as Skype and Facebook span formerly unreachable distances in an instant—and this is a good thing. I am not suggesting that this would be an example of substitutionary virtual community for the simple reason that physical community between two or more people separated across vast distances do not have the option of embodied community. In this case, the online mediation of the relationship is a necessity, not just a convenience, for any connection to grow and mature.

What I propose instead is a supplementary role, where OSNs exist to enhance already-formed instances of embodied community rather than supplant them. If a person uses an OSN to enrich face-to-face relationships, where embodied contact retains its place as the normative way of being, then these networks can have an overwhelmingly positive impact on individuals, communities, and churches. OSNs flourish as tools of connectivity. This quality is beneficial in innumerable ways. This project does not seek to belittle those benefits, yet it does remain vigilant against the over-promising of goods offered by OSNs. I simply suggest that, as societies use such technologies, it can be alerted to the following potential scenario and take the necessary steps to avoid: OSNs that encourage people to see connectivity as an end to itself, not as a means to the end of embodied life together. When this connectivity moves more and more to be the goal of the individual, depth simply cannot flourish. When one must decide between "being in the loop" and being fully present in embodied relationship, OSNs are tempting for users to choose the former.

Perhaps one way to discern whether or not virtual community has overtaken embodied community is to use a two-part rubric derived from some of the material referenced in this work. By applying this rubric, one can better understand if their use of any one network falls into the category of "substitutionary" or "supplementary." One rubric uses the spiritual gift of discernment as the feature that distinguishes these two terms. The second method is located in Bonhoeffer's understanding of sin as domination; any technology that supports a human in his/her rebellious quest to be godlike requires opposition, not support. I suggest that the application of the below rubrics will foster the necessary critical approach to one's daily interactions with digital technologies.[3]

Christian living requires a large measure of discernment. Since the world is filled with nuance, the Christian interacts with others within a confusing matrix of contexts and conditions. Therefore, God gives to his people measures of his discerning spirit that they may properly exercise virtue and character when the explicit word of God may fall silent. Paul includes the "distinguishing between spirits" as a spiritual gift (1 Cor 12:10), and the writer of Hebrews counts this exercise as a sign of Christian maturity (Heb 5:14). The practice of discernment informs the Christian's distinction between "the Spirit of truth and the spirit of falsehood" and is to be applied generously in all manners of Christian living (1 John 4:6; 1 Thess 5:20–22).

Every claim of community is subject to spiritual evaluation. Therefore, discernment may be applied to each specific OSN as a way to filter out that which is beneficial and, conversely, that which is harmful to evaluate its value in one's life. Such critical assessment allows a person to better understand the consequences of any one decision or action. How does this apply in the present discussion of the supplementary vs. substitutionary roles of OSN use? Practicing discernment affords the Christian community the ability to see which features of embodied life are lost if one chooses the substitutionary role for virtual living. This effort leads to a clearer understanding of the transaction; that is, what is being exchanged when a person substitutes digital relationships for embodied ones. This discernment should not be a wholly individual enterprise. Local church parishes can participate in the corporate evaluation of spiritual goods present or absent in any affair of Christian life. Therefore, when the congregation leads the congregants toward a biblical evaluation of these technologies, she places her members in

3. I believe this rubric works at the level of institution as well. In other words, parishes and schools can use the various frameworks I offer as a launching point for discussions about discernment and OSN use.

positions of wisdom. The resulting effect of community-based discernment is manifold. Not only do the members receive instruction on discerning an OSN's value and/or harm, the very benefits of embodied community over-and-against virtual community are being modeled in the exercise!

I earnestly see a future in which the discerning Christian can use OSNs as supplementary force to enrich embodied living. When parishes critically examine the blessings and curses of virtual community-building, its members are more likely to direct their use of programs like Facebook in ways that connect people toward the end of relationships that ring with depth, local bondedness, and reciprocal trust. Because the use of a tool is primarily in the hands of the user(s), it may also be put down, turned off, or otherwise ignored. The responsible, discerning OSN user knows when such drastic measures need to be taken. Yet within the sphere of everyday life, an individual often is not given these options. They work, relate, and connect with the aids that their vocation provides, or even demands. Discernment, therefore, can be applied in the individual encounters with social technology and draws the Christian toward an ethos of stewardship. A person has limited attention and a finite amount of energy with which to engage their social relations. The above criteria encourage the individual to practice discernment so that he/she may participate in the joy of stewarding time and social energies.

A second, separate way to discern whether or not OSNs are being used in a godly way comes from the theology of Bonhoeffer. In Bonhoeffer's anthropology, the human subject demonstrates his/her sinfulness by perpetrating acts of domination over the Other; the person becomes *sicut deus*. God is pushed to the margins, and, at the center, the individual resides in the full expression of inward looking narcissism. Divorced from his/her original disposition toward God, the human is completely alone. When an OSN moves from its role as a supplementary force for embodied living to that which encourages an individual's inclination to self-centeredness, it has crossed the Rubicon into something ungodly. The human, in this case, experiences the temptation of living outside the boundaries of his/her creaturely limit. However, if the OSN is used in a way that does not seek to defy or belittle the role of the person *qua* creature, it may in fact draw a person toward positions of empathy. OSNs are regularly used as platforms that give awareness to a variety of social and political injustices. The immediate dispersal of information can, in theory, promote benevolent action that protects and defends the weakest among society. Here, the person is bent toward the other; the inward curve of the sinful person is broken and love of neighbor can emerge.

Allow me to offer a final note on this discussion. The temporary nature of the digital landscape needs to be addressed. While it is true that technological advances, as a whole, appear to be positioned for a long and lasting life in Western culture, the same cannot be said for individual platforms. The shelf life for any one OSN in its present incarnation is remarkably short-lived. This lack of longevity seriously calls into question claims about any particular OSN's ability to foster long-term community. One might critique this argument by stating that most young people use a mosaic of different social platforms to experience virtual community, so the loss of any single website does relatively little damage to their online experience. While I acknowledge that the short life expectancy of individual OSNs does not represent a collapse in one's virtual social life, I certainly question if the transient nature of Internet itself allows for the type of long-term, permanent features that give embodied community so much of its value. The feature of temporality is yet another reason why I stress the supplementary nature of OSNs as opposed to using them as a primary (or substitutionary) mode of being.

Identifying the Community under Examination

Before these criteria are applied to the OSN phenomenon, it is important to identify as precisely as possible the OSN user I have in mind. An accurate description of the user will prevent grand generalizations about OSN use based primarily on outlier cases. I will seek to answer, "What demographic of OSN user is being observed and then called into godly discernment?" The vast majority of people in this country are, in fact, OSN users, and the differences between each are unique. Yet I believe it is possible to narrow the field considerably and approach this task of identification by readily acknowledging who the target is, both sociologically and theologically speaking. Before proceeding to these categories, I wish to first limit my evaluation by addressing Christian communities. While the effects I describe in the next chapter are not limited to Christians, this project seeks to benefit the church first and foremost. The online experience of the Christian OSN user, therefore, is substantially more useful for the church's discernment on such matters. The believer stands on the front lines of discerning that which is beneficial for the individual, the family, and greater society.

Sociologically speaking, this particular text is not attempting to address the extreme fringes of the OSN universe. The young man who devotes his waking life to his alter-ego on the massively-multiplayer online game, World of Warcraft, is not the subject of my critique. Nor is the person who devotes his virtual life to fetish pursuits with a miniscule troop of like-minded sociopaths. Using outlier cases like these can be problematic and ultimately undercuts the thrust of my project for the following two reasons. First, using an addict or extreme apologist as the test sample tends to oversimplify and overstate the dangers involved in certain types of OSN use, lifting up straw men arguments over a nuanced appreciation of the average person's interaction with digital technologies. Most people, I surmise, would describe daily 10–12 hour commitments to a video game as detrimental to the social and physical health of the gamer. Yet few people innately know when Facebook participation moves from the realm of acceptable behavior to something else entirely. My goal is to focus on the latter example, where the use of digital social technology still falls within reasonable boundaries of normal social behavior. Second, extreme cases of OSN use often involve a host of other issues not directly related to the embodied life. Social phobias, severe self-image issues, and other neuroses can, in large part, be mitigated by the anonymity found in these technologies. These abnormalities require delicate attention and are not under the evaluation offered in this text.[4]

Rather than focusing on most remarkable or rare of cases, I will address the vast majority of instances in which a person uses OSNs and other digital media for a noticeable, but not overwhelming, amount of time each day, comprising a significant portion of an individual's social experience. This narrowing of the field appreciates the fact that OSN use falls along a spectrum. I will seek to identify the OSN user as someone who falls within the middle portion of the spectrum, neither obsessed with his/her digital life nor isolationist in his/her outlook on social technologies.

This sociological angle may help us get a better grasp of the user addressed in the next chapter, but I believe this approach is significantly enhanced when one considers the human subject from a theological perspective. This approach will provide some necessary insight as to the inclinations of the human heart and the temptations which draw the person away from Christian life and worship. Three theological conditions, I believe, will ground our understanding and discussion of the OSN effects.

---

4. I would, however, issue a caution against the prejudice of "extreme cases" simply for the fact that, in many instances, reality and perceived reality are two different things. For example, the word "gamer" evokes images of teenage boys surrounding a TV with friends, or perhaps a person playing in front of a PC for hours on end. These instances appear to fall well outside of society's normative behavior with respect to these social technologies. In actuality, there are roughly 183 million active gamers (those who report playing video games "regularly"—on average, about thirteen hours a week) in the United States alone. This fact shows us the difficulty of isolating what precisely makes for an "extreme" case, since people of every age and gender commit substantial amounts of time to this enterprise. For an eye-opening description of video game popularity (and their potential benefits), see: McGonigal, *Reality is Broken*, 1–34.

First, every human being is radically impacted by sin. This condition has deep theological roots in nearly every Christian tradition, and while the nature of sin and its impact might have some varying interpretations,[5] no serious theologian (or even Christian, for that matter) believes that a person can fully escape sin's effect in daily living. Therefore, an important presupposition for the discussion to follow is that every OSN user is also, at his/her core, a sinner in need of God's restoration. No OSN user can enter into a utopian virtual community nor can he/she use discernment (even godly discernment) in an utterly pure way.

Second, every human being seeks forms of community, whether the community desired is with one another or with God. This condition is more than simply saying that humanity was created expressly for social interactions, a point I addressed in chapter 2. I am suggesting that, in line with Dietrich Bonhoeffer, the individual finds the fullest expression of his/her own humanity *in the community*. The believer seeks to know and be known; this only happens when the person is confronted by an external personal being. Applying this theological reality as a precondition to OSN use will allow us to note where human vulnerabilities lie. If the Christian necessarily craves community as a part of being human, one can expect that they will go to great lengths to meet this particular need and not feel bound to limit the pursuit to traditional forms of social living.

The third condition is extrapolated from the prior two. If every human subject is affected by sin and also seeks out forms of community, one can reasonably expect that each person will be tempted (from the various forces that comprise temptation) to seek relationships that fall outside the boundaries of godly living. The flesh desires sexual expressions that violate the marriage bond. The world offers alternative forms of community that often violate God's design for healthy communities. And lest Christians forget, spiritual forces can directly tempt a believer to substitute the short-term comforts of amusement and base desire fulfillment for a relationship of depth and trust. The OSN user is not immune to temptation. Each user, by virtue of the Internet, is afforded a measure of information and connection that is unprecedented. With this influx of information and access comes exposure to morally vague forms of individual expression and corporate participation. The challenge is to determine when/if these expressions run counter to the embodied life offered in Scripture and the Lutheran theological tradition.

5. For example, some denominations portray sin as a sickness in need of a cure, others frame sin as rebellion against God. In the first instance, it has internal, mostly individual effects. In the latter, the communal effects of sin are highlighted.

Ultimately, these three conditions effectively speak to the classic Lutheran formulation *simul justus et peccator*. The Christian, whether an OSN user or not, is identified both as a sinner and as a saint. The believer is responsible to God for his/her actions and yet receives the righteousness won on the cross, where God imputes into human nature the perfection of Christ himself. The *simul* status frees us not from temptation, but it rather provides the theological resources to offer sober judgment on all manners of Christian living. A person's "blind spots," if you will, reduce when the dual reality of the human saint-sinner existence is accepted and brought to bear on the challenges confronting the humanity. According to Luther, the Christian life is a life dedicated to repentance, as the act of humble confession is a form of obedience to Jesus' call.[6]

---

6. Luther, "The Ninety-Five Theses," 490. The first of Luther's ninety-five theses affirms this point: "When our Lord and Master, Jesus Christ, said, 'Repent,' He called for the entire life of believers to be one of penitence."

5

LOOKING FOR COMMUNITY
IN VIRTUAL SPACES

Now that criteria have been established, the remaining task is to apply
it directly to online social network use as a test of the criteria's potential
effectiveness, both in secular applications (this chapter) and in parish settings (chapter 6). The prior chapter offered three necessary markers for the
identification and maintenance of an embodied Christian community. If
one can locate the features of depth, local bondedness, and reciprocal trust
in the daily or normal use of these networks, the aforementioned fears of
a Christian theology that dangerously minimizes embodiment may prove
to only be that: a fear. If, however, the search for the three markers proves
unfruitful, Christians have the necessary resources to make discerning
decisions about the individual and corporate use of these particular technologies. Without this exercise, many of the prior claims in this paper are
ensconced in the world of theory, divorced from practical applications
to the world of digital technologies. My immediate goal, then, is to apply
the criteria to online social networks, both philosophically and practically
speaking, and offer a measured examination that is not reduced to neo-
Luddite hysteria. At the conclusion of this chapter, I will address those who
have written about OSNs in largely favorable terms as a way to situate my
conclusions in a broader academic conversation.

The penultimate section of my project begins by delving into the undergirding philosophy and use of online social networks. Earlier I offered a
working definition of such networks: An OSN is any Internet-based gathering of individuals for the purpose of creating and developing social bonds
through shared interests. But what is the nature of these bonds? In what

ways are the features of embodied community (depth, local bondedness, and reciprocal trust) present/absent in the use of these technologies?

It is possible that OSNs offer people a way to experience authentic forms of community without the explicit need for bodily presence, and if this is so, such community should be praised as the Digital Age's successful attempt to forge lasting social bonds in a remarkably complex world. However, OSNs also foster a version of social living that runs counter to the life offered by God in Scripture, a life framed in the preceding pages as an embodied theology. The connected life of the technophile may have the "appearance of authenticity, but in reality, [online social networks] may be a façade to mask the deep sense of loneliness experienced when one is sitting alone at the computer screen."[1] If this is the case, certain instances of OSN usage may: 1) offer only a limited portion of the benefits ascribed to traditional physical communities; 2) be rejected as a wholly antagonistic force that resists a godly understanding of human life and community; and/ or, 3) be subjected to a re-ordering, whereby the goods they contribute to society are placed in proper perspective within the whole of Christian life. This chapter will apply the criteria offered in chapter 4 to the phenomenon of online social networks, evaluating the degree to which they support or resist the aforementioned features of community. The undergirding question to this section is: "To what extent can an online social network complement or sabotage a community's depth, local bondedness, and reciprocal trust?"

To ascertain the answer to that particular question, it is helpful to determine what OSNs actually *do* to the human being. For the purposes of this text, I have limited the exploration to three fields of inquiry: philosophy, physiology, and sociology. First, I will lay out some initial philosophical concerns raised by scholars of technology to shed some light on the understanding of these networks. Working forward from Marshall McLuhan's seminal text, *Understanding Media*, it will become apparent that OSNs are not simply a "neutral tool" in the building or decaying of societal connective tissue. Second, since a person cannot engage the digital terrain without their own physical bodies present (e.g., real fingers are needed to insert keystrokes), it is appropriate to ask what physiological effects such networks have on the body. Recent research in the field of neuroscience suggests that digital technologies, such as OSNs (though not strictly limited to them), are remapping the neural pathways in human brains to be more efficient at collecting disjointed pieces of information at the expense of the pathways needed for sustained concentration. In turn, other areas of the brain may experience some decay as long, sustained spells of concentration

---

1. Yust et al., "Cyber Spirituality," 291–93.

are less necessary. Third, using an online social network, by definition, is an explicitly *social* enterprise. Therefore, an explanation of the various ways OSNs impact social life is both necessary and illuminating. Sociologist Sherry Turkle leads the way in this area of research; her work on social media reflects in depth on the issues of isolation, sexuality, anxiety, and social cohesion.

When taken together, these fields of inquiry will provide us with a helpful, albeit not comprehensive, look at OSNs that can then be placed against the features of an embodied theology and the crucial element of community that runs through its veins. The benefits of online social networks are numerous and important to recognize. However, I will primarily attempt to draw out the particularly harmful results of OSN use and how these results threaten the depth, local bondedness, and reciprocal trust crucial in order to call the Church into the practice of discernment as it engages these innovations.[2]

A Philosophical Primer on Online Social Networks

Before an adequate catalogue of effects is compiled, we should take care to consider first some of the philosophical foundations of technology. This text will explore two sides of the same fundamental issue: the relationship between content and media in both secular and parish contexts. First, I will use Marshall McLuhan's work to undercut the popular position that technology exists merely as a neutral aid for disseminating information; rather, media necessarily changes content. As a clarifying aid to some of McLuhan's conclusions, I will draw on the insights of cultural critic Neil Postman. Postman connects McLuhan's theory to the realities of the present media culture and their influence on social structure and political discourse. He contributes the necessary historical context for technology's current hegemony in American life and provides a clear link between McLuhan's arguments and the challenges associated with OSNs. Second, I will present some of author and theologian Shane Hipps' reflections on the ecclesial effects of McLuhan's conclusions, particularly concerning the use of social technology in Christian parishes.[3] When taken together, these authors will provide

2. Later in this chapter, I will provide a detailed analysis of those scholars who are particularly sympathetic to the online social network phenomenon.

3. Shane Hipps has written several books on the relationship between technology and theology. Formerly an advertising account planner, Hipps left his job to become a Mennonite pastor and public speaker. See his work in: *Flickering Pixels* (2009) and *The Hidden Power of Electronic Culture* (2005).

a useful platform from which to survey the landscape of social technology's effects, perceived and real.

The Medium Is the Message

Marshall McLuhan, in his foundational work *Understanding Media*, broke new ground when he argued that the primary effect being presented in any one communication event originates not from the explicit message presented, but from its accompanying medium. His oft-repeated phrase, "The medium is the message," forces one to consider the nature of the delivery every bit as much as the content of the message. McLuhan understood that all forms of mediated communication event have two central components: The message itself and the medium that dispenses it. However, he argues that the media component is far more significant because the recipient is wholly unaware of its effect, thereby assuring no barriers are erected in the conscious Self to resist its transformative power. He states, "Our conventional response to all media, namely that is how they are used that counts, is the numb stance of the technological idiot. For the 'content' of a medium is like the juicy piece of meat carried by the burglar to distract the watchdog of the mind."[4] For example, the late-night infomercial impacts a viewer to a far less degree than the medium he/she watches it on—the television. The viewer can consciously evaluate the content of the infomercial (its persuasiveness, its value, and/or its capacity to communicate information), a task that the mind performs dozens of times hourly. Yet the person is wholly unprepared to critically evaluate, even understand, the transformative power of the television which distributes the infomercial.[5] This is but one form of the manifold technologies available to the average American citizen. The overwhelming influx of media is an assault that humanity has been unable or unwilling to resist.

How do these effects manifest themselves? For McLuhan, all technology forces society to reorganize into patterns that accommodate its efficient use. Technology affects "sense ratios or patterns of perception steadily and without any resistance."[6] The formative power of such media is so deep, so vast, that McLuhan found it helpful to consider them as natural resources.

4. McLuhan, *Understanding Media*, 18.

5. Such an example would be television's use of image to evoke an emotional response. Or, alternately, the ability of the television to structure the viewer's attention span in certain time increments through advertising and programming decisions. Both demonstrate television's ability to transform the routines of a culture.

6. McLuhan, *Understanding Media*, 18.

Just as the emergence of a cash crop can realign the entire socio-economic structure of a region, the forces of modern media consumption have an all-inclusive transformative effect on those who participate. The message of the medium changes the "scale or pace or pattern that it introduces into human affairs."[7] Discoveries of contemporary neuroscience can expand on McLuhan's understanding of "human affairs" to include a person's own physiology, a topic to which I will explore shortly.

Two important observations should be made here. First, McLuhan is essentially claiming that technology necessarily transforms *both* the content of the message *and* the social arrangements of those who receive said message. The introduction of any influential technology forces the population to realign and adjust for its presence; the equilibrium is lost and, therefore, must be reestablished to accommodate the technology's presence. Second, McLuhan's initial warnings about media-based content were sounded a half-century ago, prior to the appearance of the Internet, iPad, virtual reality systems, Google, even the personal computer. Considering that the amount of information available to a connected population doubles roughly every eighteen months in accordance with Moore's Law,[8] society appears to be experiencing a state of near-constant disequilibrium. The individual can longer keep track of the various forms and frameworks by which they understand their world.[9]

According to McLuhan, technological devices are extensions of human capacity. A telephone, for example, extends the normal capacity of our ears and voices over extreme distances. While these devices are indeed tools, they cannot be viewed as neutral aids to receiving information. Social patterns emerge to accommodate new technologies; patterns that may or

7. Ibid., 8.

8. Moore's Law specifically refers to the amount of transistors that can fit on an integrated circuit; traditionally this number has doubled every two years. More recent references to Moore's Law are usually connected with information flow. The commonly established number is referenced in the above claim: The sheer amount of information available to the world doubles every eighteen months. Nicholas Carr notes several other prescient statistics of same persuasion: "Over the last three decades, the number of instructions a computer chip can process every second has doubled about every three years, while the cost of processing those instructions has fallen by almost half every year . . . Network bandwidth has expanded at an equally fast clip, with Internet traffic doubling, on average, every year since the World Wide Web was invented." Carr, *The Shallows*, 83.

9. Postman, to whom I will return to shortly, noted that this deluge of information (much of it without any context at all) is a character trait of the "Technopoly." The Technopoly is a society that no longer has the necessary institutional resources to provide certain restraints on, and therefore *proper context for*, information. Postman, *Technopoly*, 40–55.

may not be beneficial to human flourishing. Just as Narcissus wasted away under the mesmerizing effect of his reflection in a pool, a person could fall prey to the unintended consequences of uncritical media consumption, to their own detriment. McLuhan warns society to keep their collective eyes open to all of the hidden effects of technological advances.

Two different interpretations of McLuhan's work are particularly appropriate for present work. Examining some of the implications of McLuhan's thought from a secular perspective, cultural critic Neil Postman argues how technological advances have the ability to shape truth claims within a population. He particularly zeroes in on the effect that television has on public discourse, and his conclusions prophetically resonate with the Internet culture that has since followed. By contrast, theologian and pastor Shane Hipps uses McLuhan's philosophy of technology as a way to draw the Christian church into an examination of its own missiological and worship philosophies. Hipps brings McLuhan's warning to the parish. Even further, he gives an account of how media has actually changed and shaped the content of the Christian message over the centuries. Both approaches will prove helpful as one discerns the value and challenges that social technologies lay before the contemporary world, sacred and secular.

Neil Postman and the Death of Public Discourse

Truth claims are bound directly to the medium in which they are delivered. This is a central feature of Neil Postman's seminal work, *Amusing Ourselves to Death*. To understand the full ramifications of this conclusion, we would benefit by charting the connections between two particular paradigmatic media shifts in history: from written word to the television and from television to the Internet. Postman directly engages the former shift, and, by applying his central critiques, I will subject the latter to close inspection to determine the Internet's (and, by extension, the OSN's) relationship to community and truth. By examining communication shifts through the lens of truth claims, one can more readily witness what is at stake for embodied community, since all three markers fundamentally rest on the assumption of truth's presence.

Postman, in a revealing opening salvo, laments "the decline of the Age of Typography and the ascendancy of the Age of Television."[10] The Age of Typography is Postman's term for the ways of knowing that are influenced, in fact defined, by the printed page. The epistemology of the printed page forces a culture into patterns of logic and reason, for each act of reading

10. Postman, *Amusing Ourselves*, 8.

is a highly disciplined affair. For example, one must remain more or less immobile while reading and pay attention to the arguments or propositions stated within the book, constantly analyzing the meaning of terms and their related coherence to the whole of the text.[11] By contrast, the contemporary obsession with the television or photographic image is intended to evoke a certain *emotional* response; the image neither requires context nor logic for its effect to take shape.[12] Since television is primarily an act of watching images and has now become the primary means by which Americans receive their information and entertainment, Postman argues, the printed word as the central form of information distribution has receded into the background. The discipline required to read anything is under siege and often replaced with the passive experience of enduring televised forms of entertainment.

Postman's conclusions have maintained their force in the Internet era, although some augmentation may be required since the time *Technopoly* was published. First, the Internet/television line has become quite blurred with the widespread availability of streaming video. Traditional commercials are becoming a rarer and rarer sight within the household. Second, Internet-based offerings of information and amusement tend to be less passive than television. Websites barrage the user with interactive polls, games, quizzes, and hyperlinks as a way to tether a person to their delivery system.[13] These innovations have found a home in the Internet and while they do not encounter Postman's direct analysis (vis-à-vis the Internet), they certainly serve to reinforce Postman's primary point; that is, the influence of the printed page is waning. Commercial advertising may not hold the influence that it once had (both as generators of income or as a means by which television establishes attention rhythms), yet few would venture to argue that television's overall influence on culture has been seriously compromised. It still purports to be an impressive delivery system for what Postman might pejoratively call, "the news of the day."

Postman continues his argument by suggesting that "the media of communication available to a culture are a dominant influence on the

---

11. Ibid., 25.

12. No doubt, many pictures have captions with some minimal context mentioned, such details are: (1) minimal in and of themselves, providing a mere modicum of context anyways, and (2) unnecessary to capture the overall emotions being conveyed (e.g., fear, outrage, beauty, love).

13. The Internet is a haven for such entertainments. I would argue, however, that the OSN more specifically has become the ultimate breeding ground for these tethering applications.

formation of the culture's intellectual and social preoccupations."[14] Such preoccupations include education, civic responsibilities, religious affairs, and the political discourse that shapes daily life in America. More than simple influence, Postman is convinced that media "directs us *to organize our minds* [emphasis added] and integrate our experience of the world, . . . [Media] imposes itself on our consciousness and social institutions in myriad forms . . . It is always implicated in the ways we define and regulate our ideas of truth."[15] Media appears to have an all-encompassing effect in Postman's thought (a true standard-bearer for McLuhan in this regard); it has a "resonance" by which it touches most, if not all, areas of social interaction.

Whereas in the past the above topics (religion, politics, education) had been largely defined by the printed word, today the dominant culture-shaping tool is the Janus-faced titan of television and the Internet. Complex, logical systems laid out in books now have given way to the 30-second (or less) commercial. Information is processed in quick sound bites with a premium on the ability of the medium to produce an emotional response, interest or outright unapologetic entertainment value. According to Postman's argument, Americans have deluded themselves into thinking they have been receiving the same quality content that was once provided by books, oratory, and newspapers. Only the medium changed. Postman, like McLuhan before him, understands this statement to be an oxymoron. Media necessarily changes content. The OSN sits directly into the line of fire. Many users receive their daily news through the medium of Facebook or some other social website, relying on underdeveloped headlines with even shorter (and often less-than-thoughtful) user comments beneath the article thumbnail.

Postman would do well to internalize many of his own critiques at this point in his thinking. The printed page certainly enjoys particular advantages over the television (depth of material, capacity for intellectual engagement, higher degrees of reason), but this is not an across-the-board benefit. A more thorough analysis of technological paradigms would seek to uncover how the Print Age itself is responsible for, or at least contributes to, some less-than-desirable outcomes. For example, the printed book allows the individual to read and interpret meaning apart from any guidance from the community; the reader is now responsible for rendering judgments on texts that formerly required communal supervision. With this independence comes the plurality of voices that enter the fray and personal experience begins to override the wisdom of the collective. Some Enlightenment thinkers

14. Ibid., 9.
15. Ibid., 18.

found this to be a liberating experience,[16] yet this individualistic attitude defies the role of community as a stabilizing and, at times, ethical force. This individualistic disposition can threaten the ways in which embodied community manifests itself. In other words, the printed word can draw a person away from forms of local bondedness as well, since the individual's pursuit of information does not necessarily require embodied, communal support structures.

One of Postman's most significant observations is the overwhelming increase in decontextualized information, found in all forms of news-bearing media. He traces the beginning of this reality to the invention of the telegraph. Samuel Morse's discovery of electronic means of communication collapsed former boundaries of space and time. As a result, any person had access to information regardless of where they lived (as long as they had access to the telegraph) with essentially little or no delay. Such a discovery had significant costs. As Postman writes, "Telegraphy did something that Morse did not foresee when he prophesied that telegraphy would make 'one neighborhood of the whole country.' It destroyed the prevailing definition of information, and in doing so gave a new meaning to public discourse."[17] The information received lacked the necessary contextual markers that encouraged thoughtful reflection. Instead, the lines of communication now opened would not simply offer the opportunity for conversation, they would insist upon it. News agencies became infatuated with the "news of the day" as information quickly became a commodity, "a 'thing' that could be bought and sold irrespective of its uses or meaning."[18] The wealth of irrelevant information drastically and permanently altered the "information-action ratio."[19]

16. Immanuel Kant famously upholds this position in his influential essay, "What is Enlightenment?" In a summary of his thinking, Kant writes: "If we are asked, 'Do we now live in an *enlightened age?*' the answer is, 'No,' but we do live in an *age of enlightenment*. As things now stand, much is lacking which prevents men from being, or easily becoming, capable of correctly using their own reason in religious matters with assurance and free from outside direction. But, on the other hand, we have clear indications that the field has now been opened wherein men may freely deal with these things and that the obstacles to general enlightenment or the release from self-imposed tutelage are gradually being reduced. In this respect, this is the age of enlightenment." Kant, "What is Enlightenment?" 263–69.

17. Ibid., 65.

18. Ibid.

19. Ibid., 68. Postman tends to evaluate information's value by its ability to generate action. Hence, the "information-action" ratio should, in Postman's eyes, have a high degree of action per article of information received. It is unclear if he believes that information without an accompanying action has any substantial value at all. This opens a possible critique of Postman's work. Is not the pursuit of knowledge a worthwhile project in and of itself? Liberal arts education is built around the concept that important

The telegraph met its complementary match in the photograph. Information unobstructed by context allows a citizen to have access to every bit of information available, regardless of time and space. The telegraph provides the caption for such information while the picture gives it emotional value. Postman trenchantly remarks, "Here [in the invention of the telegraph] was information that rejected the necessity of interconnectedness, proceeded without context, argued for instancy against historical continuity, and offered fascination in place of complexity and coherence."[20] Consider how this speaks to the current condition of online social networks. The status update or tweet has become the new telegraph message, regularly alienating the user from context, history, and/or nuance. Value is placed on the speed in which a comment is made or affirmed (through the infamous "like" button), and much less in the objective value of the comment itself.

Postman, on this point, is accurate in pointing out the redistribution of values, but in light of my prior arguments, the above shift influences how one understands Christian community in light of the three markers outlined in the last chapter. The pressure to act instantaneously bites at the authentic community's requirement for deep, truthful living; speed, in this case, competes directly with depth. The Bonhoefferian community thrives on the intimacy that comes with long-lasting, intentional relationships. It neither values a quickness of judgment nor information for information's sake. Bonhoeffer's vision of community, in fact, requires significant levels of trust and depth for the confession and absolution of sins; quick judgment has little place in his schema. Postman's concerns may exist at a societal level, but the theological import of visual and digital technologies is even more alarming.

The endgame of Postman's prophecies, at least in the United States, is the development of the technopoly. The technopoly is a "totalitarian" world in which all forms of culture are subdued and given meaning by technology.[21] In this world, the primary value is efficiency, and efficiency is achieved by collecting, analyzing, and distributing bits of information:

> [The assumptions of the technopoly] include the beliefs that the primary, if not the only, goal of human labor and thought is efficiency; that technical calculation is in all respects superior to human judgment; that in fact human judgment cannot be

questions and seminal texts have intrinsic value and are worthy conversation pieces throughout life. When a student engages these timeless works, they are not necessarily reading the texts as the means to some action. Rather, the enterprise itself (asking big questions and reading important works) has *inherent value*.

20. Postman, *Technopoly*, 69.

21. Ibid., 48.

trusted, because it is plagued by laxity, ambiguity, and unnecessary complexity; that subjectivity is an obstacle to clear thinking; that what cannot be measured either does not exist or is of no value; and that the affairs of citizens are best guided and conducted by experts.[22]

Harrowing words, to be sure. Yet this sounds eerily prophetic of some modern-day "iGods,"[23] namely Google, whose search algorithms attempt to analyze each user by their preferences, shopping patterns, locations, and other quantifiable pursuits. Forms of local bondedness are at risk precisely because the local community no longer is given authority to ascribe meaning to the surrounding culture. Postman warns that a technopoly necessarily reduces the interdependence of fellow citizens; when this relatedness decreases, all three markers of embodied community are threatened.

Postman's work takes McLuhan's philosophy of technology to its practical end: a world in love with base amusement and disconnected information, lacking in the wisdom to discern how these things are problematic to authentic embodied communities. Nor will this influx of information necessarily lead to personal action. Postman asks, "Since we live today in just such a neighborhood (now sometimes called a 'global village'), you may get a sense of what is meant by context-free information by asking yourself the following question: How often does it occur that information provided you on morning radio or television, or in the morning newspaper, causes you to alter your plans for the day, or to take some action you would not otherwise have taken, or provides insight into some problem you are required to solve?"[24] Postman might be overstating his case here. As we consider the paradigmatic OSNs user in this project, they use a combination of media to grasp their world. The question could be returned to Postman with equal

22. Ibid., 51.

23. The term, "iGods," comes from Craig Detweiler's book of the same name. The term refers to the titans of the technology industry who get " rich by solving problems created by technology such as the complexity of the original computers, the unmanageability of the internet, and the sheer excess of information." Detweiler, *iGods*, 8.

24. The New Media (blogosphere, independent internet reporting, podcast and radio-based commentary) is forcing us to reconsider Postman's challenge in at least two ways: One, the rise of political talk-radio, while at times bombastic and agitating, has had a notable influence on the coalescing of political positions (particularly for more conservative political consumers) and thus does carry a certain measure of influence in the ballot box, or better yet, realized in the phenomena of the Tea Party and Occupy Wall Street movements, respectively. Two, OSNs have, from time to time, carried the banner of some forms of social change. Users often show solidarity to a movement by posting unified avatars or forwarding poignant videos to generate awareness for a variety of social issues.

force, "How often does the information you receive in a novel or non-fiction work cause you to alter *your* plans for the day?" Nonetheless, personal action is the result of committed men and women who feel a consistent measure of accountability to their fellow citizens, a deep commitment borne out of application of reciprocal trust: to act now, on my neighbor's behalf, will benefit me in some way in the future.

In spite of the above inconsistency Postman's point is clear. The new age of media (starting with television and extrapolating forward to the age of the Internet) more effectively permeates the market with ever-increasing amounts of disjointed information than traditional print media, disconnected from the contexts that give such information full meaning. What remains is an über-connected population looking for that which is often trite, funny, amusing, distracting, ironic, or shocking; hence, the death of the typographic form of discourse and a lifestyle rather void of the qualities found in embodied Christian communities. McLuhan's initial concerns are fully affirmed by Postman's observations: The medium is, in fact, the message. Still, Postman's observations appear to be incomplete on this point. McLuhan's axiom is indeed affirmed, but Postman's rather idealistic view of the printed medium precludes him from noticing this medium's tendency toward potentially-dangerous by-products: individualism, reason at the expense of emotion, and abstract reasoning over narrative approaches to truth. Nonetheless, Postman remarks that ignorance to McLuhan's central observation is no longer an option:

> To be unaware that a technology comes equipped with a program for social change, to maintain that technology is neutral, to make the assumption that technology is always a friend to culture is, at this late hour, stupidity plain and simple. Introduce the alphabet to a culture and you change its cognitive habits, its social relations, its notions of community, history and religion. Introduce the printing press with movable type, and you do the same. Introduce speed-of-light transmission of images and you make a cultural revolution. Without a vote. Without polemics. Without guerrilla resistance. Here is ideology, pure if not serene.[25]

Consider briefly how Postman's devastating critique of the television commercial has acquired more *gravitas* with the rise of OSNs. He laments the reduction of important newsworthy items to mere captions with pictures, acknowledging that most newspapers no longer rely on intensive investigative journalism. Postman, using USA Today as his target, notes a startling

25. Postman, *Amusing Ourselves to Death*, 157.

fact: "Here is an astonishing tribute to the resonance of television's episte-mology: In the age of television, the paragraph is becoming the basic unit of news in print media."[26] Yet today, a paragraph seems to be remarkably generous. Most news outlets, talking heads, and celebrities communicate through the use of online social media, most notably Twitter. Now, when a paragraph is too long, Twitter can communicate a thought in 140 characters or less. In fact, this is fundamental to the application's design: A person can add their own commentary to the deluge of noise in an instant.

Perhaps this is Postman's worst Orwellian nightmare revealed: a lan-guage reduced to 140 characters at a time. This type of social interaction appears to be the paradigmatic case of context-less information; the means of begetting and gathering information no longer produce the ends of knowledge or wisdom. But, in this case, individual knowledge and/or wis-dom are not the only casualties. The embodied community for which this text argues encourages a depth of conversation that largely remains absent in text-based OSNs; this depth is a central feature to the embodied life. This marker grows when conversations brim with patient interaction, and when present, contributes to the growth of the third marker, reciprocal trust. Conversations of depth afford an embodied relationship more opportuni-ties to understand one another, even in simple one-on-one conversations. For example, a face-to-face conversation involves multiple levels of com-munication simultaneously acting to produce a message. The text message only has one level: the words on the screen. If dissonance is discovered in an embodied conversation (i.e., non-verbal and verbal communication are in conflict), the tension is more easily discovered and resolved so that the relationship can continue to grow. The resulting trust that comes from such resolution is difficult to manufacture in a medium that relies mostly on a single message level.

How is Christian church-community affected by this instantaneous and near-constant flow of commentary? Pastor Shane Hipps parlays McLu-han's work on technology into a practical examination of the Church's methods and materials. If technology exists in all phases of human exis-tence, then one is forced to acknowledge that its presence has profoundly impacted the Church, as well. At the local level, a parish's use of technology implicitly shapes the congregation's expressions of faith. For example, in the Age of Print (compare to Postman's description of the Age of Typography), theological information was transferred in pages of writing: linear, black-and-white, organized. Spiritual expression mirrored the medium; Hipps argues that this is the era of history when the Church relied most heavily

26. Ibid., 112.

on propositional apologetics, individualism, and abstract doctrines to relate Christian doctrine to the people. These features of Christianity, however, are much less evident in the oral traditions of the early Church when the dissemination of faith relied more heavily on narrative, imagery, and the power of speech. What changed? The technological tool of the printing press radically redefined how Scripture was understood; in this case, the content was the same, but the media itself changed. As McLuhan prophesied, "We shape our tools and afterwards our tools shape us."[27]

Applying McLuhan and Postman to the Church

Hipps recognizes the paradigm shift happening in the postmodern, digital age. The power of the image has now superseded the influence of the written word, manufacturing a believer that is prone to more image-based, even emotional, interpretations of Scripture.[28] Hipps implores the Church to understand its predicament. For every technological tool it uses, the Church necessarily molds a new form of Christian because the story is told (and thus, received) in a fundamentally different way. While this is not necessarily an undesirable effect, it is an effect nonetheless, and the Church has the responsibility to enter into all engagements with technology with open and critical eyes, whether print or digital *for her doctrine's sake.*

Two important developments emerge here, both of which concern the nature of Christian authority. First, Hipps believes that a culture steeped heavily in electronic technologies threatens the original medium of the Scriptures: the written word. He argues that "the impact of electronic media can cause us to lose touch with a crucial source of authority for our faith— the printed medium of Scripture. Along with church, Scripture is God's other chosen medium for revelation and sending the gospel to the world. *The vitality and faithfulness of the church depends upon our understanding of a printed medium* [emphasis added]."[29] In one sense, I agree wholeheartedly with Hipps' conclusions. The shape of the present church is largely constructed by the way it reads the words of Scripture. However, I find it curious that Hipps seems to miss the connection between New Testament history and the claim above: Most of the earliest Christians did not read the encyclicals, they heard them! The apostles of Jesus were first and foremost evangelists of a message, not authors. The Gospels were compiled many years—even decades—after the events of the Passion Week. The "vitality

27. McLuhan, *Understanding Media*, xxi.
28. Hipps, *Flickering Pixels*, 74–84.
29. Hipps, *Hidden Power*, 130.

and faithfulness" of the earliest church did not depend so much on texts as the ongoing gathering of the faithful, recalling the words of Jesus Christ (and witnessing his acts, culminating with the events of Good Friday and Easter) and embodying them in faithful worshiping communities.[30] The witness of the earliest Christian community reaffirms the local bondedness that grows in embodied communities. Central to the health of the early church was the simple fact that they gathered together in physical spaces. The various communities of believers were in conversation with one another as they told and re-told the narratives surrounding Jesus, and, as a result, the intimate bonds of intentional fellowship increased in the corporate expression of Jesus' identity as the Son of God.[31]

Hipps's second concern speaks directly to the balance, or perhaps *imbalance*, of authority that remains with a world connected to the vast quantities of information. The authority of the priestly class has slowly eroded since the invention of the printing press, for information became accessible to all people at relatively low costs. Hipps notes the seismic shift: "If the age of print introduced cracks in the information dam that separated priests from the people, then the electronic age detonated the dam, obliterating nearly all information barriers."[32] This "detonation" may be an overstatement as skilled practitioners are required for the *interpretation* of the raw data, but his main point holds. The unrestricted access to information made available by the Internet connection necessarily brings about a crisis of authority. Here, he agrees with Postman's conclusions. Information without context necessarily destabilizes the controls of authority, or as Hipps puts it, "everyone is a leader and everyone is a follower."[33] This might not be a

30. The Print Age was not without consequence. As cheaper print copies of the Bible were made available to the public, the church's hegemony on matters of biblical interpretation began to lessen. Individualism increased, as did a more rationalistic view of Scripture. In at least this one important sense, the role of the community experienced a significant loss of influence.

31. I would go so far as to suggest that the telling and re-telling of meaningful narratives within a community is an extraordinarily effective strategy to build reciprocal trust, as well. The history of a people develops this way, even at the level of the family. When a member is confident of their place and role within this narrative, they perpetuate these narratives to the next generation. As a result, multiple levels of trust emerge. First, trust in the fact that these narratives accurately reflect the history of a community. Second, trust in the fact that these narratives have authoritative ethical value within the community. And third, trust that the performative act of telling these narratives binds families together in profound ways.

The print medium, then, is not without its faults, as it struggles to offer many of the social goods that oral traditions provide naturally.

32. Ibid., 129.

33. Ibid., 130.

particularly devastating development for the local church body; even Hipps recognizes that "more participatory and egalitarian forms of leadership," like those that emerge from the information free-for-all, are likely to be useful and "dynamic."[34] Still, the concern is the type of faith that is being fostered. Churches that experiment with preaching methods that include heavy imagery, conversation, storytelling, and other sensory experiences at the expense of more traditional text-based approaches risk minimizing the left-brain skills of critical reasoning, logic, and abstract thinking.[35]

For the churches that wholeheartedly embrace such technologies, Hipps predicts what type of believer emerges. "The Internet is a lot of things, but it is emphatically not a neutral aid. Digital social networking inoculates people against the desire to be *physically present* with others in real social networks—networks like a church or a meal at someone's home. Being together becomes nice but nonessential."[36] The prescription must be a balanced approach, one that blends the values of both right- and left-brain thinking. The deep, rational thought that develops in textual study allows the Christian to make appropriate judgments about Scripture's cohesion and leads him/her to interpret the Bible with faithfulness. By contrast, technology affords the Christian a view of Scripture that allows for qualities that are often times subdued in the text: its narrative character, the emotional content of faith, and freedom to explore ambiguity.

Hipps argues that technology shapes (and will continue to shape) Christian faith and practice, and he wants Christians to understand the cost of any significant shift in media. At times, it appears that Hipps prefers the oral traditions of the ancient and early pre-modern eras.[37] But all communication is subject to McLuhan's analysis; they are all forms of technology. Therefore, Hipps would be best served to expand his critique of modernity and postmodernity backwards to pre-modernism, as well. He is just one step ahead of Postman in this sense but still subject to many of the same concerns.[38] Language itself is a gift of God, used for conversation and com-

---

34. Ibid.

35. Ibid., 131.

36. Hipps, *Flickering Pixels*, 115.

37. Pre-modernism, in the context that I am using it, has some of the following characteristics: communities that rely heavily on story-based knowing, parent-to-child transmission, the collective responsibility for moral adherence, and the narrative-based understanding of Scripture.

38. Postman tends to idealize the print medium, while conveniently minimizing the ways that printing eroded the goods offered by the pre-modern or oral tradition society. Hipps, in a parallel move, acknowledges the effects of printing yet lacks an in-depth analysis of pre-modern system, holding it to no stringent critique and thereby idealizing the pre-modern worldview instead.

munity, and its self-evident worth is beyond calculation. Yet, by Hipps' own framework, one could not call spoken language a neutral aid uninvolved in the interpretation and/or shaping of theological content. Both spoken and written forms of language directly impact the way members of a society relate to one another and how they express their collective history to subsequent generations.

In conclusion, Postman and Hipps provide us with a serious accounting of Marshall McLuhan's work; they warn against treating technology as a neutral aid, uninvolved in the meta-patterns that shape human thought and action. These authors press home McLuhan's conclusions that a society's use of any medium, in the present case digital, necessitates a change in the way the user thinks and acts. These effects can be dramatic, beyond the individual levels of attaining and processing information.

How do these concerns directly impact the markers of embodied community? The philosophical underpinnings of technology, in general, and OSNs more specifically, reveal significant misgivings about an OSN's role in community-building. The above authors have laid forth a convincing case that digital technologies do, in fact, have profound impact on social life. First, McLuhan's "the medium is the message" substantiates the claim that the impact of digital technology is real and not imagined; the concerns of the neo-Luddites are not without merit. This is the ground-floor of any subsequent analysis. Second, Postman's application of McLuhan's work provides us with a helpful analysis of the paradigmatic shifts in modern communication media. The Print Age, though not without its own set of philosophical vulnerabilities, enjoys distinct advantages over the Age of Television precisely in the areas of depth and reciprocal trust. Postman blames digital media for the decline in intellectual depth in political discourse, as the emotive image has superseded the value of the written word. And, on the whole, I agree. Relational depth suffers when nuance and patience give ground to a medium that more often prizes the sound bite. If a medium (of any kind) encourages instant reaction and snap judgments, it discourages the building of any long-term reciprocal trust, as well. The reciprocal trust necessary to sustain communities is seriously challenged by the contextless information that is offered in television and Internet offerings to the detriment of the those who seek to know others and be more fully known.

New technologies initiate an effect of disequilibrium; the three markers of an embodied community move into varying degrees of flux until the effects of the medium have run their course. If any one of the three markers experiences significant decline, the possibility for a Bonhoefferian embodied community decreases. The present task, then, is to evaluate the physiological and social changes that are present in online social network use, and then evaluate these changes in light of the aforementioned essential characteristics of embodied community: depth, local bondedness, and reciprocated trust.

The Physiological Effects of Using Online Social Networks

As a former advertising consultant, Hipps has been uniquely attuned to the effects of OSNs and other visually-oriented technologies. These effects are not isolated to buying patterns, of course. In one instance, he references a study by the American Academy of Pediatrics which warns against the use of television before age two and links said behavior with "an increased risk of Attention Deficit Disorder, autism, aggression, obesity, and possibly dyslexia."[39] He goes further by implicating these technologies as neurologically transformative:

> While these studies may be on to something, my concern has more to do with the subtle and invisible consequences of television. These consequences have nothing to do with the programming—whether you've got a Baby Einstein video playing or the latest abomination in reality TV, it's the *medium*, not the *content*, that changes us. Believe it or not, *the flickering mosaic of pixilated light repatterns neural pathways in the brain* [emphasis added]. These new pathways are simply opposed to the pathways required for reading, writing, and sustained concentration.[40]

Hipps acknowledges how human patterns of thinking are under constant transformation at the molding hands of technology. The effects of social technologies cannot be dismissed as irrational fear or a set of conspiracy theories without evidence. Their use has physical consequences, particularly in the area of neurology.

The intersection of physiology and the Internet is a relatively recent phenomenon in contemporary scientific inquiry. The importance of such research, however, should not be underestimated, as it may draw society closer to understanding better how culture shapes the very ways people think as well as give individuals the necessary resources for making responsible decisions. The more contextual information a population has at its disposal about a particular service or product, the more familiar people become with the consequences of using it. If one can ascertain the effects of

39. Ibid., 78.
40. Ibid.

digital media on the body, then the culture may self-adjust to accommodate a more balanced use of such media.

Of particular interest to this project is brain physiology. It would hardly be considered controversial if a person made the claim that the Internet has had a formative role in American culture. Few would argue against the great impact of the nearly instant information offered by websites such as Wikipedia, Yahoo!, and Google; the applications for education, medicine, and technology are nearly limitless. Remarkable changes, however, are happening at the level of the individual user's brain. For hundreds of years, neurologists had worked under the assumption that the adult brain was essentially fixed. Whereas a child's mind offered malleability as it grew and developed, the neural connections of the adult brain were assumed to have minimal flexibility, if any at all.[41] The prevailing view that an adult's brain is a "concrete structure" relatively incapable of significant internal modification has been significantly challenged in the past 50 years, however. The most contemporary model maintains that the brain can literally restructure itself to meet the contextual needs of the person; it demonstrates a remarkable degree of plasticity. This plasticity is not relegated to isolated areas of function.[42] Nicholas Carr speaks of this expanding horizon: "The brain's plasticity is not limited to the somatosensory cortex, the area that governs our sense of touch. It's universal. Virtually all of our neural circuits—whether they're involved in feeling, seeing, hearing, moving, thinking, learning, perceiving, or remembering—are subject to change."[43] If an individual's brain is experiencing ongoing change to facilitate efficient processing based on the demands placed upon it, and further, that each generation is confronted with new media by which to make sense of the world, one can extrapolate that any significant environmental change would necessitate measureable transformations in the way people process information. In short, the brain physically evolves with every input it receives.

41. Carr, *The Shallows*, 20.

42. Pascual-Leone, Amedi, Fregni, and Merabet, "The Plastic Human Brain Cortex," 377–401. This article goes so far as to suggest that there is no baseline state of one's brain. Since every input shapes brain circuitry, it is impossible to determine a "beginning point" for research (379). The article later notes, "We should think of the nervous system as a continuously changing structure of which plasticity is an integral property and the obligatory consequence of each sensory input, motor act, association, reward signal, action plan, or awareness. In this framework, notion such as psychological processes as distinct from organic-based functions or dysfunctions cease to be informative. Behavior will lead to changes in brain circuitry, just as changes in brain circuitry will lead to behavioral modifications" (379).

43. Carr, *The Shallows*, 26.

How does this new research shed light on the effects of OSN usage? Carr argues that the brain builds neural connections to support the activities the brain uses most. Since most websites, including OSNs, attempt to attract users with graphics, images, and headline-length sentences, an individual develops neural pathways that facilitate such a media bombardment. Past generations would use the newspaper as their primary medium for interaction with global politics, forcing the reader to: 1) Have a substantial amount of savvy in socio-political issues, and 2) read most, if not all, of the article to absorb the information. Here, Shane Hipps' earlier observations are particularly prescient; the newspaper is logically laid out, individually consumed, and requires considerable thought to absorb the necessary information. Today someone could simply move from topic to topic on any one of a thousand discreet news websites, pursuing hyperlinks, videos, and images to his/her heart's content. One could glean all the essential information without devoting any sustained concentration to one train of thought.

Using the Internet as a source for information, while convenient, necessarily shapes the brain's ability to process various stimuli. In other words, the human brain is constantly developing new and more efficient neural connections to make sense of the media that is placed before it. The effect is multiplied when one considers how young people, in particular, feel the need to be engaged in multiple media sources at the same time. Often called "multi-tasking," the use of more than one medium at a time forces individuals to split their attention across various platforms, something that is proving to be somewhat difficult, if not impossible. After extensive research on the multi-tasking habits of young people, Dr. Rene Marois from the Human Information Processing Laboratory at Vanderbilt concluded that, "our brains, it turns out, are not wired to process dual information simultaneously."[44] Another study suggests that those who regularly employ a high degree of media multi-tasking perform considerably *worse* in activities that require simple task switching where the individual's concentration must transfer from one set of activities to another. Several reasons for this somewhat unexpected result are offered, including: a reduced ability to tune out "interference" from an irrelevant task set and the inability to disregard and/or filter insignificant "representations in memory."[45] Postman foresaw this difficulty with clarity. Information that comes without safeguards or context would claim an individual's attention until he/she had lost the ability to distinguish irrelevant data from actionable information (i.e., information that can be used for individual or social improvement).

44. Quoted from Detweiler, *iGods*, 66.
45. Ophir, Nass, and Wagner, "Cognitive Control," 15, 583–87.

The above research is revealing a notable tension. On one hand, the brain's malleability allows it a certain measure of coping skills needed to withstand the significant pressures of media bombardment. On the other hand, the above research seems to indicate that any sustained success in the area of media multi-tasking appears to be fleeting, perhaps even impossible. The brain appears to have certain fixed limits of concentration when multiple media-based stimuli are involved, in spite of its uncanny capacity to restructure its own neural pathways. Or, perhaps a better way of summarizing this research is to say that the brain has a limited (although quite high) ceiling by which to facilitate the efficient reception and organization of electronically-delivered information. The floor, by contrast, may not be as fixed.

In the negative sense, the brain's ability to take in long, in-depth exchanges has decayed. Since fewer people sit down hours on end to read literature of any kind, the neural connections required to perform such a task actually erode in the brain's attempt to allocate resources to other areas where such connections are most needed. Carr suggests that the practice of long, sustained concentration is slowly becoming a physiological hardship. If a person fails to practice behaviors that require such reflection, the neurons in their brain responsible for such activities fall into disrepair. While the individual experiences this on a day-to-day level, Carr argues that meta-patterns develop as society uses some technologies at the expense of others:

> Between the intellectual and behavioral guardrails set by our genetic code, the road is wide, and we hold the steering wheel. Through what we do and how we do it—moment by moment, day by day, consciously or unconsciously—we alter the chemical flows in our synapses and change our brains. And when we hand down our habits of thought to our children, through the examples we set, the schooling we provide, and the media we use, *we hand down as well the modification in the structure of our brains* [emphasis added].[46]

Since the cultural appetite for online technologies continues to increase at a break-neck pace (all the while maintaining its steady diet of television[47]), the consequence appears to be all but a foregone conclusion. The individual's brain will continue to foster the necessary connections needed for

---

46. Carr, *The Shallows*, 49.

47. Ibid., 86–89. The assumption that Internet use is replacing the television is, for the moment, false. Carr cites research that demonstrates that even as Internet use has increased, television viewing has either held steady or increased itself.

an image-based society at the expense of deep concentration. The digital society is literally learning itself out of its ability to think deeply.

Based on this research, one can make some startling conclusions about the nature of an OSN and its ability to impact humanity at the most basic of levels. The physiological effects of the OSN reinforce a Self that excels at scanning massive amounts of material at the expense of deeper interaction with the text. Users become adept at gleaning the central point, yet often fail to see the nuances that make an article (or person, by further extrapolation) truly unique and worth reading. The OSN entices the user to sacrifice internal reflection and relationship-building for the gold ring of constant connectivity and immediate (if not constant) gratification.

More importantly, this research holds significant ramifications in the quest to establish embodied communities of depth, local bondedness, and reciprocal trust. First, no OSN user is immune to the aforementioned neurological effects because these changes happen without the subject's conscious direction. The soccer mom who browses the Internet on her free time is every bit as susceptible to neural transformation as the most dedicated of technophiles. This realization disallows one from taking the position that media only benignly extend human sensory capacities, for media also form new neural connections (and discard unused ones) with every stimulus. The body is undergoing direct change as a result of these technologies, and therefore, they have significant import for this book. One of the central features of embodied theology, after all, is the presence of a physical body. When the human physical form is manipulated, the effects are not isolated to the individual but rather extend to the level of community. I believe that Carr's work can be used to suggest something rather disconcerting: neural change by way of OSN use directly impacts the community's ability to experience depth, local bondedness, and reciprocal trust. If, as Carr indicates, OSN use facilitates shallowness over depth, judgment over trust, and connectedness over bondedness, a Christian may be forced to recognize that digital worlds offer only a facsimile of the intimacy available to physical communities of Word and Sacrament.

Second, this branch of neurological research better illuminates the relationship between two of the critical markers in the above embodied theology. In this case, the relationship between depth and reciprocal trust is significant. They are correlated, as an increase in one directly leads to an increase in the other. Since Carr suggests that the human capacity for deep interactions is waning with the rise of the image-based digital world, so the foundation for reciprocal trust becomes less sure. Much of this is due, yet again, to the forms of communication that shape person-to-person interaction. Those relationships that have deep roots typically exhibit several different forms of communication: verbal, written, non-verbal, use of space and time, and simple physical presence. Each of these communication modes serves to support the structure of the relationship, like buttresses that support a towering cathedral. If one particular mode falls into disrepair, the relationship can still stand without immediate risk because each person has grown to trust the *overall depth of the relationship that has been provided by other forms of communication in their totality.*

Bonhoeffer understood the power of communication latent in the confessor/absolver relationship. The one-on-one communication (in all of its modes) he promoted fostered not only a depth of spirit between the two participants, but it contributed to the overall trust present in the broader community of faith. By contrast, in a digital relationship primarily mediated by only one or two forms of communication (e.g., Facebook is essentially text and pictures) the risk of relationship collapse is greater simply due to the limited ways in which the participants communicate (and repair mis-communications). Fewer buttresses make for a less-stable cathedral. Stability is not simply desired for its own sake; rather, it is the crucial feature that promotes an atmosphere of disclosure and trust that, in turn, increases the strength and durability of the community. In this way, stability provides an excellent feedback loop for the increase of the church-community's reciprocal trust.

The third and final observation I wish to draw from brain research is the potential for reversal. Norman Doidge, in *The Brain that Changes Itself*, catalogues a fascinating set of test cases in which patients who suffered significant brain trauma or genetic neural abnormalities experience remarkable degrees of recovery through the intentional rewiring of their neural patterns through prolonged therapy.[48] Changes, he argues, can happen in any direction—for harm or healing. Doidge's research reinforces the position that brain plasticity itself has no motivation to build a particular brand of human thinking. If by repetition one can develop neural connections that readily absorb digital media, one can also reverse this trend toward relational intimacy. An individual who commits himself/herself to a life of reflectivity and patience will be rewarded with a brain that facilitates such behaviors. Rich interpersonal experiences, built on trust and bondedness, promote the necessary physiological changes that support communities of trust and depth. Since there is no such thing as a brain that "stands still," any conscientious member of a community can limit the ways in which OSNs have purchase on his/her time. Or, better yet, such a person can use OSNs

48. Doidge, *The Brain that Changes Itself.*

in ways that supplement and support, not overtake, the embodied relationships already present in his/her life.

In summary, the above description of the physiological ramifications of OSN usage appears to be a significant threat to the depth that is required for authentic Christian communities to flourish. Using the language of the criteria offered in chapter 4, neurological effects could lead to human behavior that subordinates the values of "depth and accountability" to the convenience of "superficiality."[49] If the primary mode of relating to one another is mediated through an OSN, the relationships may bear the marks of a superficiality that has been *physiologically* ingrained into each participant. The community's best option, based on the above research, is to use OSNs in restrained amounts—never as a substitute for life together, but as means to connect with one another for the purpose of significant, deep, and embodied contact.

The Christian community can certainly put instant information to good use as a faithful participant in the life of the church-community. Consider how the image of a starving child, forwarded from one Facebook user to another, has the potential to move people (and parishes) to action. If, however, society's acceptance of OSNs is so extensive that it struggles to function at a deep, thoughtful level, the skills for the intensive work of building the fundamental characteristics of embodied community could prove difficult. The apostle Paul exclaims, "Oh, the depth of the riches of the wisdom and knowledge of God!" (Rom 11:33). The embodied individual flourishing in the midst of authentic community recognizes the call to receive the beauty of this depth and falls prostrate before it; the person who sacrifices depth for perpetual connectivity may fail to recognize the goods that emerge from God's wisdom and knowledge!

The Sociological Effects of Using Online Social Networks

The effects of online social networks have, without question, a broader impact zone than just simple individual physiology. As the ubiquity of OSNs spreads to digitally uncharted regions of the world, an important evolution is taking shape. The user's identity in the digital world no longer remains isolated from one's "real life." In fact, the blending of real and virtual worlds marks a new world order; humanity lives in two worlds simultaneously with no hard-and-true distinction between them. Clay Shirky, in his *Cognitive Surplus*, notes the paradigm shift:

49. Refer to the criteria outlined in chapter 4.

> The old view of online as a separate space, cyberspace, apart
> from the real world, was an accident of history. Back when the
> online population was tiny, most of the people you knew in
> your daily life weren't part of that population. Now that com-
> puters and increasingly computerlike phones have been broadly
> adopted, the whole notion of cyberspace is fading. Our social
> media tools aren't an alternative to real life, they are part of it.[50]

Sociologist Sherry Turkle agrees with this fundamental fact: "We are all
cyborgs now."[51] Turkle refers to the ease in which contemporary Internet
users weave in and out of their various identities (digital and "real"), blurring their own boundaries of identity.

If human identity is at stake and this new identity is not restricted to
merely private spaces, then it follows that a variety of significant social re-
percussions follow. This section will highlight three of the more significant
social effects that have emerged from the OSN culture: 1) The physical isolation of the individual from the broader society; 2) the evolving boundaries
of sexuality in the virtual realm; and 3) the disappearing distinction between
public and private acts. Each of these effects will substantially impact how
we perceive OSNs vis-à-vis their ability to function as forms of authentic
community.

Isolation and Social Capital

The first fundamental sociological effect of OSN usage is its propensity to
isolate the user from broader physical engagement with others. At a base
level, this effect makes a great deal of sense. The only way to interface with
an OSN is to interact (at some level) with a digital device, yet this engagement most often happens when one is physically alone. Or, at the very least,
the person is focused on the device at the expense of those who might be in
the user's company.[52] Without trying to sound overly nostalgic, time spent

50. Shirky, *Cognitive Surplus*, 37.

51. Turkle, *Alone Together*, 152. Turkle's full quote: "Within a decade, what had
seemed alien was close to becoming everyone's way of life, as compact smartphones
replaced the cyborgs' more elaborate accoutrements. This is the experience of living
full-time on the Net, newly free in some ways, newly yoked in others. We are all cyborgs
now."

52 As L. Gregory Jones notes, loneliness should not be conflated with "being
alone." Nor should the presence of other souls constitute a firewall from loneliness.
Some studies suggest that online social network usage has no demonstrable effect on an
individual's sense of loneliness. This project is not dealing with the issue of loneliness
as much as isolation. I argue that physical isolation is not to be considered normative

in front of a computer screen is time that past generations may have used to foster embodied relationships. Such relationships (that is, prior to the popularity of the personal computer) had a notably physical character to them, in at least two distinct ways: One, people who sought community were forced to be in physical proximity to one another due to the lack of alternative options. Two, the physicality *of the space in which they participated in community had significant importance in and of itself.* The actual place used for social gathering often gave shape and direction to the type of community taking place. People did not simply come to a building to find an adequate place to talk. Rather, physical activity was constitutively built into the communal experience: drinking beer at the pub, watching a sporting event, or taking part in civic experiences like social clubs and political events. Community was expressed through the shared experience of activity, and activity required physical people and places.

Robert Putnam's classic, *Bowling Alone,* chronicles the loss of "third places" where citizens come together for civic experiences. These places exist outside of home and/or work and provide the necessary cohesion for a community in the shared acts of service and recreation. As urban sprawl, pressures of time and money, generational overhaul, and other factors contribute to the decline of such civic participation, citizens are less inclined to experience close ties to their neighborhoods and/or the broader community.[53] Instead of joining their neighbors at these third places, each person retreats to their private enclave of HD TVs, iPads, and "No Soliciting" signs. Putnam recognizes the significant strain that individualized mass media has placed on the availability of face-to-face interactions.[54] OSNs, as a physically isolating experience, contribute to this landslide in a significant way. Virtual third places cannot provide nearly the same social capital as physical locations, for one simple reason: A person who visits a physical third place immerses themselves in the *local* population; a digital third place could contain people from all over the world. Thus, the *local* community is strengthened when *local* community members are present and engaged in trustworthy relationship-building.

One rather significant social good that grows from local communities is a developed sense of accountability. Each member of the local community is responsible to maintain the mores and values of community as a whole; those who deviate from these shared values experience forms of social

---

behavior in the context of authentic Christian community and embodied living. Jones, "You're Lonely," 35.

53. Putnam, *Bowling Alone,* 183–88.

54. Ibid., 216.

rejection or perhaps explicit reprimands. By contrast, the digital world cannot provide the fullness of face-to-face communication or the necessary accountability to create and sustain social capital; the users can simply "log off" from the communication altogether and without consequence.

The plate tectonics of American social life continue to shift. To what degree are online social networks providing the proper resources for healthy interpersonal relationships to flourish amidst these changes? Putnam believes that social capital, the glue that binds societies together, emerges when connections of "reciprocity and trustworthiness" arise between individuals. Putnam offers a definition for reciprocal action based on trust: "The touchstone of social capital is the principle of generalized reciprocity—I'll do this for you now, without expecting anything immediately in return and perhaps without even knowing you, confident that down the road you or someone else will return the favor."[55] Reciprocity implies a transactional relationship, yet this should not be confused, at least in Putnam's eyes, as behavior done for the sole purpose of self-interest. Trustworthiness develops out of the expectation and fulfillment of reciprocal action and essentially "lubricates the inevitable frictions of social life."[56] Putnam elaborates on the benefits of reciprocal trust, noting the effect it has beyond the person-to-person relationship:

> Other things being equal, people who trust their fellow citizens volunteer more often, contribute more to charity, participate more often in politics and community organizations, serve more readily on juries, give blood more frequently, comply more fully with their tax obligations, are more tolerant of minority views, and display many other forms of civic virtue. Moreover, people who are more active in community life are less likely (even in private) to condone cheating on taxes, insurance claims, bank loan forms, and employment applications. Conversely, experimental psychologists have shown that people who believe that others are honest are themselves less likely to lie, cheat, or steal and are more likely to respect the rights of others. In that sense, honesty, civic engagement, and social trust are mutually reinforcing.[57]

Putnam draws the necessary connections between the individual and the community. Each act of civic participation not only benefits the person as they await some future reciprocated benefit, the community itself

55. Ibid., 134.
56. Ibid., 135.
57. Ibid., 136–37.

experiences meta-benefits that reinforce the behaviors that contribute to the common welfare. The community-building characteristics noted above have at their very foundation an assumption of generalized reciprocity grounded in trust. One particularly useful point to remember is that, in Bonhoeffer's framework, the believer is only able to offer themselves to the neighbor by God's grace. The inward turn of the individual ego is broken by the liberating act of God's justification. Christian freedom *is* freedom-for-the-other. Therefore, the very act of reciprocity becomes possible through God's grace; the neighbor is finally viewed as an end and not a means and trustworthiness increases.

Yet OSNs do not require trustworthiness in the same way a civic group or physical network does. In fact, the situation may be quite the opposite. Facebook, for instance, invites users to instantly "like" a friend's statement, post, or status; this action is a snap judgment that requires neither serious intellectual engagement nor accountability. Since trustworthiness develops from the repeated fulfillment of one's responsibilities, the lack of accountability in any interaction should cause one to question the social value of the above Facebook click. Admittedly, targeting the "like" button is plucking the low-hanging fruit. Facebook can also be a place where deep and lasting friendships begin to take root and can be a medium of edifying conversation. Yet if the lion's share of social interactions on any OSN *do not require or encourage* a sense of accountability or consequence, trustworthiness appears to be a luxury in the world of OSNs, not a prerequisite for their use.

Other scholars believe Putnam's conclusions may be misguided. S. Craig Watkins disagrees with Putnam when the latter asserts that "one of the main culprits of [the] declining sense of community among Americans . . . is the growth of media in our homes."[58] First, Watkins argues that the forms of domestic media are inherently different from the Putnam's whipping boy, the television. The Internet offers a type of interactivity that former household media (radio, television) simply did not have.[59] By consequence, online engagements allow a form of social mobilization that Putnam either failed to predict or considered too insignificant at the time of his work. Second, Watkins recognizes that social capital emerges when a community takes an active role in the political process, much like Putnam. Yet Watkins is convinced that these benefits can be conferred through the OSN medium. He chronicles the 2008 Barack Obama presidential campaign as the exam-

58. Watkins, *The Young and the Digital*, xviii.

59. This interactivity reaches its pinnacle in online gaming experiences where large numbers of otherwise disconnected people play in remarkably detailed and aesthetically immersive worlds. Players are often known by their personas developed over (potentially) thousands of hours in these virtual environments.

ple *par excellence* of a digital populace creating social capital in the political process. Watkins argues that one of the central reasons for Obama's victory came as a result of a superior online effort by supporters, volunteers, and the candidate himself. His conclusion flies in the face of Putnam's assertions: Household media can mobilize citizens in the political process like never before.

Yet one may ask: Does involvement in the political process (and mobilization for a candidate) contribute to a population's sense of community, or does the example of the Obama campaign merely demonstrate the power of the Internet with regards to its *communicative* function?[60] While the Internet facilitates the dispersal of political ideas, foments activism, and/ or aids in the promotion of a particular candidate, does the use of this tool *necessarily* strengthen civic bonds? At this point, I am hesitant to agree with Watkins' critique, mostly due to the ambiguity in the terms at the core of the discussion: "involvement" and "participation." If these terms are used in their broadest sense, then community is unlikely to receive any particular growth in strong bonds. For example, the "liking" of a candidate's Facebook page may constitute involvement (again, in the weakest sense of the word) in the political process, yet it offers little if any true contributions to the local social capital that Putnam believes are essential for healthy communities. If, however, Watkins' definition of participation/involvement implies action—in particular, *physical* action—then his conclusions gain significant strength. The political process takes on a more anthropological character; that is, person-to-person contact becomes the undergirding feature of the process. Despite these nuances, both Putnam and Watkins foresee significant changes in the macro, or large scale, cultural horizons that result from OSN usage, changes that will affect the vast majority of OSN users, not simply the fringe users.

Ultimately, these authors are contesting the nature of isolation. Putnam argues that isolation occurs as a result of domestically available technologies, discouraging the average citizen from broader (yet still local) communal engagement. Physical isolation becomes the norm, not the exception, for the man or woman who feels like their needs can be met with minimal neighborly contact. Watkins, on the other hand, encourages us to see technology through the eyes of the users: "Technology, first and foremost, *is social and communal in their world* [emphasis added]. Further, young people use social and mobile media to manage nearly every aspect

60. Watkins, I surmise, is correct when he states that civic involvement generates a fair amount of social capital. Yet I would tend to say that social capital is best experienced at the most local of levels. A team of dedicated volunteers, for example, may experience a long-lasting kinship in a small city or town.

of their lives—being digital is simply the way they live. Importantly, teens and young twenty-somethings use technology to share their lives with each other."[61] I imagine Putnam would ask Watkins, "But what type of lives remain?" A youth who uses technology no doubt is using them for a social purpose, but as we have seen in earlier chapters of the book, the word community has some added baggage. Subjectively speaking, a person can interpret a host of external forces as beneficial (or, in this case, communal), yet this interpretation does not necessarily make it so. If authentic community truly is an experience of the three markers, then Watkin's rhetoric certainly calls into question what he believes to be the function of community and what separates it from base connectivity.

The lacking dimension in Watkin's understanding of community may be intimacy. Earlier in this text, I suggested that embodied life, in part, is the "intimate experience of related creatureliness." When placed in the broader context of life together, person-to-person intimacy strengthens the relationships within the community as the commitment to each respective participant necessarily increases. But Watkins tends to view the social experience of humanity as something in need of *management*. Management evokes images of a bureaucracy whereby a complex system is brought into order by a person with decision-making capacity. The term itself implies a certain measure of instability that must be brought under control. While this terminology might be minimally useful to describe the complexity of human interactions, it fails to pick up on the intimate quality constitutive to Christian communities. Christian intimacy is not born of utopian dreaming but the closeness that is found at the baptismal font and the table of the Lord's Supper, distributed *to* and shared *by* the saint-sinner community of faith. It is the intimacy of limitation and closeness that results from realization that we are sinners yet completely forgiven; it cannot be located in the breadth of one's contact list on Facebook or Instagram. Bonhoeffer readily understood how human limitation brings about an intimacy that cannot be manufactured in non-physical settings. In his anthropology, part of the joy of human experience was located in the fact that man and woman, husband and wife, creature and fellow creature could joyfully bear with one another precisely because of their shared limitation. Partaking in this sort of creaturely existence continually reminds the believer of his/her dignity and orientation as a creature, freed forever from sin to look upward in worship to God and outward in service to neighbor.

---

61. Watkins, *The Young and the Digital*, 198. The Christian OSN user falls squarely into Shirky's analysis as well. I know of no study that suggests young Christians use OSNs in a manner qualitatively different than the rest of society.

Isolation and the Device

Many scholars prefer to examine the potentially isolating effects of OSN usage on the micro level. Rather than focus on many of the significant changes that occur at the cultural level, this approach concentrates on the technological item itself *as a device*, as well as the item's impact on the individual user. Such an examination has the benefit of avoiding broad sweeping generalities about the culture as a whole. The precision of the micro view, already demonstrated above in the section on brain physiology, provides us with data that affects each user personally. For this reason, the micro view, in my estimation, is more likely to generate behavioral shifts.

Noted philosopher and technology critic Albert Borgmann argues that the technological device, by definition, allows for a certain disengagement or anonymity for the user. Over time, the device is not seen as a means to a particular end; rather, the device "conceals" itself as it is taken for granted, allowing for the ends (i.e., the final product) to be used without any concern for the process which brought the product into reality.[62] Borgmann surely would have considered both the personal computer and OSNs themselves as such devices.[63] Formerly social enterprises such as harvesting or construction have been overhauled by the use of machinery that largely renders the human component obsolete. The devices that replace human work, while increasing any one individual's production level, has the unintended effect of reducing the social goods of interdependency. Intentional, even necessary, embodied relationships dissolve as the need for communal support in the production of goods dwindles.

The technological device, by virtue of its ubiquity, has become an assumed and relatively unnoticed reality that has contributed to the isolation of the individual. Nowhere is this more evident than the Internet, where anonymity rules the day.[64] Users can enter and retreat at a moment's no-

62. Borgmann, *Technology*, 42.

63. For example, a man who uses central heating for his home is not required to exert social energies in the finding, chopping, and/or transportation of firewood with his neighbors. The device (central heating) makes the commodity (heat) an assumed reality and creates further physical alienation from one's neighbors.

64. Defining anonymity in the Digital Age may require some elaboration. There are many OSN users who are known precisely by their online personas—even enjoying a degree of widespread fame. For example, Johnathan Wendel is an online gamer who is known mostly for his pseudonym, "Fatal1ty." Based on his ability to play online games (one form of OSN) at a high level in professional competitions, he has been able to amass a small fortune branding Fatal1ty products. Johnathan Wendel is largely anonymous, but Fatal1ty, his persona, is not. This is certainly the exception to the rule. Wendell intentionally decided to make his real-life identity known for the purposes of fame and financial gain. The point is this: OSNs and the Internet are near perfect places

tice, fully camouflaged by a dense fog of avatars[65] and online personas. If a person remains willfully anonymous in their interactions with society, it becomes logically impossible for a community of authentic persons to exist, since authenticity requires a substantial measure of honest self-disclosure.

Anonymity can certainly come as a result of prolonged physical isolation. Such isolation, however, is not simply an *unintended* consequence of digital social technologies. The use of certain OSNs, particularly texting and tweeting, often expresses an essential desire *to be* isolated. Whereas phone calls and hand-written letters require time to consume, process, and understand, the message given in a text, for example, allows the recipient to remain unencumbered by sustained concentration or emotional investment. The benefit of isolation certainly increases personal privacy (a particularly American value), but when one intentionally seeks this isolation as their preferred form of communication, the depth and bondedness that Christian life together requires necessarily decreases. Sherry Turkle notes this turn toward intentional isolation in the example of an answering service:

> [The answering machine was] originally designed as a way to leave a message if someone was not at home, . . . a screening device, our end-of-millennium Victorian calling card. Over time, voicemail became an end in itself, not the result of a frustrated telephone call. People began to call purposely when they knew that no one would be home. People learned to let the phone ring and "let the voicemail pick it up."[66]

A device invented for the purpose of enabling person-to-person communication through voice has evolved into a receptacle for messages, to be accessed at the will of the recipient. The general avoidance of two-way, real-time conversation is exacerbated in the age of the Instant Message (IM). Turkle argues that IMs are conversations caught in "staccato texts" in an attempt to avoid substantive, concrete communication—communication that requires time, energy, and concentration.[67] Borgmann calls this the "paradigm of the device." A technological device is primarily understood as a division between a commodity and the machinery used to deliver it. In this case, answering services essentially divorce the embodied message of

---

to practice the anonymity of the real-life self, yet even in these digital worlds virtual identities have the capacity to be known in their own ways.

65. An avatar is any digital representation of an OSN user. It is how the person is represented to those they come in contact with in virtual worlds.

66. Turkle, *Alone Together*, 207.

67. Ibid.

the caller (i.e., the commodity) from the mechanical apparatus of the answering machine.[68] For Borgmann, this has some interesting consequences:

> [Devices] dissolve the coherent and engaging character of the pretechnological world of things. In a device, the relatedness of the world is replaces by a machinery, but the machinery is concealed, and the commodities, which are made available by a device, are enjoyed without the encumbrance of or the engagement with a context.[69]

Few computer users fully understand the inner workings of their machine, and computer companies, for their part, attempt to make the operating systems as user-friendly as possible without the encumbrance of an enormous user's manual. The result is manifold: One, no user fully understands the digital tools he/she uses to manipulate the world and, therefore, remain unaware the manipulation they experience at the behest of the device.[70] Two, the fact that the overwhelming majority of computer users are ignorant to the inner workings of their machines creates the need for specialized expertise.[71] Borgmann and Turkle are essentially arguing the same point from different angles: Many of society's most valued technologies are contributing to the individual's overall sense of isolation. Whether the isolation comes as a result of a conscious decision to conceal oneself in a text/voice message (Turkle) or as the *unconscious* result of the device's own complexity (Borgmann), the average user forgoes real-time physical conversations with their neighbor—an explicit experience of multiple communication techniques combined with accountability[72]—for the power to address the other at his/her convenience.

68. Borgmann, *Technology*, 4. See also 40–48.

69. Ibid., 47.

70. This manipulation is at the heart of Marshall McLuhan's conclusions earlier in this chapter.

71. One might argue that the existence of specialized experts (in the way I have been describing) is a necessity for any vocation. I am not willing to go that far. A car mechanic, for instance, has a level of expertise that far exceeds the average driver. However, many people who own cars can at least recognize the various pieces of equipment and their function to the whole driving experience. They know where the engine is, why oil is needed, where the coolant goes, among other things. The computer, by contrast, is exceedingly technical. The complexity of the machine exponentially outpaces the ability of the user to understand its inner workings. How many people can find their computer's video card? Its on-board memory? Can they explain the how memory caching works in a straightforward way? It would be safe to say that the majority of computer/OSN users would be at a loss to answer these questions.

72. I am using accountability in the sense that direct, real-time conversations require a measure of responsibility. A face-to-face conversation, unlike a OSN post or

These forms of isolation have significant theological implications, particularly as we revisit the criteria for embodied community. I have pressed for an understanding of embodied Christian community with certain distinguishable features that separate it from mere connectivity. In this case, the feature of local bondedness is at stake. A device (whether an answering machine or the Internet) that is used a substitutionary form of physical presence hides the importance of the individual's local relational matrix, for such devices increase the user's ability to stall, ignore, or outright undermine the communication messages that are received from the neighbor. Embodied communities, by contrast, recognize the value of immediate physical presence precisely because such presence brings about the accountability necessary to debunk lives of "cheap grace." Bonhoeffer's *The Cost of Discipleship* was written, in part, to forge a corrected understanding of the person in relationship with the call of Christ. Discipleship rejects personal isolation. "Costly grace," as Bonhoeffer terms it, assumes an obedience to the call of Christ; in this sense, all community starts first by the individual's relationship with Jesus Christ himself. Accountability, not isolation, is the hallmark of the Bonhoefferian community, and this accountability is utterly bound to Christ: "For its own sake, as well as the sake of the earth, the salt must remain salt, the disciple community must be faithful to the mission which the all of Christ has given it."[73] Hence, the call of the Christian in community is an ordering to the mission of Christ, a faithful "disciple community" that expresses the bondedness of presence and *telos*.

In summary, devices have the capacity to reduce "the relatedness of the world," substituting esoteric machinery for contextual relationships that many, if not most, people take for granted. As artificial intelligence critic James Barrat writes, "Every step toward inscrutability is a step away from accountability."[74] Isolation increases as devices make commodities widely available without the necessity *of* and accountability that is offered *by* the physical community. While many might laud this societal development, people who once relied on their neighbors to survive now rely more heavily on machines, prompting some to question if the benefit is worth the cost.

Physical isolation is a common, yet unfortunate, result of many OSN experiences. This observation leads us to make the following conclusion: OSNs, when used as a substitute for face-to-face interactions, threaten the

---

text message, includes adherence to social norms (attentiveness, responsible use of language, eye contact) that are not required in the forms of communication that Turkle and Borgmann are describing. There is no option for simply "logging off" or offering the excuse, "I didn't get the message!"

73. Bonhoeffer, *The Cost of Discipleship*, 130.

74. Barrat, *Our Final Invention*, 75.

local bondedness that is a critical component of embodied community. In a sense, the inherent nature of an OSN encourages communication on a global scale, far beyond the circumscriptions of the local community: The global marketplace (Amazon, eBay) overruns the local businesses, global news (Drudge Report, CNN) overruns the community happenings (local newspapers and civic groups), and global access found in a computer or smartphone overruns one's neighborly obligations for friendship and mutual security. Each of these innovations certainly benefit the individual who maintains a deep commitment to his/her local context as a supplementary force, yet the temptation remains to use these innovations *at the expense* of local, physical relationships. This temptation is present for Christians, as well, as intentional isolation has a particular appeal to the sinner who may wonder how the church-community will respond to his/her personal struggles. The believer may feel the pull to isolate themselves from the herd, so to speak, and therefore distance themselves from the worshipping, sacramental community. Embodied third places, for the Christian racked with a guilty conscience, become just another opportunity to experience some form of shaming and/or reprimand and are subsequently avoided. While the digital community could offer such a person the ability to visit digital third places (e.g., chat rooms or gaming sites) to mitigate *virtual* isolation, the potential for miscommunication and/or the using of such online sites as replacements for face-to-face life together remains significant enough to generate concern that the markers of embodied community may not have much purchase in the digital community. OSNs, when used as a substitute for physical conversation, simply cannot be a considered a firm foundation for local bondedness. Authentic embodied communities use local third places precisely because these venues offer a type of bondedness that, more often than not, eludes cyberspace.

Rethinking Human Sexuality

A second sociological issue emerging from OSN usage is the changing landscape of human sexuality. To catalogue all of the various ways sexuality is understood in the academic sphere would be remarkably tedious (and, often times, contradictory). Therefore, I will introduce the shifting boundaries of sexuality through two particular distinctions. First, the biological sex of the subject plays a critical role in many online interactions that involve sexual identity, intimate relationship-building, or role play. By this I mean that one's biological sex is more or less fixed and not subject to fluctuation based on social influences.[75] This biological fact has direct impact on a subject's activity within virtual social worlds in several ways. One, a person's biological sex usually is considered to be the foremost indicator of one's gender. Males tend to demonstrate masculine traits; females tend to exhibit traits of femininity. The online world, while certainly opening up the possibilities for experimentation, still affords the user at least some measure of confidence that an interaction with another user who has a masculine avatar would correspond to a male in real-life. This is becoming a less certain enterprise, as I will demonstrate shortly. Two, a user's sex ultimately determines the truthfulness of a social interaction when they claim, either explicitly or implicitly, to be male or female. This is no small issue, since many critics of online relationship-building argue that this medium necessarily promotes an element of deception.

The second way in which online social networks potentially affects a person's sexuality is at the level of gender. Gender may be understood as a subject's self-identification within the spectrum of masculinity/femininity and includes one's behavior and preferences in the world in accordance with that identification. At this level, many OSNs invite a certain amount of gender exploration. When a user creates an avatar (again, the online presentation of oneself), the person is given a buffer between the real and virtual necessarily providing the user with a high degree of anonymity. The avatar shrouds the "real" person. Therefore, experimentation with various gender identities happens simply by changing the avatar and acting the part.

In the vast majority of physical human interactions, each person's biological sex is explicitly obvious. While one's gender or sexual preference may be somewhat less transparent, their behavior and physical appearance provide the public with clues as to the individual's self-identification. A person's clothing, use of make-up (or lack thereof), behavior, and speech patterns tend to reinforce the reality of his/her biological sex or gender. To engage the world as the opposite sex (e.g., cross-dressing) requires a great deal of deception and skill, lest the individual be found out by society as a fraud. In the online world, however, it is quite simple to "present" as a member of the opposite sex.

75. I am aware of the arguments that reject this view of biological sex. Many scholars argue that even the binary terms "male" and "female" are socially constructed and that there is no safe ground by which to say that one's biological sex is unchangeable or fixed. This is not an argument I will engage here. Rather, I will proceed on the assumption that a human with male sex organs can be called a male and one with female sex organs can be called a female. Those exceptional circumstances where biological sex is ambiguous or in transition via surgery will be bracketed as boundary cases.

In her second book, *Life on the Screen*, Sherry Turkle introduces a series of complex sexually-centered issues that emerge from participation in OSNs.[76] Turkle observes the ease by which users drift between sexual identities in cyberspace and warns of several potential problems. First, virtual "gender-swapping" is psychologically complex. She explains, "Taking a virtual role may involve you in ongoing relationships. In this process, you may discover things about yourself that you never knew before. You may discover things about other people's response to you. You are not in danger of being arrested, but you are embarked on *an enterprise that is not without some gravity and emotional risk* [emphasis added]."[77] While a user is allowed to explore various, undiscovered aspects of the Self, relationships formed in this way require a constant self-monitoring in order to keep one's "story straight." Online social networks allow for such exploration, yet the pull to experiment the boundaries of one's sexuality (even virtual sexuality) often results in high degrees of confusion and anxiety.[78]

Second, a user who presents as the opposite sex invites a host of questions regarding the integrity of his/her online interactions, particularly interactions that result in some sort of personal disclosure, prompting the most basic of inquiries: How can any meaningful interaction take place if a core deception lies at its heart? This is not to argue that bonding cannot take place in online arrangements; rather, the bonds that happen in the midst of such behavior are not consonant with the bonds required for authentic Christian community. Other, more complicated, questions follow when outside parties are allowed access to sexual talk, flirting, and/or online forms of sex itself.[79] What is the moral import of a married man who presents himself as a female (or, vice versa) in an OSN for the purpose of initiating a sexual encounter and how does this behavior contribute/disassemble the three markers of Christian community? What about virtual sexual encoun-

76. Turkle's book was written in 1995, about 10 years before the rise of online social networks. Her work, however, prophetically lays out many of the issues that OSNs would usher in a few years later.

77. Turkle, *Life on the Screen*, 213. My emphasis. I would add that the threat of arrest is now emerging as a topic of legal conversation, at least in certain circumstances. Much attention has been given to online predation: for example, a man "presenting" as a girl on Facebook for the purposes of meeting, then abducting, an unsuspecting target.

78. The widespread frequency of the above experiences should not be underestimated. For example, a significant percentage of online video games allow a person to determine the sexual identity of the user's virtual character, even allowing for the manipulating of the physical features of the character.

79. "Sexting," for example, is an online conversation that includes back-and-forth description of sexual acts toward the goal of a mutual sexual experience often with accompanying pictures.

ters of any kind outside of the husband/wife relationship? At first glance, these examples appear to be outliers, far outside the norm of acceptable behavior in American society. This conclusion would, however, be misleading. Turkle suggests that new definitions of marital fidelity are evolving to account for such activities, partly because they are becoming more and more common. Many of the key questions that inform such boundaries have no easy answers. She asks, "Is infidelity in the head or in the body? . . . The fact that the physical body has been factored out of the situation makes these issues both subtler and harder to resolve than before."[80] Many Christians, as well, experience temptations that deal with sexuality, infidelity, and the role of the physical body. Turkle is hitting at the core of the issue here. When the physical body is removed from the equation—when it ceases to be seen neither as a force for influence nor as an object to be influenced itself—the person acts without grounding in the concrete world.

Turkle rightly identifies the various consequences of exploring one's sexuality in OSNs, but she limits her exploration to the effects located in the individual and his/her immediate relations. How is the community at large affected by such behavior? Issues of communal trustworthiness move to the forefront when this meta-examination takes place. A community, whether Christian or secular, is constructed of individual agents; the behavior of the one will, without fail, exert an influence on the whole. Therefore, it is fruitful to explore how these changes in human sexuality and identity affect the oft-cited cornerstone of a healthy and stable society: the marriage. Infidelity is not restricted to the fringe elements of American society, of course, so it is important to remember that Christian men and women are not isolated from this grave temptation. In many ways, the general temptation to commit adultery increases when one is confronted with innovative ways to hide extramarital engagements that begin online.[81] Again, the presence/absence of reciprocal trustworthiness is the primary issue. The wife who must confront her husband over his virtual identity and behavior is not concerned with his physical infractions outside of marriage per se, but she may express anger over his lack of honesty in his virtual activities.

Ultimately, the virtual world forces society to reexamine questions of authenticity and deception, faithfulness and adultery. For more optimistic

---

80. Turkle, *Life on the Screen*, 225.

81. In one particularly disturbing example, there are now websites committed to connecting married people to one another for discreet sexual encounters. While not accessed for this project for obvious reasons, www.ashleymadison.com is an example of such a site, using a tag line, "life is short, have an affair." Such sites, unsurprisingly have been the target of many conservative-leaning AM talk radio stations and other family values media outlets.

OSN users, self-representation in any world, digital or real, *necessarily re-quires* a certain amount of shape-shifting. After all, is not every single social interaction, digital or otherwise, marked by a certain amount of withhold-ing and/or experimentation? A young single man, for example, may meet an attractive woman at a bar, and in an attempt to impress her, may stretch the truth about some of his exploits (e.g., where he's traveled, who he knows, how much he earns). Exaggerations, even flat-out mistruths, are not exactly uncommon in embodied attempts at courtship. Yet even in the mistruths of an over-eager suitor, his body cannot be hidden in the embodied exchange; at least one important piece of truth (in this case, what he looks like, his biological sex, and probably his gender) forces its way into the exchange. No such information necessarily makes itself known in the online world. Culture critic Howard Rheingold argues this point well:

> It is easy to deceive people on-line: for nasty people to wear a polite mask and for nice people to pretend to be nasty. We all wear masks in our lives. We all play many roles at home and work and in public. But on-line discourse is nothing *but* masks. We can never be sure about our knowledge of another person when that knowledge is based solely on words on a computer screen.[82]

Rheingold's observation cuts deeper when one considers that sexual inter-action probes deeper than mere conversational relationship building. In this more extreme example, the stakes are higher. When a person misleads another into a sexual encounter, the situation is often given the label, "sexual predation." Yet, in the online world, such behavior is either willfully ignored or outright accepted as normative behavior. For typical OSN users, by con-trast, the digital world is a place with its own languages and social norms; users must confront the online world with these cultural codes in mind. While average users may not pursue relationships by presenting as the op-posite sex or experiment with sexual deviancy in online environments, they understand that sexuality profoundly shapes identity. The Christian user, in particular, knows how sexuality is tied intimately to God's design for the

---

82. Rheingold, "Virtual Communities," 119–20. On this point, Rheingold may be going too far when he says that online discourse is "nothing but masks." One can, I believe, have an honest interchange in an OSN that exhibits characteristics of respect, honesty, and accountability—but this presupposes a pre-existing embodied relationship in place before the exchange. Rheingold is, I think, speaking to the online propensity for conversation between two persons who know nothing at all about one another. In these cases, no external trustworthiness is available to the parties since they rely solely on the words of the interchange as the sole basis for the relationship.

man-woman relationship, a relationship of complementarity and mutual love.

The central issue appears to be trustworthiness, because trustworthiness itself seeks to clarify, not obfuscate. To make evident, not hide. Turkle argues that, in many cases, online social network users seek out the ambiguous online life "with the intention of playing it in precisely this way."[83] The way Turkle refers to is the actions that allow one to remain hidden or disguised in the virtual universe. The lack of accountability allows for the user to hide in the anonymity of cyberspace; he/she can escape vulnerability and judgment by being completely camouflaged. Yet for Turkle (and ultimately, for the Christian), such bold deception in something as central to the conception of the self as sexual identity is remarkably problematic. Deception blows apart the first and most important element to strong, cohesive communities: trustworthiness. For the believer, God commands truth-telling from the tablets of the Ten Commandments and Paul reminds the church at Philippi to think about "whatever is true, what is noble, whatever is right" as a significant part of Christian practice (Phil 4:8). Even Jesus prefaced many of his most important monologues by stating, "I tell you the truth" as a way to emphasize the fundamental reality of his teachings.

At a secular level, trust creates the social capital necessary to build strong civic bonds, forging communities that are loving, protective, and healthy. No matter how strong a particular OSN association is, it cannot provide the degree of love, protection, and/or health that exists in embodied communities. At the level of Christian community, the church proclaims God's gift of sexuality to be exactly that: a gift. God imparts upon humanity the ability to physical unite with another human being, where the two "will become one flesh" (Gen 2:24). Therefore, in each healthy act of sexual expression, the crucial feature is not simply two people engaging in intercourse. Rather, the context for the union requires the reciprocal trust of the marriage bond and implies a depth of intimacy gained through the shared experience of embodied married life. Out of this relationship flows the necessary social benefits that keep a community stable and healthy. The common bond of the community is most fully realized when that bond does not require mediation over a wireless network.[84] By contrast, reciprocal trust

---

83. Turkle, *Life on the Screen*, 228.

84. Perhaps this observation of a required connection (i.e., bandwidth via a modem or satellite) has deeper meaning than I imply. Stanley Hauerwas once remarked, "The problem with technological forms of community is that when the technology fails, there is often no community left" (Carondelet Lecture at Fontbonne University, October 17, 2011). If a community needs a medium in the first place, does this, by necessity, cause problems in the sending and receiving of messages—and by extension, cause problems

within a community erodes when accountability has a less prominent function and the reliability of exchanged information is more readily questioned.

Distinguishing Public and Private Acts

A third significant social effect this project wishes to highlight is the blurring of the public and private domains. While an OSN user can control his/her immediate followers and thereby construct a private world of his/her making, this description is overly simplistic and rather incomplete. An aforementioned tension exists. On one hand, OSN users can, to a large extent, control their audience by "friending" people they know (or want to know). On the other hand, the very existence of an audience changes the user's behavior; each digital act is exposed to the public for consumption, without filter or accompanying explanation. Joshua Meyrowitz sensed this effect in other forms of electronic media almost thirty years ago with his important work, No Sense of Place. Relying heavily on the work of Erving Goffman, Meyrowitz carefully articulates the difference between "expression" and "communication." Expression refers to the myriad "gestures, signs, vocalizations, marks, and movements produced by the *mere presence* of a person in an environment."[85] While such behavior does not constitute the primary message being delivered, information about the message-giver is being communicated nonetheless. The rolling of the eyes, a nervous facial tic, or a verbal stutter are all unconscious mechanisms by which the communicator is more fully known.

Communication, by contrast, means the use of language and symbol to convey any particular message. This form of information transfer can be divorced from the physical idiosyncrasies of the sender. For example, an articulate newspaper editorial about the goods of capitalism may completely mask the various insecurities of an author who has a social neurosis. The sender's expressions do not get exposed to the audience; only the communication event gets transmitted. Because digital technologies tend toward multi-sensory experience, including a heavy reliance on the visual, the private areas that print media afforded the author now recede. The Digital Age brings forth a new generation of communication and information technologies couched in videos, pictures, and new language tools that attempt

---

for maintaining a common bond? Perhaps the inverse to Hauerwas' statement would also be cause for concern. What if the technology succeeds too well and becomes the primary (and preferred) expression of communal life into the future?

85. Meyrowitz, No Sense of Place, 94.

to communicate facial expressions.[86] Ultimately, this multi-dimensional approach changes an individual's behavior. If a person feels like they are being watched, the individual adjusts his/her behavior to be more socially appropriate; or, in some cases, the person modifies their behavior to be more edgy or socially dangerous.

In the present context, the Millennial Generation *assumes* it has an audience; every post or status update is formed under the given that the message will show up on dozens of front pages.[87] Taken at face value, this statement rings true for generations of adolescents and young adults, many of whom imagine a personal entourage as they "organize [their] inner worlds."[88] This self-reflective "organization" can be interpreted as a healthy expression of their social maturation. What marks this generation as unique, however, is the fact that youth have access to a technology that allows them to manifest this assumption without limit. An online social network "offers us a spotlight, a microphone, and a stage as vast as cyberspace from which to act out our assumption—with our legion of friends serving as an invisible entourage."[89] As a result, the average teenage OSN user experiences many of the same benefits and anxieties of the celebrity life. It is the life of a public figure where privacy is a truly rare commodity.

Every online interaction is neither wholly public, since a user can initiate, at the very least, some minimal boundaries on who can see what in certain conversations, nor wholly private, since no user can truly know if the intended recipient actually receives the message at the other end of the connection. Perhaps a better way to conceive of this public-private dichotomy is to consider that the OSN user is under constant threat of eavesdropping. Each online post or musing online has the potential to become social fodder, and while this is a potential problem in an embodied conversation (e.g., someone eavesdrops on your conversation in a restaurant), such face-to-face conversations are not exposed to the whole of your online community, often hundreds of contacts strong.

---

86. Emoticons are text-based tools to communicate certain facial expressions or attitudes. With the advent of the smart phone, images and videos become a form of social currency. Instragram allows you to share some of your private moments to your circle of friends through the use of a single image. Some applications, such as Snapchat, use the near-instant exchange of photos as the primary medium for the message itself. Videos are uploaded to Facebook, *en masse*, for the purpose of making some of which was formerly private, public.

87. Front pages, or "news feeds," greet Facebook and other OSN users as their opening webpage. They brief the user on the activities of their friends since their last log-in.

88. Rice, *The Church of Facebook*, 111.

89. Ibid.

Eavesdropping happens at the macro level, as well. In the United States, for example, the National Security Administration has been under severe criticism for some of its domestic surveillance program. The constant watching of America is defended as a necessary inconvenience to battle various national security threats, yet many citizens find the audio and video forms of surveillance as an affront to their privacy. Even more disturbing, mega-companies like Google and Amazon use complex algorithms to track their customers' purchases for the purpose of understanding their spending habits, cultural pursuits, and recreational hobbies. Personal information appears to be a nearly oxymoronic term. Rather, all this information has but a single purpose: to determine which online advertisements will draw the most profit for the company. Google, for instance, employs a vast array of user tests at any one time, attempting to create the most efficient search engine possible.

> Google continually introduces tiny permutations in the way its sites look and operate, shows different permutations to different sets of users, and then compares how the variations influence the users' behavior—how long they stay on a page, the way they move their cursor about the screen, what they click on, what they don't click on, where they go next.[90]

All of this effort is devoted to the core values of efficiency and profitability. Yet this is not the work of a benevolent company trying to offer vast resources to the public for progress's own sake. Each click allows Google to penetrate the individual customer, guiding his/her searches to produce the most monetary gain. The user loses a measure of humanity and becomes, in the eyes of the algorithm, a series of preferences and habits to be used for Google's gain. At this juncture, it is relatively easy to discern how major corporations are tempted to use people as a means to an end. After all, the United States' collective wealth is due, in great part, to the advances of free market capitalism. The challenge remains for the individual who must decide how and when to participate in this economy, where such invasions of privacy can threaten the reciprocal trust necessary to build cohesive communities. The sinful act, in the Bonhoefferian system, is a move of unbounded power where one entity imposes itself on the physical and psychological integrity of another; such an act is an exertion of power. In a similar sense, the person who has lost a sense of privacy experiences, in no small way, a violation of their humanity. Trust cannot abide violation.

What separates companies like Google from brick-and-mortar buildings is the medium. A convenience store can only offer advertising that

90. Carr, *The Shallows*, 151.

points to the store's own goods; each customer assumes this fact and understands this tactic as the business's explicit request to receive patronage. The online algorithm of Google, however, effectively becomes an advertisement for all stores simultaneously. Google controls the advertisements the user sees and collects data on all surfing, searches, and purchases. The online world promotes the radical de-personalization of the user, and even more so, demonstrates how easy it is to strip them of their private worlds. As Nicholas Carr astutely remarks, "Google doesn't believe that the affairs of citizens are best guided by experts. It believes that those affairs are best guided by software algorithms."[91] As these algorithms continue to expose the customer, perhaps it is time for society to ask itself to what degree it remains complicit in its own exposure. Jaron Lanier, in his probing *You are Not a Gadget*, cuts to the chase with the following observation:

> You can't tell if a machine has gotten smarter or if you've just lowered your own standards of intelligence to such a degree that the machine seems smart . . . People degrade themselves in order to make machines seems smart all the time. We ask teachers to teach to standardized tests so a student will look good to an algorithm. We have repeatedly demonstrated our species' bottomless ability to lower our standards to make information technology look good. Every instance of intelligence in a machine is ambiguous.[92]

Lanier subtly notes how each digital attempt to uncover more personal information occurs with the implicit consent of the user. Such consent renders the user prone to such unwelcome penetrations into his/her private lives. Lanier's warning may be well-heeded by the Christian user. Without practicing discernment, the Christian OSN user uncritically surrenders his/her privacy for the sake of convenience. Yet this is not the way of the embodied life. The church-community, at its heart, is a fellowship which experiences the intimacy of being in Word and Sacrament together. Intimacy cannot be taken; it is offered from one person to another in an extraordinary demonstration of reciprocal trust and privacy. Can an OSN protect the intimacy of individual if every exchange is catalogued by some algorithm?

An interesting tension has emerged. On one hand, an OSN user can choose to "go full black." That is, they can disappear into various social websites as a social wallflower or as an active participant who is camouflaged by their avatar, essentially anonymous. A person's embodied existence, in this case, is completely unknown. On the other hand, many OSNs (such as

91. Ibid., 152.

92. Lanier, *You are Not a Gadget*, 32.

Facebook and Instagram) encourage mass levels of self-disclosure that allow for a user to upload more and more material about his/her life: photos, notes, and status updates. An individual's information is broadcast across the Internet without prejudice or security concerns. As a result, the user weaves between being completely unknown and being known by too many (people and corporations, alike). This is the tension between constant hiding and equally constant over-exposure.

This public-private blurring effect is exacerbated by the current wave of technological advances. The iPhone, for instance, allows a person to be at a private event (e.g., a daughter's wedding rehearsal dinner), yet engage simultaneously in the affairs of the public workplace (e.g., check email). The gratification of "always being on" overrules a person's tendency to make a distinction between social settings; the smart phone remains ready to serve both public and private domains. As S. Craig Watkins quipped, "We have evolved from a culture of instant gratification to one of constant gratification."[93] The need to be connected forces many users to disregard their reservations against the breaking down of one's social roles. The most pressing implication of this new lifestyle is the breakdown in relational depth. The person who blends the worlds of work and home life risks distributing his/her social resources in unhealthy shares. In one all-too-common example, the professional who allows his work to penetrate his home life on a regular basis diverts energies away from the relationships that make up his private world and toward the needs of his profession, sacrificing his marriage and family in the process.

The public-private dichotomy of years past is failing. Formerly private expressions have been thrust into the public sphere for mass consumption. Yet this is exactly what some researchers are decrying as the central problem. Christine Rosen lays out the primary issue with public forms of relationship-building:

> Friendship in these virtual spaces is thoroughly different from real-world friendship. In its traditional sense, friendship is a relationship which, broadly speaking, involves the sharing of mutual interests, reciprocity, trust, and the revelation of intimate details over time and within specific social (and cultural) contexts. *Because friendship depends on mutual revelations that are concealed from the rest of the world, it can only flourish within the boundaries of privacy; the idea of public friendship is an oxymoron* [emphasis added].[94]

93. Watkins, *The Young and the Digital*, 160.
94. Rosen, "Virtual Friendship," 26.

Rosen's work suggests that the traditional features of friendship are eroding. Privacy allows for relationships to grow in low stress conditions, where
reciprocity and accountability forge a trustworthiness that cannot be dupli-
cated by the ever-public world of the OSN. Her observations complement
Bonhoeffer's understanding of embodied community. For an authentic
Bonhoefferian community to thrive, the mutual consolation and conversation of the brethren is central. This includes the remarkably personal and
vulnerable acts of confession, empathy, encouragement, and compassion.
For example, Bonhoeffer suggested that the public confession of specific
sins[95] would invite discord among the brethren, eroding the trustworthiness that served as the foundation for flourishing Christian community. By
contrast, the act of consolation emerges primarily in private settings, where
the intense emotions of grief and anger can be brought forth without fear
of judgment. Such ministering behavior, in this instance, is an intimately
shared experience that necessarily brings about higher levels of reciprocated
trust.

The sociological effects of OSNs consistently undercut the Bible's vision for authentic, embodied Christian community. First, God condemns
isolation as the normal mode-of-being from the first chapters of Genesis: "It
is not good for man to be alone" (Gen 2:18). He constructs human society
around the union of man and woman as family, bound together for the joy
intrinsic to social relationships, sexual unions, and the mutual consolation
that human existence often requires. Second, Christians confidently proclaim that a person's sexual identity is a gift from God. Not only do men
and women have different roles within the context of life and marriage, they
are warned not to trade in these roles for prohibited sexual deviance (Rom.
1:26–27). Biblical marital fidelity is both of the body and mind and contributes to the community's need for depth and trust (Matt. 5:27–28). An OSN
that encourages men and women to cheat, even "virtually" cheat, on their
spouses violates at least two central pillars of the Decalogue: "Thou shalt
not commit adultery" and "thou shalt not bear false witness." Third, Jesus
himself understood the balance of public life versus privacy. He sought to be
alone (Luke 5:16). He urged Christians to pray alone (Matt 6:6), for certain
affairs of the heart are known to the Holy Spirit alone (Rom 8:26–27).[96]
These times of solitude offer the Christian more than peace of mind; they
allow the body to recover from the variety of physical and social demands

---

95. As opposed to a general confession offered in many worship settings.

96. Intentional isolation of this kind is, without doubt, manifestly different than
isolation as a mode-of-being. Rather than isolating oneself to avoid an embodied presence within a community, this temporary isolation gives a person the peace and focus
necessary to re-enter the community as a flourishing, contributing partner.

placed upon it. By contrast, a person who needs to be in the public spotlight at all times bears resemblance to the hypocrite who loves "to pray standing in the synagogues and on the street corners to be seen by men" (Matt 6:5). Some of the most substantial effects produced by OSN usage stand in direct contrast to Word of God. Therefore, one is forced to conclude that the vital elements of depth, local bondedness, and reciprocal trust are found lacking in the uncritical use of OSNs.

The three sociological effects I have listed above certainly do not constitute the totality. They are, however, effective categories by which one can evaluate the overall worth as well as the potential damage OSNs afford their users. To this point, I have focused primarily on the negative effects of OSN use without offering a balanced look at their benefits. This section will currently consider the scholars who express optimism in the current turn toward virtual life together.

In Defense of the Online Social Network

Many scholars assert that online social networks, far from being a societal detriment, contribute to human well-being on a variety of levels. They tend to argue that OSNs facilitate new forms of human bonding and ultimately hold the power to change the world for the better. Such conclusions are not isolated to starry-eyed futurists, although certainly futurists tend to have a great deal of optimism regarding technology. Rather, they come from a variety of academic and cultural disciplines: biology, economics, political science, just to name a few. First, I will examine some secular works by three notable authors who are sympathetic to the innovations of the Digital Age, including the online social network itself. Yochai Benkler, professor of law at Harvard University, speaks of the online network as ground zero for the changes happening in the global economy. He argues that a return to a commons-based society where information is accessed by all citizens could be an economic catalyst that increases across-the-board production and profit. Clay Shirky, noted New York University writer and cultural observer, hails the wealth of new participants in the information economy by stressing how collaboration, the ultimate result of the aforementioned participation, positively influences the political process, culture-making, and civic life. Finally, Andy Clark, distinguished professor at Edinburgh University, illuminates how the human mind is predisposed to use external aids for life betterment, even when these tools obscure the distinction between human and machine. He describes this affinity for mind-machine interface as humanity's proclivity to be a "natural-born cyborg."[97] The brief survey of these authors is not meant to be exhaustive yet should provide us with paradigmatic thinkers in significant secular fields who represent a necessary counterpoint to many of the claims above. This survey will culminate with an examination of the futurist view on human development, the gold standard of society's optimistic perspective on online technologies. After outlining some of the above authors' reasoning and contributing my own brief critiques, I will turn to two Christian authors, Jesse Rice and Leonard Sweet, who share many of the same forms of optimism but succumb to many of the same philosophical difficulties.

The Commons-based Approach to Economics

Online social networks have, without a doubt, led many secular disciplines into a golden age of innovation. In the field of socio-political economics, scholars are pointing to the power of online networks as a resource for the free and rapid distribution of information as well as for political change. Economist Yochai Benkler, in his *The Wealth of Networks*, lauds the rise of "networked information economy" as the harbinger of multi-class prosperity in liberal societies.[98] Future economies, he suggests, may use freely distributed information as a way to build strong economic structures without the encumbrance of legal entanglements emerging through copyright and patent law.[99] This "free-sourced" information changes the game by "decentralizing" those who are in authority over a project or resource.[100] In other words, when information is widely and freely distributed, it cannot be contained by an elite few, and this diffusion of authority paradoxically leads to greater production, revenue, and social impact.[101] If nothing else,

97. Clark, *Natural-Born Cyborgs*. Clark's work precedes many of the most influential online social networks, yet his work has deep applications for those seeking to draw conclusions about social life in the age of the Internet.

98. Benkler, *The Wealth of Networks*.

99. In much of his work, Benkler implies that connectivity found in online social networks drives much of conversation and dissemination of new ideas required to build such economies.

100. Ibid., 59–63.

101. Ibid. I say "paradoxically" here because past models of economic gain require a person to think of an idea, develop it, then patent it for his/her own protection of intellectual property. With the patent, the entrepreneur secures the ability to offer his product to the market for profit. Offering one's innovation to the public through Benkler's "commons-based approach," by contrast, appears to forfeit the individual's ability to profit from his/her idea. However, Benkler argues that significant obstacles in production and finance are overcome by the public's willingness to modify and

the online social network provides the perfect opportunity for people to introduce, debate, and modify various ideas and/or products. This process cannot but lead to innovation, fostering the networked society that benefits both citizens and businesses.[102]

Benkler's work is both engaging and insightful. The value of online social networks as a platform for developing new products and/or as a sounding board for the testing of new ideas is patently obvious. My instinct is to endorse these methods of conversation wholeheartedly. I imagine criticisms may come from more conservative circles that tend to question innately any scholar who suggests that intellectual property is best served when it is given to the public without direct recompense. While I am sympathetic to this criticism in principle, the concerns (not without a little irony) can be fully articulated (and thus, debated) in social networks, among other media that promote public conversation. Ultimately, the debate whether a commons-based approach or individual property approach is more economically successful is not under the purview of this project, nor is it my particular area of expertise. I seek to evaluate OSNs *as a form of community*—particularly regarding its potential as an effective substitute for embodied Christian community—and I do not find Benkler's work as directly threatening to physical forms of sociality. The ongoing critiquing of ideas, no matter from what intellectual sphere they emerge or from which medium, positively impacts society and is a fundamental pillar of political liberalism. The conversation itself seeks not to be a recreation of authentic community, but a place where such critical interactions can be had with the thousands (perhaps millions) of people who may be affected by the proposed idea/product. Benkler's social networking is better suited to the metaphor of the laboratory rather than a community, where experimentation is performed, data is collected, and conclusions given for the betterment of the whole. His ideas do not seek to supplant the necessity of physicality.

---

improve products without direct labor costs to the entrepreneur, and many of these improvements have the potential for significant social impact because no one person or company has control over the information needed to get such a product to market.

102. Benkler believes that work done by a group of peers without the supervision of a managerial hierarchy may be the way forward. This "commons-based peer production" allows the multitude of Internet participants to engage in tasks that are important to them. Clay Shirky is optimistic about Benkler's conclusions, noting that the "increase in our ability to create things together, to pool our free time and particular talents into something useful, is one the great new opportunities of the age, one that changes the behaviors of people who take advantage of it." Shirky, *Cognitive Surplus*, 119.

The Collaborative Effect on Political and Cultural Life

Economies are largely constructed and augmented by the various political powers and processes that be. These processes are also experiencing significant transformation in the Digital Age. Clay Shirky points out the positive effects that OSNs can have on the political process, particularly for those nations who have had a history of suppressing political dissent. As a recent case in point, much of coordination and publication of the Arab Spring movement in Egypt (2010–12) coalesced due to the protestors' use of social media; in many occasions, they "live-tweeted" the revolutionary events as they unfolded, beating traditional news outlets to the story time and time again. Shirky's book, *Cognitive Surplus*, outlines how mass participation in digital media allows for a radical devaluing of any single piece of information. Just as resource becomes less valuable as it increases in availability, so information becomes a commodity for the many, not just the elites. The protestor on the streets of Cairo, to use the above example, has equal access to the available information as the government under siege. As a result, the "cognitive surplus" of digitally connected citizens creates an atmosphere of experimentation and innovation for all manners of political, cultural, and civic life. The result appears to be a trend toward freedom and autonomy, since governments no longer have the singular ability to utterly restrict and/ or control a population's access to information. With this foundation, Shirky appears to take Benkler's commons-based approach and apply it to social change.

In 2003, South Korea implemented a ban on American-imported beef since several sources of beef were contaminated with mad cow disease.[103] Five years later, Korea and the United States signed a trade agreement that reopened the Korean market to American beef suppliers. When the Korean public found out about the reintroduction of American beef, the reaction was uniform and instantaneous—outrage. Weeks of protests and vigils continued to grow in size and influence, yet these protests were not the work of organized labor parties or special interests. Rather, teenaged girls organized and mobilized a sizable majority of the dissent. They communicated through various online social networks, including through a fan site for a Korean boy band named Dong Bang Shin Ki, discussing the various health and political issues that emerged with the reopening of Korean markets. The results were profound. So much political pressure was brought to bear on the Korean administration that President Lee Myung-bak nearly lost his

---

103. Scientifically known as bovine spongiform encephalopathy.

power after seeing his formerly high popularity plummet.[104] Ordinary citizens, in this case teenage girls who could not even vote, harnessed the power of online social networks to give attention to government abuses (perceived and real) and use this attention to affect significant political change.

Political change appears to be a genuine achievement of the digital native generation; it is unclear, however, whether or not such achievements in politics are uniformly desirable.[105] On one hand, the individual autonomy to either condone or condemn a political system, whether national or local, is a crucial feature of free societies. On the other hand, empowering the masses with "context-less information" (as Postman calls it) does not necessarily lead people to pursue forms of government that promote freedom, equality, and stability. Online social networks could generate the necessary groundswell for both representative democracies *and* theocratic authoritarian regimes, depending on how the networks are put to use.[106] In this sense, the medium has no controlling interest in which idea gets promoted for mainstream assimilation.[107]

Shirky's work also demonstrates that online social networks do not necessarily lead to a significant decline in face-to-face contact; in the Korean case, the opposite effect was generated. As Shirky notes, "digital tools were *critical to coordinating human contact and real-world activity* [emphasis added]."[108] Yet concerns exist. First, if citizens use online social media as the overwhelming choice of medium for their political and civic partici-

---

104. Shirky, *Cognitive Surplus*, 35.

105. Ibid., 37. In the example of South Korea, the beef protests eventually led the South Korean government to push forth measures that require citizens to use their real names online. The balance of power between the government and the people continues to ebb and flow and reactionary measures (by both sides) push the boundaries of what is appropriate in political discourse.

106. The rise of Islamic extremism may be a case in point. The Syrian-Iraqi group ISIS appears to be gaining at least some measure of local support for their gains in Iraq while promoting strict Sharia Law and anti-democratic ideals. News stories are beginning to emerge about Western women who have learned of the political movement through OSNs and have traveled to Syria and Iraq to join the ranks of ISIS.

107. This claim may arouse some suspicion. Proponents of OSN as a tool for political change may argue that online social networks, by their very existence and function, promote the free distribution of ideas and therefore, more readily support political systems that share those characteristics. I find this possible, but not totally convincing. History shows us how those in power readily manipulate technology, any technology, to advance certain messages to manipulate the public. Propaganda is one obvious example of such a message. If a government or some other authoritarian body has access to an online social network (or worse, the censorship controls), it has an opportunity to shape the nature of the communication therein, at least to some degree.

108. Ibid., 38.

pation, I question whether or not this can lead to sustainable and healthy communities, not just as a quickly coordinated response to some crisis. Putnam believed that the political process that is done by proxy representation (e.g., contributing money to a political cause rather than physically volunteering) creates a false sense of what constitutes civic responsibility, and, therefore, community ties are weakened, not strengthened. If political discourse is reduced to chat rooms and discussions on OSNs, then the very *nature* of the political discussion will take on the flavors of OSN communication. To paraphrase McLuhan yet again, the tools are actively shaping the tool-makers. The ultimate victory in the political arena will be the sound bite, witty and biting phrases that are memorable but not contributing to thoughtful discourse. In other words, political discussions in a "140-character world" are a threat to genuine, serious dialogue. This is Neil Postman's worst nightmare. In the Korean example, Shirky himself admits that it is unclear whether or not the policy shift was a good thing or not; his interest remains in the catalytic efforts of the online cadre that manufactured such changes.

A second potential issue flows from the first. The danger with any political movement, for better or worse, is that such action can lead to outright revolution. Political revolutions are prone to mob-like behavior; one action acts as the precipitate for collective action without regard for consequence, often taking on a violent character. This appears to be a common characteristic of the online social network, albeit that text-based vitriol is commonly substituted for actual physical violence. While these networks retain the uncanny quality of distributing information to vast numbers of people in short order (e.g., a "viral" video), they also shape public thought and opinion *prior to the act of public discourse itself.* The mob mentality is such that an idea or action gains almost immediate traction with a large segment of the population without a measured consideration of the potential collateral damage. The typical Christian OSN user is not sheltered from this temptation; the pull to act rashly and judge too quickly is a sinful force that must be reckoned with every day. Shirky recognizes the social and political change that can be generated by social technologies, but his analysis would be significantly more balanced if he included a sober rendering of the potential harm inherent in their use.

The specific context of the Christian community might also be subject to some of these same features. While not necessarily causing more extreme scenarios like revolution, grassroots movements from within the church may gain traction to the wider public through the use of OSNs. Many church bodies use these digital networks precisely for the reason of generating public awareness and action. The need for discernment, then, remains vital as church bodies measure how doctrine can be applied (and sometimes, misused) to great effect in local communities.

Clark and the Natural-born Cyborg

Earlier, I offered two general perspectives on the online social network phenomenon. Macro-effects shape how the individual interacts with society and culture, while micro-effects are those that impact the individual at the level of the person. Andy Clark explores the latter approach. He argues that human beings are unique to nature due to their ability to generate meaning from external cues, whether natural, technological, or other. A cyborg, he argues, is not some product of science fiction where man and machine are melded into one monstrous abomination. Rather, the very nature of human intelligence is biologically designed to facilitate "looping interaction between material brains, material bodies, and complex cultural and technological environments."[109] The human is perfectly structured to be a cyborg. Clark fully embraces Carr's notion of the highly plastic brain, essentially arguing that the "empowering web of culture, education, technology, and artifacts" to "build our own mental circuitry" is, in fact, the very thing that makes humans, human.

Clark argues that mind-machine interface has been happening since the dawn of humanity, at least to some degree. Rather than traditional "machines," however, Clark simply states that the human mind has needed (and has used) external thinking prosthetics—external aids by which to acquire and interpret information. He envisions a future world in which social technologies are embedded into our very bodies by surgical implantation. I suspect Clark is right on both counts here. The human brain, without question, consistently uses external aids to make sense of the physical world that surrounds them. Human brains create culture complete with artifacts of every kind, then, in turn, culture changes the very structure of human brain activity. The loop is continually supported and reinforced by all forms of culture, digital technologies included. Nor is it a leap to believe that the surgical embedding of microchips or sensory-enhancement devices will become (eventually) cheap and ubiquitous. The question might be whether or not there is resistance to such procedures from the fields of philosophy and/or theology. The central objection that might be posed is that such "enhancements" actually erode the very nature of humanity itself. If one defines humanity as Clark does, no significant qualms need surface from the use of

109. Clark, *Natural-Born Cyborgs*, 11.

technologies that transcend human finiteness. But this obviously begs the question, is his definition of human uniqueness sufficient?[110]

Clark addresses the concern of embodiment directly in the concluding remarks of *Natural-Born Cyborgs*. He believes that many disembodiment fears spring from an anachronistic view of the OSN user: a young man sitting alone at a computer, punching in keyboard strokes.[111] The contemporary citizen has access to these social networks, he argues, while being physically social in the world. The image of an isolated OSN user is no longer applicable. Clark anticipates a future when individuals experience "multiple embodiment and social complexity."[112] Yet this approach seems to miss a central point of critiques like mine; that is, being present physically with another person while on an online social network does not serve as an adequate endorsement of embodied behavior![113] The very nature of an online social network means that the individual must split their attention between those whom with he/she is physically present and those whom demand his/her attention in the digital realm. Intimacy, a critical feature of embodiment, necessary decreases when a person cannot be *fully* present. While physical presence sans technological device is no guarantee of intimacy, it remains the best way for "intimate experience of related creatureliness" to take shape.[114]

Perhaps Clark's view should not surprise us, considering his understanding of the Self. "There is *no self*, if by self we mean some central cognitive essence that makes me who and what I am. In its place there is just the 'soft

110. Clark reveals his understanding of human uniqueness in his introduction to *Natural-Born Cyborgs*. "Our brains, more than those of any other animal on the planet, are primed to seek and consummate such intimate relations with nonbiological resources that we end up as bright and as capable of abstract thought as we are. Is because we are natural-born cyborgs, forever ready to merge our mental activities with the operations of pen, paper, and electronics, that we are able to understand the world as we do" (6).

And later, "It is our special character, as human beings, to be forever driven to create, co-opt, annex, and exploit nonbiological props and scaffoldings. We have been designed, by Mother Nature, to exploit deep neural plasticity in order to become one with our best and most reliable tools. Minds like ours were made for mergers . . . My goal is not to guess at what we might soon become but to better appreciate what we already are: *creatures whose minds are special precisely because they are tailor-made for multiple mergers and coalitions* [with external symbolic aids]" (6–7).

111. Ibid., 190–92.

112. Ibid., 194.

113. As stated earlier, my definition of embodiment requires "shared intimate experience." Such intimacy is a mirage if one of the subjects is physically present yet socially and intellectually absorbed in an OSN.

114. See chapter 1 for my definition of embodiment.

self': a rough-and-tumble, control-sharing coalition of processes—some neural, some bodily, some technological—and an ongoing drive to tell a story, to paint a picture in which 'I' am the central player."[115] This view should raise some red flags for Christians, beyond what has already been noted. If Clark's definition is correct, a person requires certain mental processes or actions in order for the self to materialize. But this would suggest that those who do not exercise such mental faculties do not, in fact, possess a self with inherent dignity. The Christian conception of self, by contrast, claims that God gives humans their life and dignity by external fiat; the role of "central player" has always been reserved for God and God alone. Therefore, human value exists regardless of an individual's capacity for neural processes or his/her desire for a meaningful role within the narrative of their life. At the very least, Clark's vision of human flourishing should give the critical Christian pause. He may be prophetic in the ways of future technologies, yet his analysis of the human component in human-machine interactions diverges from biblical anthropology. The three markers of Christian community, at best, are difficult to see in the Clark's visions for the future.

Abundance Theory and the Futurists

Perhaps the most optimistic rendering of a future that wholeheartedly accepts online social technology comes in the work of futurists like Peter Diamandis, Steven Kotler, and Ray Kurzweil. Proponents of what can be described as "abundance theory," these innovators charge that human life in the next century will be markedly improved from public health to economic prosperity, thanks to "change agents" that are having unprecedented impact at local and global levels.[116] Health, economics, and national relations will all benefit from intellectual gains in other fields, providing an abundance of resources for future generations. To give one example, water purity is a challenge for a significant portion of the world's population. Right now, cheap (yet high-volume) water filtration systems are being implemented in many of these regions. The cascading effect of such technologies includes: lower incidents of water-borne illness, decrease in infant mortality, higher nutrition, and other collaborative benefits. As survival rates and general health improves, the more intellectual power is preserved and diverted to address other issues and increase regional productivity. Many of the most difficult

115. Ibid., 138.
116. Diamandis and Kotler, *Abundance*, 9–10. See also Kurzweil, *The Age of Spiritual Machines*.

issues facing the world can be solved by the combined force of these tech-nologies precisely due to their capacity for benefits across a variety of fields.

Futurists such as these have impressive track records when it comes to applying Moore's Law to cultural changes; they predict upcoming technolo-gies with uncanny accuracy at times. This history of success is impressive in itself, but more importantly, it lends credibility to the central claim of their work: Solutions to many of the world's most treacherous ailments are within reach. I am particularly hopeful with the advancements that Diamandis and Kotler report in the fields of environmental and medical sciences. With the former, food production can increase with the emergence of soil-less crop systems (often called, "hydroponics"), allowing for healthy food to be grown in areas traditionally considered to be dead for agriculture, such as urban areas and deserts. With the latter, health care innovations have brought life-saving medicines to a wider swath of poor and distant populations, bring-ing Diamandis to celebrate the "rising billion."[117] No longer under threat of many devastating illnesses, the Global South can offer their own collective brain-power to the significant problems of this generation. The common undercurrent for many of these innovations is the steady communication of ideas through online social networks.

Yet the futurists seem to missing the mark in at least crucial aspect—namely, the meaning of humanity in this technological golden age. While I do not consider the role of OSNs (as Diamandis and Kotler perceive them) to be particularly threatening to community in matters of information dis-tribution, broader philosophical concerns of the abundance movement do exist. Their work tends to gloss over the area of technology that is most pressing (to me, at least) and most directly stands in contrast with some of my prior conclusions. One, they articulate a future that often borders on unabashed utopianism, which forces an astute observer to raise a concern over such blatant Hegelian optimism: Abundance theory assumes that all progress is intrinsically good. In other words, futurists earnestly believe that progress for progress's sake will usher in a world without the socio-political challenges that have forever plagued the human race. Proponents may argue that, by removing the primary sources of conflict (sickness, income inequal-ity, scarcity of resources), one can create a just and peaceful society built on the backs of technology. Yet to the Christian, placing hope in some future utopian system is folly. No amount of social and/or political manipulation can repair that which has been ingrained in humanity from the Fall: the problem of sin. Other critics may point out, in response, that these attempts to build a common good, whatever the cost, were the justification and

117. Diamandis and Kotler, *Abundance*, 140–52.

intent of communism—both in Leninist and Maoist forms. History's cruel response to Hegelian optimism, ultimately, was the outright devastation of the two World Wars where humanity introduced new and terrible forms of technology that shook the staunchest proponents of a technologically-driven utopia to their foundation. How can Diamandis and Kurzweil avoid the same fate? Only time will tell if their vision of a "society of abundance" comes to fruition, yet without a firm assessment of humanity's propensity for domination—particularly when it comes to securing natural resources and foodstuffs—the worldview they describe in their works seems, at times, to be bordering on naïve.

Two, futurists often excel at the logical ordering of technological achievements.[118] That is to say that they can see how one technology can lead toward multiple streams of human benefit. However, this skill appears to be restricted to societal implications only, leaving out the impact online social technologies generates at the level of the person. Or worse, some authors (Kurzweil, in particular) see visions of a post-human scenario, where all human social interactions are effectively online, but find little or no cause for concern as humanity marches ever-closer toward non-physical consciousness. Flowing from this, the ethical questions that emerge are substantial: What does it mean to be human in this particular future? This is an essential question, as it informs society in the quest to define a better future. Kurzweil offers a definition of humanity that is scarcely distinguishable from that of the hardcore naturalist:

> In my view there is something essentially special, after all, about human beings. We were the first species on Earth to combine a cognitive function and an effective opposable appendage (the thumb), so we were able to create technology that would extend our own horizons. No other species on Earth has accomplished this.[119]

Kurzweil appears to tie the definition of humanity directly to its acts. In other words, the accomplishment of parlaying technological advances into the expansion of human horizons makes us uniquely human. If we, as a race, were unable to complete this task (e.g., have tools that merely aid our survival), it appears that our unique identification as humans would be lost.

118. Ray Kurzweil himself is adept at drawing conclusions about where technology is headed 10, 20, and 50 years into the future, with alarming precision. For example, in 1999, he predicted, among other things, that 2009 would include: high speed wireless Internet access, personal computers the size of a thin book, and intelligent course-ware as a common supplement to traditional institutions of learning—all realized. See Kurzweil, *The Age of Spiritual Machines*, 277.

119. Kurzweil, *The Singularity is Near*, 433.

Kurzweil is implying that nothing intrinsic makes us uniquely human; our transcendence is only afforded to us through our technological ability *to* transcend. Yet this appears short-sighted to me. The very act of considering a future in the first place, to apprehend a greater purpose and to apply one's efforts towards achieving that purpose, strikes me as singularly human—an act that (even while Kurzweil does it himself) may not qualify as human by his own definition.

Summary

In chapter 1, I defined embodiment as the intimate experience of related creatureliness made most fully possible by physical immediacy or presence. The body plays a central role in the person's identity as a creature as well as the individual's identification within the broader community. Bonhoeffer's theology shored up the connection between the person as a creaturely, sacramental, and eschatological being with his/her participation in the church-community. The Christian is necessarily embodied and necessarily social. In chapter 4, I proposed three intrinsic characteristics that can be found in Christian embodied communities; they are constitutive markers that can be used as bellwethers to determine the presence or absence of embodiment in other claims of community.

The philosophical underpinnings of modern technologies reveal the complex nature of any one communication event; there is both the message being conveyed by the medium and the message of the medium itself. The latter, according to McLuhan, is substantially more impactful (and perhaps, more dangerous) simply for the reason that it eludes a person's conscious evaluation. The power of the technological device, therefore, should not be underestimated as it can affect wide swaths of everyday life. Postman applies McLuhan's theory to political discourse, arguing that the world of television has had deleterious consequences on intellectual and political thought in the last few decades. Modern social media (as it relates to Western political discourse) is becoming increasingly superficial while maintaining the guise that such tools can, in fact, deliver the important news with the appropriate amount of context and insightful, nuanced commentary. If Postman's conclusions are correct, and I believe they are, the first part of the criteria (concerning the nature of depth) has been violated. When an OSN "values superficiality at the expense of deep, accountable relationships," it cannot be considered helpful to the church-community. The discerning Christian can, however, search for those OSNs that offer an affirmation of deep, accountable thought (rare as those may be) and use them in a supplementary way with a clear conscience.

The impact of OSNs is not restricted to their influence on human thought as a theoretical concept. Physiologically speaking, a person's neural hardware is in an ever-transforming state of plasticity, building for the brain the resources it needs to process scattered information across digital platforms. Yet scholars like Carr and Doidge suggest the payment for such skills may be too steep. As the neural pathways for OSN use increase and strengthen, the connections that were once used for deep processing, sustained thought, and nuanced conversation now fall into disrepair. Once again, depth is sacrificed. When OSNs are used in high quantities, they no longer facilitate the depth constitutive in embodied communities because they encourage the brain to devote its resources elsewhere. In addition, this research suggests that the marker of reciprocal trust may be at risk, as the "environment of authentic communication" becomes less of a reality. Authentic communication, as stated in the criteria, implies that an ability to understand the neighbor in his/her respective fullness is present. To this point, I am not convinced that the physiological effects of OSN use are promoting this environment in a meaningful way.

The sociological effects of OSN use are manifold. Three consequences of OSN were outlined in this chapter: physical isolation (unintended or otherwise), the changing nature of sexual identity and behavior, and the blurring of public and private worlds. When these effects are directly placed beside the criteria, one can see some deficiencies. For example, when an OSN user prefers to communicate via texts over-and-against embodied conversations per Turkle's observations, developing locally bonded communities becomes quite a challenge. The person, wittingly or not, is participating in an act that contributes to his/her isolation from the broader community. The criteria points out, "The use of an online social network that . . . suggests face-to-face interactions have limited benefit . . . cannot edify the community *qua* community." Yet this limited benefit is exactly what extensive texting implicitly creates: a minimal appreciation for the physical contact between community members as the desire for isolation increases.

In terms of human sexuality, a fine line must be walked. This category of effects has a wider spectrum of behaviors, some more socially acceptable than others. In the case of those who use OSNs as a vehicle for sexual identity transformation or illicit sexual engagements, the criteria operate in full force. These instances directly affront the embodied community as opportunities to "intentionally deceive or mislead" and should be treated with the utmost seriousness. For the common Christian saint-sinner who uses OSNs to explore more socially acceptable nuances in his/her sexuality, the criteria acts as a guide for healthy behavior. If no deception is involved and the biblical examples of godly sexuality are not offended, OSNs may offer a somewhat safe environment with which to recognize the goods of human sexuality in all of its proper manifestations. In this case, honest reflection on one's physical identity can be pursued—even uplifted—within virtual worlds and online conversations.

The third and final sociological effect referenced in this work concerned the blurring of the private and public worlds. The typical OSN user is caught in the middle of a difficult tension. On one hand, the user is likely to publish large quantities of personal information for public consumption in the forms of status updates, pictures, and videos. On the other hand, OSNs afford the ability to move around anonymously in wastelands of cyberspace, using the virtual world as a buffer from being ever really known by those they interact with. How do the criteria give the Christian guidance in the midst of this challenge? In the depth portion of the criteria, accountability is held up as an important value. The person who offers, without discretion, the whole of his/her life in commentary and pictures without any member of the community speaking back, accountability is lacking. No embodied community grows from this one-sided release of information. Likewise, if an OSN user moves in and out of virtual conversations like a social butterfly and does not allow for the other person to challenge his/her ideas, this also contributes little to the growth of embodied relationships. However, those who use OSNs in ways that promote the open expression of ideas, as well as encourages responsible accountable conversation, uses these technologies in a good and trustworthy manner.

As a substitutionary embodied community, the online social network fails on multiple fronts. The solution is not to stuff a square peg into a round hole. That is to say that the Christian should not be finding ways to manipulate social networks to artificially meet the requirements of the criteria. Rather, the call of this book is to call for the measured practice of discernment. If discernment is the operating principle, then it can be applied consistently into the future regardless of what permutations of OSN emerge. Discernment gives the Christian church the ability to determine whether or not a social technology is serving in a substitutionary or a supplemental role.

6

LOOKING TOWARD THE SINGULARITY

ALL THAT REMAINS IS to bring the criteria's gaze directly upon the local Christian parish. In broader strokes, this project challenged the physiological and sociological changes brought about by even a normal amount of OSN use. This evaluation would not be complete, however, unless it directly engaged the community of Christ in concrete settings. For the Christian, community is largely located in the sacramental life of the parish where believers experience grace and fellowship at the Table, supplying each communicant with the necessary strength to engage their homes and businesses. This grace extends outward to each person's respective vocation; forgiveness becomes the *modus operandi* for the individual's life in the world outside of worship.

The traditional understanding of community now finds itself at a crossroads. The introduction of digital life together calls into question the foundations of the embodied, sacramental life. This chapter will drive toward a sharp evaluation of those in Christian circles who would offer up OSNs in enthusiastic terms. Local Christian churches have been woefully unprepared to discuss many of the concerns I raise in chapter 5; yet for the good of the Body of Christ, these criteria should be properly turned inward. That is to say, the parish's uncritical use of OSN is not shielded from critique simply because they offer corporate worship and the sacraments. Application of an appropriate theory should always be "for us" and not just, "for everyone else."

Online social networks have a unique and growing hold on Christian communities. The temptation exists to treat virtual environments as places that offer forms of depth, local bondedness, and reciprocal trust, a temptation that is not isolated to teenage video gamers or Facebook junkies. In a society that values efficiency, the OSN allows contact between friends separated by miles, money, and/or time. The convenience of joining a discussion without the difficulties of travel and time commitments often trumps the hassles of participating in the embodied life, where accountability and intimacy are present with all of their demands.

Discernment is required, nonetheless. The above analysis of the OSN phenomenon compels me to bracket these innovations as supplementary features of the embodied life. On their own, OSNs do not provide the measures of depth, local bondedness, and reciprocal trust that Christian communities require. The neurological changes that come with OSN and/or Internet use challenge the assertion that relational depth can be achieved in the virtual world. The isolation that often results from their use threatens the possibility for local bondedness and trust, as the task of knowing another person (and being known) becomes more and more problematic. Even matters of sexuality and gender identity become less clear when an OSN user is afforded the shroud of anonymity present in many of these networks.

The saint-yet-sinner Christian community, however, maintains a responsibility to one another. The mutual participation in the sacraments joins the believers together in dual-fold recognition: first, that they are sinners together; and second, they are forgiven creatures together. This solidarity promotes a common kinship, the bondedness in Christ, which becomes the foundation for life together. Because this bondedness is largely present in local communities of faith, the final application of the above criteria will target the OSN's role within the church. More specifically, I will examine two authors' disposition toward the OSN phenomenon and present some challenges to their arguments. The difficulty will be to determine how OSNs can serve the embodied community in a ministerial capacity without driving it toward a view of community that minimizes "the intimate experience of related creatureliness made most fully possible by physical immediacy or presence."[1]

The Christian Church and the Online Social Network

The optimism outlined in the previous chapter is not restricted to secular fields. Christian denominations are attempting to make sense of the OSN phenomenon as well. Many pastors and theologians are using social technologies as a way to speak the gospel to a generation that has been largely unchurched. In one more peculiar example, postmodern guru and pastor, Leonard Sweet, regularly accepts live tweets during his Sunday messages

1. A reference to my definition of embodiment found in chapter 1.

and responds to them mid-sermon. Others, while not as overtly optimistic about a future saturated with social technologies, simply hold that these realities are the new norm and as such require the Church's adjustment to the new world order. Jesse Rice may serve as the example *par excellence* for this point-of-view. He acknowledges that social networks have forced society into wholesale changes, changes that have prompted both secular and sacred communities to spontaneously readjust as a new equilibrium establishes itself. Since Sweet and Rice represent large populations of pastors, theologians, and youth ministers, respectively, it behooves us to consider what each has to say in more detail. First, I will briefly note the stance of Jesse Rice, who keeps a rather neutral approach to online social networks and their effect on Christian community; he treats the Digital Revolution as an inevitable process that requires the Church to modify its language and practice. Second, I will turn to one of the more influential practical theologians in the United States, Leonard Sweet, to examine his particularly enthusiastic disposition toward technology and those who use it as the latest form of relationship-building.

Jesse Rice, in his *The Church of Facebook*, examines the most popular online social network in the world as a phenomenological force, capable of forcing significant changes in the way humans interact with each other. He frames his discussion with a tripartite statement about reality: First, there are forces that are "capable of synchronizing a large population in very little time, thereby creating spontaneous order." Second, "this spontaneous order can generate outcomes that are entirely new and unpredictable." Finally, "these unpredictable outcomes require the affected population to adapt their behavior to more adequately live within the new spontaneously generated order."[2] The aforementioned case of tainted beef in South Korea may serve to illustrate Rice's framework. OSNs allowed for the near-immediate dissemination of information and the organization of protests by the Korean people, generating an order that was utterly unpredictable. This order forced the South Korean government to shape their policies (eventually) in service to the people's will, thereby adapting their behavior to better fit a world in which all of their citizens are hyperconnected. Online social networks, in Rice's view, are not only capable of generating social changes, but their impact can be felt in the world of Christian theology.

Rice makes it a point to avoid overgeneralizations, but my observation is that he is trying to walk a very thin line. On one side of the fence, he carefully points out many of the flaws that are present in online social

---

2. Rice, *The Church of Facebook*, 20–21.

technologies: tendency toward judgment, narcissism, even fear.[3] On the other side, he rejects a view that presupposes embodied community as qualitatively better than virtual community.[4] On this count, Rice may be inadvertently directing the reader toward a Lutheran epistemology. Core to the Lutheran understanding of theology is the acceptance of and appreciation for paradoxical tensions: *simul justus et peccator*, Law-Gospel dynamics, the doctrine of Real Presence and others. I suspect he is trying to strike a balance between the difficult consequences of uncritical OSN use and yet support the efforts of the present generation who use certain digital technologies for social benefit. Rice runs a particular risk with this tension. He appears unwilling to carry his significant reservations about uncritical OSN use to the end of explicitly endorsing embodied community as the better alternative. I tend to think his position is borne of a belief that real and virtual identities are intertwined, with no possibility of examining one without the other. This belief is not so removed from Clay Shirky's position noted earlier. While I agree that the virtual identity of a person impacts an individual's senses of identity and belonging, I still believe that Christians retain the ability (and responsibility) to adjudicate between different forms of identity and community building. This ability comes through the practice of Christian discernment of which I have been advocating. Each user can practice a measure of discernment as they use these networks, limiting his/her use when OSNs begin to command a too large a portion of the individual's participation in social affairs. This is not to say that embodied community has perfected human-to-human interactions or provides some nebulous vision of utopian society. Rather, this understanding of community maximizes the opportunity for depth, local bondedness, and reciprocal

3. Ibid., 197.

4. Ibid., 163–70. Rice recounts a fascinating interchange between several prominent Christian thinkers on the subject of technology and community, including Shane Hipps, Scot McKnight, and Anne Jackson. Hipps initiated a small controversy when he described virtual community as such: "It's virtual, but it ain't community." Rice challenged Hipps on the presupposition that embodied community is of more value than mediated forms of sociality found online. Rice notes, "[Shane] Hipps's response to those questions represents an assumption commonly held that there is something called 'real' community and quite another thing called 'online' or 'virtual' community. This assumption presupposes that the two are very different in terms of quality and style, and that one ('real') is certainly better than the other ('virtual'). While Hipps is right on the money in describing the benefits of 'real' relationships, the problem is that his is an assumption shared by fewer and fewer of us in the Facebook universe. To us the real and virtual are intertwined" (164–65). Anne Jackson, author of *Mad Church Disease*, later contributed to the discussion with her own prescient insights, saying that online interactions are meaningful but that such communication is *connection*—not community.

trust to flourish. Rice plays the part of the realist—unwilling to claim that embodied community is substantially more edifying (and less problematic) than virtual reality—in the face of the inherent dangers that OSNs make manifest.

Is there a moral dimension to Rice's conclusions at all? He describes Facebook as one of these forces that spontaneously generate a new world order, yet it is unclear if these forces mandate a Christian resistance or outright rejection. Rice raises certain concerns about the rise of Facebook, particularly as it concerns self-identification in the avatar. He acknowledges: 1) That the avatar is often a serious distortion of reality;[5] and 2) The online persona often breeds a certain form of narcissism where the user assumes he/she has an omnipresent audience.[6] Yet Rice's concerns on these fronts do not prompt him to make broader conclusions about online technologies as a whole. His contention is "that the gospel (literally, 'good news') of Jesus is particularly well suited for helping [Christians] understand, adapt to, and even thrive among the challenges of living within a hyperconnected culture."[7] This implies a certain measure of acceptance, or at least acquiescence, to the reality of OSNs. Rice's neutral stance toward OSNs may simply be a form of pragmatism; these technologies are not going anywhere soon and so the Church must be prepared to present the Gospel in the midst of these cultural seismic shifts. Or, he may be again allowing a tension to remain in place, where he asks users to ready themselves for some of the potentially harmful effects of OSN use while, at the same time, promoting a freedom to use these technologies when beneficial to already embodied relationships. While authors like Rice see technology as an inevitable reality both now and in the future, proclaiming to the Church a message of understanding and assimilation, other authors see more possibility in the OSN phenomenon. Foremost among these thinkers is Leonard Sweet.

Sweet and the Culture-Technology Relationship

Leonard Sweet is one of the more popular Christian pastor-scholars engaged in the topics of postmodernism, technology, and ministry—and how they interact with each other. His work largely focuses on the substantial cultural and philosophical changes that have occurred in the last thirty years. For Sweet, the seismic shifts in worldwide communication are largely driven by the technologies referenced in his useful acronym: TGIF (Twitter, Google,

5. Ibid., 95–102.
6. Ibid., 111–14.
7. Ibid., 22.

iPhone, and Facebook).[8] These tools of connection and communication reorient the world in unprecedented ways and have the potential reshape an individual's understanding of authentic Christian community. Yet these innovations do not, in Sweet's framework, conflict with the church's historic message or practice—quite the opposite. Sweet argues that his way forward is paradoxically *backward*-looking:

> The greatest symbol for the inherent "doubleness" of the Christian faith is the cross: the intersection of the horizontal and vertical, the overlap of the divine on the human, the interface of the ancient and the future.

> A cross Christianity, a faith that is both ancient and future, both historical and contemporary, . . . is an attempt to show the church how to camp in the future in light of the past. [This book] argues that the Bible outlines a double procession of rejection and affirmation in terms of culture: a movement away from the world to God is followed by a movement back to the world as we love what God loves and do what Jesus did.[9]

By tracing this outline, Sweet is arguing that the prescription for many of the challenges that confront parishes today can be solved by using ancient techniques, grounded in an early Christian worldview.[10] He suggests that the postmodern generation may have a certain affinity with these practices, as they share many of the same concerns and desires. For example, the postmodern is highly suspicious of individual truth claims, grounding all reality in the subjective experience found in community. This rings familiar to the earliest church communities of Acts, where individual Christian expression was remarkably scarce, if present at all. The foundational forms of early Christian life were radically communal.

Sweet certainly understands the richness of the Christian imagination; he rightly notes that the participatory and connected qualities of the ancient church offer this (and every) generation a way to receive Jesus that is meaningful and rich. Online social networks provide a medium that facilitates the ecclesial methodology Sweet endorses: The OSN is the paragon of the

---

8. Sweet, *Viral*, 15–17. I find these four categories useful in light of each technology's overwhelming popularity and social impact. The OSN user under examination probably has a great deal of familiarity with most, if not all, of these applications.

9. Sweet, *Post-Modern Pilgrims*, xvii.

10. Sweet is certainly not alone in this "ancient-future" approach. Robert E. Webber, Doug Kimball, Alan Hirsch, and Brian McLaren have, to one degree or another, promoted this tactic.

experiential, participatory, image-based, and connected life.[11] In a future cast by innovations that make connecting easier than ever, Sweet's prescriptions for evangelism appear to be well-situated for the parish-culture interaction that is to come.

Nowhere is Sweet's optimism more apparent than in his most recent text, *Viral*. Here he uses two paradigmatic technologies, the printing press and the Internet search engine, to distinguish older ecclesial worldviews from more relevant, contemporary ones.[12] The "Gutenberger" (by which, I believe, Sweet means by the "modern" era of philosophy) is "unapologetically grounded in text," where words are "on a par with living out one's beliefs."[13] They find relationship-building a secondary activity, behind the drive to apply oneself and accomplish goals. Not surprisingly, they openly criticize the Millennial generation—who Sweet refers to as "Googlers"—for being "shallow, obsessed with games, narcissistic, and irresponsible."[14] Googlers, according to Sweet, openly seek out community in all of its various forms, devoting massive amounts of time and energy to build networks that offer "no payoff beyond engaging with other people."[15] Their virtual lives have significant meaning and are seen as another conduit to their first priority: creating a community. Technology is a tool that promotes "networking, sharing, connecting, belonging, and letting others get to know you."[16] Sweet's argument essentially calls the Church to heed the call of the Googler; technologies that these Millennials embrace how the power to reinvigorate the Church as well as educate the individual about certain subtleties present in the Christian journey.[17] Sweet, no doubt, believes that

11. Sweet, in *Post-Modern Pilgrims*, creates another acronym, EPIC, to describe the postmodern ethos. Churches that accentuate the (E)xperiential, (P)articipatory, (I)mage-based, and (C)onnected life tend to have greater success ministering to the postmodern generation.

12. Sweet, *Viral*, 13–24. Sweet uses a similar bifurcation in *Postmodern Pilgrims*. For those churches ensconced in the modern worldview, he uses the term, "Old World Churches." Conversely, those parishes who embrace the postmodern emphasis on the EPIC features of Christian living he calls, "New World Churches." This overly simple division has its problems as most overly simplistic categories tend to create. I would offer that the contemporary individual resides in an undistinguishable blend of these competing worldviews; Gutenberger-centric at times and Googler-centric at other times. Ironically, Sweet later undercuts his own categories by saying, "As in most things of life, the choice between simplicity and complexity is not an either/or proposition. It is both/and, and also, one and the other" (45).

13. Ibid., 6.

14. Ibid.

15. Ibid., 7.

16. Ibid.

17. Sweet perhaps reaches his most controversial point when he suggests that

the Church can benefit through a wholesale adoption of social technologies; the Googler, in fact, acts as the exemplar of relationship-seeking in the noise of the contemporary world. What is Christianity if not the pursuing and receiving of a relationship with Jesus and others?

Some notable inconsistencies emerge from Sweet's work. One, he is careful to keep a safe distance from postmodernism, suggesting that the philosophy is better suited at "faking reality than at fixing reality."[18] He notes, "Christians should not embrace a postmodern worldview; we must not adapt to postmodernity."[19] This, however, can be problematic when one considers that all worldviews are essentially culturally determined. In other words, culture forms how a society thinks about itself (i.e., its philosophy). Yet culture is constructed by the whole of meaning-making materials available to the population, whether it is art and symbol, song and text, and/or *by its technologies*. The technological advances of any generation directly inform how its members conceive of their place in the surrounding world.

The online social network is not just a product of technological innovation; it serves as an artifact, both passive and active. Every technology is passive in the sense that it captures the innovation and imagination of any one group of people, as a snapshot from a camera can permanently record a moment in time. However, technology is also active in that it re-enters culture as a force to either support the philosophical and communal structures in place (as a buttress for the status quo), or tear them down (as a tool for resistance). The online social network, then, cannot be seen as separate from the worldview from which it emerges; its presence and ongoing use actively support a certain way of knowing. Sweet cannot, therefore, successfully divorce worldview from technology as he desires to do. Christians actually embrace a technologically-dominated worldview every time they turn on a personal computer or iPad. Sometimes this embrace is done grudgingly, other times with great enthusiasm. But it is impossible to claim that technology and worldview are completely isolated concepts. With each introduction of the latest social technologies, the prior understanding of community (and the markers which compose the type of community I have been advocating) undergoes evaluation and revision.

Twitter can make the reader a better Christian, claiming that the OSN had already had a profound effect on his own faith journey. This is certainly possible, I surmise, but this enthusiasm for Twitter could be abused. I suggest that Sweet may be using a form of inductive reasoning that is questionable; he assumes that his experience with the OSN can be universalized rather easily. In reality, I imagine that a great many people use Twitter for less-than-enlightening reasons. Ibid., 61–88.

18. Sweet, *Post-Modern Pilgrims*, xix.

19. Ibid., xvii.

As my book argued, the features of depth, local bondedness, and reciprocal trust fluctuate in accordance with the various pressures acting on the community. If a technology increases deception within a community, the reciprocal trust necessarily lowers. But much more than that, if the technology is widely accepted as the best available interpretation of community life, the community will revise (even overhaul) its prior definition(s) of social responsibility. The process comes full circle. A technology threatens an established population by challenging a definition. If successful, the new definition is accepted and the population accommodates it accordingly. Finally, the definition becomes a crucial feature of the population, requiring yet another challenge (if and when it arises) to upset the new-found equilibrium. Worldview and technology, then, are deeply intertwined.

A second, and perhaps more important, inconsistency in Sweet's work emerges when he references the goods of the connected life in ways that superficially appear to be in sync with the biblical model of common life together. Indeed, his "ancient-future" model for Christian mission and practice accords with the earliest of Christian communities in Acts 2 and 4. However, Sweet commonly assumes that connectivity is the same thing as relationship and therefore loses the essential thrust of the embodiment laid forth in this text. He earnestly believes that he shares authentic community with his legions of Twitter followers, yet this again defies the role of the body within Christian community. This is particularly troubling when he acknowledges first that:

> Christianity is not a vague, amorphous, ethereal religion; nor is it a prescribed set of ritual practices, whether they be liturgical or litigious, religious or political. You can try to get rid of flesh and blood and make Christianity into a religion of excarnation, but you will fail. Christianity is and always has been a religion of incarnation. It puts on flesh and blood. As a living and breathing faith, it is inescapably material, physical, and cultural.[20]

But what does he mean by "inescapable" here? Based on his endorsement of the virtual community in all of its manifestations, I have to assume he means one of two things: 1) The plan of salvation offered in Scripture is inescapably physical. In other words, Christianity rests on the Incarnation of Jesus Christ. Or, 2) Christian life together must be about real people, not just a series of abstract doctrines or documents. Yet both of these possibilities have nothing to say about the defining features of community itself. Is the Christian, simultaneously an individual and community member, to conceive of himself as "inescapably material?" Sweet goes so far as to

20. Sweet, *Viral*, 28.

suggest that, "*Social media* is a term that means, 'community.'"[21] If this is so, he implicitly belittles the critical relationship between embodiment and communal life together.

Ultimately, I reject Sweet's view of the community for reasons that emerge from his own work; Christianity cannot be constructed excarnationally. But the statement has broader implications in this project than Sweet's own work. For Sweet, the Christian practice of worship and ritual must be physical in nature. I am suggesting that Christian life itself, both individually and communally conceived, is *necessarily physical*. The connectivity offered in tweets and Facebook posts, while having some limited benefit, cannot be considered a primary expression of Christian community precisely because it lacks at least one feature that which makes us distinctively human—our human bodies.

Uncharted Paths

This text has attempted to critically engage the online social network phenomenon as a form of community-building through the lens of embodied Lutheran theology. This subject, I suspect, has the potential to give birth to other academic pursuits in the fields of theology, technology, and cultural studies. While embodied Lutheran theology may continue to generate some tangential interest in scholarly circles here or there, I suspect that the bulk of new material related to my work will emerge in the areas of social technologies and culture. This is a pursuit well worth engaging, as OSNs may prove to be more influential than the inventions of the printing press and television, as brash as that proposition sounds. Since online social networks are positioned as communication tools in a vast number of cultural disciplines, I believe that these technologies will continue to impact sacred and secular institutions and therefore require ongoing examination. In particular, I would encourage future research in the following three areas: sexuality, worship, and historical theology.

In chapter 5, I introduced how online social networks are transforming how society thinks about sexuality and gender. For the purposes of my project, this topic required but a brief analysis of this overwhelming field of study. However, I believe it would be fruitful to examine how online social networks have specifically impacted expressions of sexuality and gender identity from a neurological perspective. Plenty of scholars have successfully demonstrated how OSN use transforms sexual norms, some of which are mentioned in this book, but have mostly restricted their studies to how

21. Ibid., 146.

digital society shapes one's views on sexuality *as a social construct*. What is more original, in my estimation, is examining evolving forms of human sexuality through the lens of brain plasticity. Does the neural reorganization that happens with excessive OSN use directly affect how an individual conceives himself/herself as a sexual creature? To what degree does a person's gender/sexuality evolve due to the brain remapping that happens at the behest of screen technologies? While this has no direct bearing on the sacred disciplines, such research might shed some light on how people conceive of their self, their body, and the social function of sexuality in general. Indirectly, this research may then allow the Church to articulate more precisely a vision of godly sexuality that responds well to the challenges of ever-evolving social norms.

A second issue for further exploration would be how online social networks are directly impacting our methods of worship, pan-denominationally. If our society is increasingly drawn toward online forms of sociality, one could surmise that the Church would move along a spectrum between two polarizing positions. The accommodationist position, on one pole, might press for future forms of Christian worship that place less of an emphasis on the embodied features of worship and/or ritual and more on the connectivity of the members. In such a scenario, online social networks appear to be the platform best situated to fulfill this vision. This leads me to question whether or not the features of sacramental theology, in these experimenting parishes, have been lessened or outright abandoned in favor of a more tech-savvy evangelism project. The alternate polar position would be somewhat counter-cultural. In an effort to offer something distinctly different from the way of the world, worship becomes hyper-sensory. Worship, from this perspective, would overwhelmingly emphasize a five-sense experience of God and would tend to minimize forms of Christian practice that are abstract or disembodied.

A third and final area where I believe extended research may prove fruitful is an in-depth look at electronic media and its impact on matters of church orthodoxy. Are doctrines themselves evolving as a result of the OSN phenomenon? Better put, can we trace the evolution of doctrine (in denominational Christianity) to the social networking phenomenon—and can we expect new anthropology in Christian doctrine as a result of the approaching landscape of transhumanism? This might seem a bit rash, as Christianity has come to expect a remarkable sense of continuity over the past two millennia. I am not discounting the reality of historical theology here, either; I am merely noting current evolutions in doctrine might be emerging directly as a result of technological innovations as opposed to formulations that combat heresy[22] or highlight particular contextual theologies. My above interaction with Marshall McLuhan and Shane Hipps should serve as a warning about underestimating the influence of any technology. I suspect that a traditionalist's worst fears are already being realized: Christian doctrine has changed and will continue to change as a direct reflection of the dominant social technology of the time. I can only imagine what shape Christian theology and practice will take in the possible worlds of the abundance theory advocates and/or futurists.

For the Christian, embodied theology stands as the cornerstone of reality. God becomes man in Jesus Christ to reconcile the relationship that was broken in the earliest hours of human history. Yet man and woman were made in the image of God; they *also* bear the designation of being incarnate. More than that, their physicality bears the hope of the Gospel, as Paul writes to the Corinthians: "We always carry around in our body the death of Jesus, so that the life of Jesus may also be revealed in our body" (2 Cor 4:10). In a theology of incarnation, the image is made flesh. This stands in direct confrontation of today's secular philosophy of *excarnation*, where the embodied-ness of the person is forfeited for an image, an avatar. Excarnation stands as the greatest risk to embodied theology, not simply because it challenges the goodness and sovereignty of the Creator, but because excarnation shrouds the individual from being fully known. Depth is lost because little or no embodied communication takes place through bandwidth. Local bondedness suffers when individuals isolate themselves in smart phones rather than patronize the local pub or gymnasium. Trust necessarily decreases because the image presents but a poor reflection, a facsimile, of the neighbor. Excarnation need not be a threat, however, if Christians continue to discern the dangers of wholesale acceptance of digital technologies.

If the above criteria is consistently successful, Christians (whether individually or as parishes) can be judicious that the social technologies they use do not invite more dangerous issues down the road. Whether this framework is applied by individuals or communities, families or parishes, sober judgment will be required. One of God's most precious gifts to humanity is the physical body, and, by extension, the embodied community. Perhaps the next wave of online social technologies will be met with serious scrutiny, informed by Lutheran theology, and laid out for our communities

22. Arianism comes to mind here. Before the Council of Nicea in AD 325, the dual nature of Christ was largely unchallenged, at least across broad portions of Christendom. The Council ultimately defeated Arius' teachings on the subordination of Jesus and refined Christian doctrine through a creed that more thoroughly defined his dual nature.

to see them for what they are, good and bad. Bonhoeffer once wrote, "God is the God of living persons."[23] To live is to be under God's authority. In a spirit of submission, then, the common goal of Christian living can be this: Live joyfully as embodied souls in authentic community with one another.

23. Bonhoeffer, *Sanctorum Communio*, 288.

BIBLIOGRAPHY

Althaus, Paul. *The Ethics of Martin Luther.* Translated by Robert C. Schultz. Philadelphia: Fortress, 1972.

————. *The Theology of Martin Luther.* Translated by Robert C. Schultz. Philadelphia: Fortress, 1966.

Athenagoras. *A Plea for Christians.* In *The Ante-Nicene Fathers* 2, edited by B. P. Pratten. Grand Rapids: Eerdmans, 1977.

Augustine of Hippo. *Confessions.* Translated by R. S. Pine-Coffin. New York: Penguin, 1961.

Barrat, James. *Our Final Invention: Artificial Intelligence and the End of the Human Era.* New York: Thomas Dunne, 2013.

Benkler, Yochai. *The Wealth of Networks.* New Haven: Yale University Press, 2006.

Berger, David O. "Cybergnosticism: Or, Who Needs a Body Anyway?" *Concordia Journal* 25 (1999) 340–45.

Bethge, Eberhard. *Dietrich Bonhoeffer: A Biography.* Edited by Victoria J. Barnett. Minneapolis: Fortress, 2000.

Bonhoeffer, Dietrich. *Act and Being.* Edited by Wayne Whitson Floyd, Jr. Translated by H. Martin Rumscheidt. Minneapolis: Fortress, 1996.

————. *Christology.* Translated by J. Bowden. London: Collins, 1966.

————. *The Cost of Discipleship.* Translated by R. H. Fuller. Revised edition, New York: Macmillan, 1949.

————. *Creation and Fall; Temptation: Two Biblical Studies.* New York: Touchstone, 1959.

————. *Ethics.* Edited by Clifford Green. Translated by Reinhard Krauss, Charles C. West, and Douglas W. Stott. Minneapolis: Fortress, 2009.

————. *Life Together: A Discussion of Christian Fellowship.* Translated by John W. Doberstein. New York: Harper & Row, 1954.

————. *No Rusty Swords.* Edited by Edwin H. Robertson. Translated by Edwin H. Robertson and John Bowden. New York: Harper & Row, 1965.

————. *Sanctorum Communio: A Theological Study of the Sociology of the Church.* Minneapolis: Fortress, 2009.

————. *A Testament to Freedom: The Essential Writings of Dietrich Bonhoeffer.* Edited by Geoffrey Kelly and F. Burton Nelson. Translated by John Bowden. San Francisco: HarperCollins, 1990.

————. *The Way to Freedom.* Edited by Edwin H. Robertson. Translated by Edwin H. Robertson and John Bowden. New York: Harper & Row, 1966.

Borgmann, Albert. *Technology and the Character of Contemporary Life: A Philosophical Inquiry.* Chicago: University of Chicago Press, 1984.

Bosanquet, Mary. *The Life and Death of Dietrich Bonhoeffer.* New York: Harper & Row, 1968.

Brown, Peter. *The Body & Society: Men, Women, & Sexual Renunciation in Early Christianity.* New York: Columbia University Press, 2008.

Brunner, Emil and Karl Barth. *Natural Theology.* Translated by Peter Fraenkel. Eugene, OR: Wipf & Stock, 2002.

Bynum, Caroline. "Why All the Fuss about the Body? A Medievalist's Perspective." In *Beyond the Cultural Turn,* edited by Victoria Bonnell and Lynn Hunt, 241–80. Berkeley: University of California, 1999.

Calvin, Jean. *Institutes of the Christian Religion.* Vol. 1. Edited by John T. McNeill. Translated by Ford Lewis Battles. Library of Christian Classics 20. Philadelphia: Westminster, 1960.

Carr, Nicholas. *The Shallows: What the Internet is Doing to Our Brains.* New York: W. W. Norton, 2011.

Clark, Andy. *Natural-Born Cyborgs: Minds, Technologies, and the Future of Human Intelligence.* New York: Oxford University Press, 2003.

Cooper, John W. *Body, Soul & Life Everlasting: Biblical Anthropology and the Monism-Dualism Debate.* Grand Rapids: Eerdmans, 1989.

Davidow, William H. *Overconnected: The Promise and Threat of the Internet.* Harrison, NY: Delphinium, 2011.

Detweiler, Craig. *iGods: How Technology Shapes Our Spiritual and Social Lives.* Grand Rapids: Brazos, 2013.

Diamandis, Peter H. and Steven Kotler. *Abundance: The Future is Better Than You Think.* New York: Free Press, 2012.

Doidge, Norman. *The Brain that Changes Itself: Stories of Personal Triumph from the Frontiers of Brain Science.* New York: Penguin, 2007.

Dyrness, William A. *The Earth is God's: A Theology of American Culture.* 1997. Reprint, Eugene, OR: Wipf & Stock, 2004.

———. *Themes in Old Testament Theology.* Downers Grove, IL: InterVarsity, 1977.

Ebeling, Gerhard. *Luther: An Introduction to His Thought.* Translated by R. A. Wilson. Philadelphia: Fortress, 1970.

Elert, Werner. *Eucharist and Church Fellowship in the First Four Centuries.* Translated by Norman E. Nagel. St. Louis: Concordia, 1966.

Ellul, Jacques. *The Technological System.* New York: Continuum, 1980.

Godsey, John D. *Preface to Bonhoeffer; the man and two of his shorter writings.* Philadelphia: Fortress, 1965.

Green, Clifford J. *Bonhoeffer: A Theology of Sociality.* Grand Rapids: Eerdmans, 1999.

Hauerwas, Stanley. *Performing the Faith: Bonhoeffer and the Practice of Nonviolence.* Grand Rapids: Brazos, 2004.

Hipps, Shane. *Flickering Pixels: How Technology Shapes Your Faith.* Grand Rapids: Zondervan, 2009.

———. *The Hidden Power of Electronic Culture: How Media Shapes Faith, the Gospel, and Church.* Grand Rapids: Zondervan, 2005.

Irenaeus of Lyons, *Against the Heresies*; vol. 1 of *The Ante-Nicene Fathers.* Edited by Alexander Roberts and James Donaldson. Reprint, Grand Rapids: Eerdmans, 1979.

Jerome. *Against Jovinianus.* In vol. 6 of *The Nicene and Post-Nicene Fathers*, Series 2. Edited by Philip Schaff and Henry Wace. Reprint, Peabody, MA: Hendrickson, 1999.

Johnson, Luke Timothy. *The Writings of the New Testament: An Interpretation.* Minneapolis: Fortress, 1999.

Jones, L. Gregory. *Embodying Forgiveness: A Theological Analysis.* Grand Rapids: Eerdmans, 1995.

———. "You're Lonely, I'm Lonely." *Christian Century*, January 26, 2010.

Kant, Immanuel. "What is Enlightenment?" In *Philosophical Writings*, edited by Ernst Behler, 263–69. New York: Continuum, 1986.

Kolb, Robert. "Luther's Hermeneutics of Distinctions: Law and Gospel, Two Kinds of Righteousness, Two Realms, Freedom and Bondage." In *The Oxford Handbook of Martin Luther's Theology*, edited by Robert Kolb, Irene Dingel, and L'ubomir Batka, 168–86. Oxford: Oxford University Press, 2014.

Kolb, Robert, and Timothy Wengert, eds. *The Book of Concord.* Minneapolis: Augsburg Fortress, 2000.

Kurzweil, Ray. *The Age of Spiritual Machines: When Computers Exceed Human Intelligence.* New York: Penguin, 1999.

———. *The Singularity is Near: When Humans Transcend Biology.* New York: Penguin, 2005.

Lanier, Jaron. *You Are Not a Gadget: A Manifesto.* 1st ed. New York: Vintage, 2010.

Lindsay, Mark R. "Bonhoeffer's eschatology in a world 'come of age.'" *Theology Today* 68, (October 2011): 290–302.

Lutheran Church—Missouri Synod. "Together with all Creatures: Caring for God's Living Earth." A Report of the Commission on Theology and Church Relations, April 2010. https://www.lcms.org/document.fdoc?src=lcm&id=341.

Luther, Martin. *Luther's Works*, American Edition. 56 vols. St. Louis: Concordia, 1955–86.

———. "Bondage of the Will." In *Martin Luther: Selections From His Writings*, edited by John Dillenberger, 166–203. New York: Doubleday, 1962.

Lutheran Service Book. St. Louis: Concordia, 2006.

Mathews, Kenneth A. *The New American Commentary.* vol. 1a. Nashville: Broadman & Holman, 1996.

McGonigal, Jane. *Reality is Broken: Why Games Make Us Better and How They Can Change the World.* New York: Penguin, 2011.

McLuhan, Marshall. *Understanding Media: The Extensions of Man.* Cambridge: MIT Press, 1994.

McLuhan, Marshall, and Quentin Fiore. *The Medium is the Message: An Inventory of Effects.* San Francisco: HardWired, 1996.

Mellor, Philip A. and Chris Shilling. *Re-forming the Body: Religion, Community and Modernity.* London: Sage, 1997.

Metaxas, Eric. *Bonhoeffer: Pastor, Martyr, Prophet, Spy.* Nashville: Thomas Nelson, 2010.

Meyrowitz, Joshua. *No Sense of Place: The Impact of Electronic Media on Social Behavior.* New York: Oxford University Press, 1985.

Moltmann, Jürgen. *God in Creation: A New Theology of Creation and the Spirit of God.* Minneapolis: Fortress, 1993.

Moltmann, Jurgen and Jurgen Weissbach. *Two Studies in the Theology of Bonhoeffer.* Translated by Reginald H. Fuller and Ilse Fuller. New York: Scribner, 1967.

Ophir, Eyal, Clifford Nass, and Anthony D. Wagner. "Cognitive control in media multitaskers." *Proceedings of the National Academy of Sciences of the United States of America* 106, (September 15, 2009) 15583–87.

Ott, Heinrich. *Reality & Faith: The Theological Legacy of Dietrich Bonhoeffer.* Philadelphia: Fortress, 1972.

Palfrey, John, and Urs Gasser. *Born Digital: Understanding the First Generation of Digital Natives.* New York: Basic Books, 2008.

Parker, T. H. L. *Calvin: An Introduction to His Thought.* Louisville: Westminster John Knox, 1995.

Pascual-Leone, Alvaro, et al. "The Plastic Brain Cortex." *Annual Review of Neuroscience* 28 (2005) 377–401.

Postman, Neil. *Amusing Ourselves to Death: Public Discourse in the Age of Show Business.* New York: Penguin, 1985.

———. *Technopoly; The Surrender of Culture to Technology.* New York: Vintage, 1992.

Putnam, Robert D. *Bowling Alone: The Collapse and Revival of American Community.* New York: Simon & Schuster, 2000.

Putnam, Robert D. and Lewis M. Feldstein. *Better Together: Restoring the American Community.* New York: Simon & Schuster, 2003.

Rheingold, Howard. "Virtual Communities" in *The Community of the Future,* edited by Frances Hesselbein, Marshall Goldsmith, Richard Beckhard, and Richard F. Schubert, 115–22 . San Francisco: Jossey-Bass, 1998.

Rice, Jesse. *The Church of Facebook: How the Hyperconnected are Redefining Community.* Colorado Springs: David C. Cook, 2009.

Rosen, Christine. "Virtual Friendship and the New Narcissism." *The New Atlantis,* Summer 2007, 15–31.

Ross, Susan A. "God's Embodiment and Women." In *Freeing Theology: The Essentials of Theology in Feminist Perspective,* edited by Catherine Mowry LaCugna, 185–210. New York: HarperCollins, 1993.

Sasse, Herman. *This is my Body: Luther's Contention for the Real Presence in the Sacrament of the Altar.* Adelaide, S. A.: Lutheran Publishing House, 1977.

———. *We Confess the Church.* Translated by Norman Nagel. St. Louis: Concordia, 1986.

———. *We Confess Jesus Christ.* Translated by Norman Nagel. St. Louis: Concordia, 1984.

———. *We Confess the Sacraments.* Translated by Norman Nagel. St. Louis: Concordia, 1985.

Schlink, Edward. *The Doctrine of Baptism.* Translated by Herbert J. A. Bouman. St. Louis: Concordia, 1972.

Shirky, Clay. *Cognitive Surplus: How Technology Makes Consumers into Collaborators.* New York: Penguin, 2010.

Smith, James K. A. *Who's Afraid of Postmodernism? Taking Derrida, Lyotard, and Foucault to Church.* Grand Rapids: Baker Academic, 2006.

Sweet, Leonard. *Viral: How Social Networking is Poised to Ignite Revival.* Colorado Springs: Waterbrook, 2012.

———. *Post-Modern Pilgrims: First Century Passion for the 21st Century World.* Nashville: Broadman & Holman, 2000.

Turkle, Sherry. *Alone Together: Why We Expect More from Technology and Less from Each Other*. New York: Basic Books, 2011.

———. *Life on the Screen: Identity in the Age of the Internet*. New York: Touchstone, 1995.

———. *The Second Self: Computers and the Human Spirit*. New York: Simon & Schuster, 1984.

Watkins, S. Craig. *The Young and the Digital: What the Migration to Social-Network Sites, Games, and Anytime, Anywhere Media Means for our Future*. Boston: Beacon, 2009.

Webber, Robert E. *Ancient Future Faith: Rethinking Evangelical for a Postmodern World*. Grand Rapids: Baker, 1999.

Weiss, Gail and Honi Fern Haber. *Perspectives on Embodiment: The Intersections of Nature and Culture*, edited by Gail Weiss and Honi Fern Haber, xiii. New York: Routledge, 1999.

Wingren, Gustaf. *Luther on Vocation*. Translated by Carl C. Rasmussen. Eugene, OR: Wipf & Stock, 1957.

Wolff, Hans Walter. *Anthropology of the Old Testament*. Mifflintown, PA: Sigler, 1996.

Wright, N. T. *Surprised by Hope: Rethinking Heaven, the Resurrection, and the Mission of the Church*. New York: HarperOne, 2008.

———. *The Challenge of Jesus: Rediscovering Who Jesus Was and Is*. Downer's Grove, IL: InterVarsity, 1999.

———. *The Resurrection of the Son of God*. Minneapolis: Fortress, 2003.

Wright, William J. *Martin Luther's Understanding of God's Two Kingdoms: A Response to the Challenge of Skepticism*. Grand Rapids: Baker Academic, 2010.

Yust, Karen-Marie, et al. "Cyber Spirituality: Facebook, Twitter, and the Adolescent Quest for Connection." *International Journal of Children's Spirituality* 15 (November 2010) 291–93.

Made in the USA
Columbia, SC
20 February 2021